Ouida

The Tower of Taddeo

A Novel

Ouida

The Tower of Taddeo
A Novel

ISBN/EAN: 9783337029357

Printed in Europe, USA, Canada, Australia, Japan

Cover: Foto ©Thomas Meinert / pixelio.de

More available books at **www.hansebooks.com**

THE
TOWER OF TADDEO

BY
OUIDA
AUTHOR OF "UNDER TWO FLAGS," ETC.

WITH ILLUSTRATIONS BY HOLLAND TRINGHAM

LONDON
WILLIAM HEINEMANN
1896

[All rights reserved]

LIST OF ILLUSTRATIONS.

	PAGE
BELDIA ON THE TOWER	*Frontispiece*
THE PALAZZO VECCHIO	10
THE CHURCH OF SAN JACOPO	46
DANTE'S HOUSE	88
SAN MICHELE	126
FLORENCE	158
THE PONTE VECCHIO	207
'GOOD PEOPLE, WHAT ARE YOU DOING THERE?'	254

THE TOWER OF TADDEO

CHAPTER I.

It was a high square tower, brown and gray, standing in a narrow street; one of the oldest of the once numerous towers of Florence. It was of great height, and dark with age, and rose above the lofty houses which surrounded it; its machicolated roofs and its iron vane and wooden flagstaff looked black against the sky. But warlike, and stalwart, and austere as it was, it had been given both grace and poetry by its builders, who had belonged to that age in which men knew so well how to unite the useful and the beautiful, how to harmonize the lovely with the formidable, and how to use the sports of peace to hide the strength of war. For it had been built by the great builder of its neighbour, the Jeweller's Bridge, and it was called now, as it had been called in the days of its rising, the Tower of Taddeo.

Tradition indicated it also as at one time his residence, but this rested only on rumour; that he had been its architect the archives of the city proved beyond any doubt. He had built it as he built and painted so much else that was beautiful. Beauty in those days was necessary as air to those men, so much greater in every art than are the men of these days; and the makers of all these mighty mediæval streets of Italy loved to decorate them with marble and majolica and terra-cotta, and to put niches in them for Madonna's shrines and statues of the saints, and allegorical devices, and inscriptions in the Latin tongue and iron scrollwork made by hand into the utmost delicacy of flower and foliage.

This tower was rich in all such decoration, and was sometimes called as well the House of the Loves (Casa degli Amorini), from the winged children, by Luca della Robbia, which clustered together over its archway, and held aloft the shield of the great family for whom it had been built, a Tuscan branch of those Brancaleone who once were lords of Cesena and Imola.

Above their shield was a shrine, with the Virgin and Child seated beneath a canopy, which had, it was said, wrought a miracle in the plague, and a framework of white and green lilies was around them. Above these were other winged children, and other garlands of lilies, and above these, again, was the figure of a bishop with a lamb at his feet; and all this ornament went upward, upward, upward, until figures and flowers mounted as high as the lines of the battlements, and were full of bright colour, and wholly unspoiled, although four centuries, if one, had gone by since they had been placed there to brighten the dark and gruesome walls, which were pierced with ogive windows and kneeling windows, barred with iron gratings, while below these were iron rings for torches, and iron sconces for lamps, and one massive oaken iron-studded door.

A narrow and dark staircase of stone, very steep, went from top to bottom of the tower; half its lower chambers served as a store place for oils, cheeses, and pastes to a chandler; and a seller of fuel had the other half filled with his charcoal wood and pine cones; on the narrow mezzanina above lived a cabinet-maker, a tailor, and a shoemaker, whilst the first, second, and third floors were occupied by a bookseller and librarian, and were known in the quarter as the Libreria Ardiglione.

On these floors every yard of space was filled to overflowing with books. There was a little kitchen, a little sitting-room, two little bedrooms, mere closets; and all the rest served as storage for books, books, books, nothing but books—and old books all of them, moreover—for their owner would no more have sold new books than he would have sold daily newspapers; either were abominations in his sight. A place of business might easily have been put in a more accessible locality than the Tower of Taddeo. But his father had been there before him, and his grandfather also; and if the dark, steep, breakneck stairs deterred customers from mounting them, its present proprietor, Francesco Ardiglione, commonly called Ser Checchi, had more leisure time in which to pore over his treasures, and chase the mice away from them, and add to them by visits to bookstalls in the town, and to any remote ancient rural place where it was known that there were any volumes of interest or age to be purchased. Books, even choice and antique ones, fetch but little in

Italy; and many scores of valuable volumes rot away in old rooms or granaries, or cellars, no one noticing them except the rats. In the country which once produced the noblest literature in the world, books are in the present era the least esteemed, are read the least, and are regarded with the most indifference and contempt.

Ardiglione was a man of some sixty-five years old; he had the true scholar's stoop of the throat and shoulders, and the true scholar's eyes, luminous and benign and dreamy; his head was fine, with white hair which fell softly off a broad and noble forehead, and a complexion smooth, pale, and delicate, of the faint yellow hue of old ivory. In stature he was short, and in build frail and spare. His clothes were always very shabby, and his gait was awkward; but no one who looked on him could doubt that he had gentle blood in his veins and vast learning in his brain.

Everyone called him Ser Checchi, which is the Tuscan diminutive of Francesco, and he was the jest of the neighbourhood for his absence of mind and his simplicity in money matters; but no one, not the boldest and most impudent little rascal of the streets, would have dared to joke at him to his face, and the rudest rough of the populace stood aside respectfully to let him go by on the curbstone.

He had married late in life, but his wife had long been dead, having bequeathed to him a ceaseless regret and two young children—a son, Cirillo, and a daughter, Beldia. Cirillo was a cause of trouble, Beldia was a perennial spring of joy. Their mother had been a German Swiss from the Canton of Freiburg, and they and her great-grandmother, a woman of Leyden, had given to the girl her sweet serenity of temper, as well as her fair hair, her fair skin, and her fine health. The boy had gone back for his type to far-off ancestors of more violent and headstrong temper, and had the dark brows, the black close-curling hair, the olive skin, the olive face, the slender limbs, of the young men of Luca Signorelli. In bygone days the Ardiglione had been amongst the territorial nobility of the Casentino, wild and arrogant people, riding out from their own castle gates, and holding their own against the Pope and the devil. In recent generations their impoverished descendants had become harmless, plodding, laborious citizens, tradespeople, and the like, living quietly, plainly, and honestly; but Cirillo seemed to have soared high over the heads of these his nearer progenitors, and to have come straight down from the days of the free lances and the mountain lords.

'Race is a strange thing!' said Ser Checchi, whenever he looked at his young son. 'You may bury the warrior's seed in a trader's till for centuries and centuries, and at the end of them it will start up armed, and cry for blood.'

He was sorely troubled by his son; and shaken by his exorbitant demands out of that peaceful, dusty, fragrant atmosphere which surrounds those who live amongst old books. Beldia, on the contrary, never had given him a moment's uneasiness since her babyish limbs had been strapped down in her swaddling clothes, and laid out in the sun by her country nurse, amongst the honeyed figs and the drying tomatoes on the bench of a farmhouse door in the southern hills.

Despite the infantine captivity of her swaddling bands, she had grown into a tall and gracious woman, very finely formed, and having the more massive muscle of her mother's race and her mother's sunny hair and milk-white complexion. On her reposed all the government of the family: the domestic direction, the tutelage of the youth who helped to carry on such business as was done, and all matters great and small appertaining to the Ardiglione household and to the small country place lying to the south of the city which belonged to her father. All larger financial questions were settled by Ser Checchi himself, but all smaller ones were the affair of Beldia; and even at seventeen years old her hands and her mind were full, and her thoughts as busied as though she were a matron of fifty. She had a single servant who cooked, swept, ironed and dusted; a sturdy widow, by name Veronica, who did the marketing, saw to the linen, and cleaned as much as the presence of so many books allowed to be cleaned; but this was all the help which Ser Checchi's daughter ever had, and she worked diligently and cheerfully herself all the year round.

It was she who set the flowers in fresh water under the Madonna's shrine every morning, who kept pots of geraniums and clove pinks and lemon verbena growing behind the broad casements, who on the flat roof behind the battlements had a little garden of young lemon-trees and rose-bushes, mignonette and sweet herbs, protected by matting in winter-time from the north winds which sweep down the Apennines. It was Beldia who freed the mice from the traps which Veronica set, and cherished the swallows who built beneath the machicolations, and petted Lillo the warehouse mastiff, and her own white Maremma dog Folko; and threw crumbs to the sparrows perching among the plants on the roofs, and carried carrots, and crusts, and cabbage-leaves to the charcoal-seller's mule, who was stabled in the basement.

'If she were not so clever, one would say she was daft,' said Veronica, a good-natured soul, to whom, nevertheless, a sparrow only existed for the spit, and mice for the cats, and the food of a dog and the provender of a mule only concerned those who owned them.

Beldia had inherited from her mother one of those benignant and tender souls whose compassion is as wide as the sea, and whose kindness embraces all earth's creatures.

'The heart of St. Francis came back into the world in your body,' her father said to her once, seeing her standing on the roof in the sunshine amongst the young lemon-trees, with the pigeons and sparrows and swallows flying about her.

'Beldia was only a nurse, not a saint,' she said, with a smile. Her namesake was nurse to Santa Fina, of San Gemignano, and so has a humble place in Hagiology.

'It is well for me that I shall have you to be mine,' said Ser Checchi, thinking that the day might not be so far distant from him when he should grow dull of sight, and stiff of limb, and able only to sit and dream of books long read, and days long dead, as Petrarca used to sit in the loggia at Arqua.

At present, however, he was, though of slight frame, strong, and active after his own serious and leisurely fashion, and his physical and mental strength had been little impaired by his sedentary habits and his preference of the study to the air. His daughter incessantly meditated on and provided for his comfort and safety; and dry shoes after a muddy walk, warm possets after a chilly day, well-aired linen, and well-cooked food, had not a little to do with his excellent enjoyment of health.

When he always found his coffee ready at six in the morning, his dinner ready at mid-day, his linen fresh and whole, his papers arranged and docketed, his beloved books classified as far as he would permit such classification to disturb their chaos, he owed it all to Beldia, but it never occurred to him that it was so.

'Good child, good child!' he said sometimes to her dreamily, and she was more than content.

'He never sees that the signorina is letting all her youth and playtime go by for his sake,' the servant Veronica grumbled to herself. 'He thinks a sight more of that graceless, heartless, devil-may-care spendthrift, Cirillo.'

Yet it was not that Ser Checchi thought little of his daughter: he thought much of her, but he was so used to rely on her, to turn to her, and to have all his material necessities forestalled by her, that he noticed what he owed to her no more than most people—alas for them!—notice the beauty of sunshine and sky.

Beldia was esteemed by the few, the very few, who knew her as a grave, strong, energetic maiden, careful as to pence, watchful as to waste, thinking constantly of the little clerk's misdemeanours, the price of fish and meat, the cost of clothing, the rise in charcoal, the wear and tear of linen. But underneath that prosaic surface there were in her a musing and poetic nature, an imagination which was mute, but none the less vitally and quickly touched to fine excess. When she sat in the dusk of the early evening, or in the faint lamplight of the later night, whilst her father was busied amongst his books below her, and the serving-woman in her kitchen above, she would let her work drop on her lap, and the shadowy spirits of the past come about her.

As a little child she had been brought up on their farm in the Casentino; and those early years had filled her with a need of and longing for country sights and sounds, wide landscapes and broad skies. But the tower was still more dear to her, too, in its own way, and when the wood burned on its hearth, and the lamplight flickered on its grated windows, and its oaken chests, and its dusky ancient pictures, it had for her the warm, deep, abiding charm of home: that charm of which those of her generation usually understood nothing.

It is a charm which takes most hold, and can best be felt, in ancient houses, where many generations have lived and loved, where the suffering of birth and of death has gone on for centuries, where the painted angels on the ceilings have looked down in pity on so many beds of pain, and the bright cherubs on the walls have laughed through their maze of flowers on so many lovers whose bones have mouldered for so many years; in ancient houses, whence emanates a sense of multitudinous life, of sacred and softened death, of ghosts who come tenderly and in affection amongst the living who have replaced them; and in such houses there is a sanctity which endears them to the dwellers in them, if these have eyes to see the unseen, and souls tender enough to venerate the dead.

The back of the tower rose above the Arno amidst red-roofed and brown-roofed buildings, gray and moss-grown with age, with terraces on which linen was blowing, and wallflowers were blossoming, and weather-vanes of all kinds and colours and shapes were shifting about to the winds. From her own platform at the top of the tower Beldia could see the river-reaches to right and left of her, and the beautiful lines of the mountains; the cool dark woods of the Cascine and the shining marbles of San Miniato; and across the water, above the palaces on the opposite quay, the dome of the cathedral and the lantern-tower of the Palazzo Vecchio. It was her supreme happiness and recreation to stand there at sunrise or at sunset, and look up at the glad and glorious sky above, and the gliding stream beneath, now green, now brown, now dun coloured, with the reflections of the lights trembling on its surface, and all the sounds of the city softened and spiritualized by distance.

There were so many of those towers once in this city; and now they are nearly all levelled and destroyed by people who prefer factory chimneys with their hellish stench, and the frightful follies of the

jerry-builder. Dante would have sat quite content amongst its book-lined walls, and Fra Angelico would have painted happily at its barred casement, and Leonardo would have drawn and modelled joyfully on its flat roof so near the clouds, amidst the pigeons and the bells; but what could any one of them do in a machine-room or in a modern villa?

The old tower dated far back to the earliest days of the Republic. It had felt iron and lead and flame. It had seen combat rage and blood flow like water down its narrow street. It had known all that full, rich, various, splendid life which came with the effulgence of the Renaissance. It was itself a part and parcel of all that noble and splendid existence, and as such it was doubly dear to this quiet maiden, deep down in whose heart was the reverence for all great things, and heroic lives, and beautiful creations.

She could make a fritter ably, and could iron like a clear-starcher, and could see quickly when the butcher and the baker tried to cheat her; but all the same she honoured art and nature, and when she saw them outraged she was herself ashamed. She had been born with the eyes which see, and the ears which hear, and the scholarly and historic atmosphere in which she had been reared from her babyhood made her perceptions clearer, and her thoughts finer, than are those of most women. She loved these things which were around her; and she knew why she loved them, which was more.

For an unintelligent love, whether for man or for nature, is of little benefit to either, because it knows not what it does; and so does ofttimes more harm than good, and only tortures when it seeks to serve.

When she had leisure to dream, she liked to lay her head back against her chair, and close her eyes, and think of all those scenes on which the iron torch-rings and stanchions and the dark and gruesome walls had gazed. Full many a time must they have seen their creator, Gaddi himself, watching them in their rising, his fine straight profile like a cameo against the light, and the woollen lucco wrapped about his head to keep out the north wind.

She had a great reverence for the elder Gaddi; it seemed to her that he had never got his full meed of fame. He built the Campanile, and it is called Giotto's; he built San Michele, and it is called Orcagna's. True, those masters did design both belfry and church; but he built them, and all alone he both designed and built the Ponte Vecchio, the Goldsmith's Bridge, which has no rival anywhere except the arch named after the *alta Riva* of Venice, and which has stood the sieges and floods and storms of six hundred years, and will stand six centuries more unless the accursed greed of municipal speculation seizes on its stones. Taddeo Gaddi led one of the loveliest, happiest, manliest lives ever led on earth, such a life as it is impossible to lead now, because the atmosphere which then made it possible nowhere now exists. But of fame in the mouths of posterity he has not had his full portion. Of the many thousands who every season pass over his bridge, scarce one Florentine, or one foreigner, in a million remembers its architect.

In old times the tower had been a fortress, and

had felt the tramp of steel-clad feet and the roar of discharging arquebuses; many a dead body had been flung or dragged down its stairs, many an awful night of flame and fury had settled darkly down upon its roof: torches had flared in its rings to light many a mortal combat, and many a foeman had fallen stiff and stark upon its stones. It had stood there in the Borgo San Jacopo ever since A.D. 1230, the date carved on the stone of its threshold, and the whole course of Florentine history had passed through the deep and narrowed street on which its frontage looked. Like its street, it had seen the citizens in mortal feud with the mercenaries, and the artisans in fierce struggle with the ducal or imperial soldiers; and had seen also many lovelier, happier, gayer scenes, when the white palfreys had ambled with a nuptial party beneath its walls, and the carnival masques had danced and rioted. It had heard the rousing calls of trumpet and bugle; and the mellow rhythm of chant and anthem: the hiss of burning oil and the shriek of ravaged women; the resounding tread of the warhorse and the sweet singing of the Virgin's litany. It had beheld the Conte Verde pace gaily over the bridge, and the standard of justice rise in Michel di Lando's hand, and Cosimo de' Medici sally out with his attendant dwarf to the siege of Siena, and Tasso pass on his tired horse, travelling from Ferrara, and Bianca Cappello go by with her fatal beauty, and Boccaccio hasten daily on his visits to his friend and scribe Francesco Manelli; and the Bardia's Dianora watch for her lover with her silken rope; and Ariosto and his lady of the golden palms come forth from the

Hospice of the Knights of Malta and walk in peace together.

Once, tradition said, Saint Catherine had come up these very stairs when on her visit hard by to Nicolo Soderini; and Charles VIII.'s superb entry and stealthy exit had both passed along under it, and troops of wild condottiere had ridden past in festal bravery, and ladies' silken litters had been borne in gay procession, and painters and singers had sung May-day lays and Christmas carols to their mistresses in the moonlight; and it had seen the green maio blossoming and swinging in its doorway; and on the night of the Fierucolone had been alive with sparkling, waving, fiery tow; and the rusty big bell which hung below its flagstaff had added its voice to the clamour of the Carmine chimes ringing in the rising of the Ciompi; and Francesco Ferruccio had run about under its shadow, a bright, bold baby with fearless eyes and sturdy limbs; and its stones had been hot with the reflection of the fires burning the Bardi palaces and towers; and Baccio della Porta and Giovanni di San Giovanni had passed by there in gentler times, going to their studios by the Romano Gate; and in the little church of San Jacopo close at hand the nobles had once met to defend their rights and demand their share of government; and in the greater church of Santo Spirito hard by Piero Capponi had been brought to his burial with torches and banners countless, and the whole magistracy and populace weeping for his loss.

For anyone deeply versed in the traditions of the past, and amorous of their beauty, as she was, the dead arise and live again in such historic and hero-haunted precincts.

To the fool, to the vain, to the puffed-up ape of modernity, they are but dark walls, narrow ways, dumb stones, closed portals: but to those who love them with humility and tenderness they are full of eloquent and undying life.

Beldia dreamed of these dead people often in her rare enjoyment of unoccupied time, and when she lay in her bed in the narrow chamber under the roof they came about her, smiling gladly or weeping wearily, and telling her many things.

CHAPTER II.

But her moments of leisure were few and always brief, for she had a great deal of various work to do, and when she was not actively occupied her father gave her many papers to copy, and manuscripts to write out clearly, for he loved to pen learned dissertations on disputed points of history or archæology, and printed some of these at his own cost for the small, very small, number of persons who were interested in the abstruse subjects which interested himself.

Those square, solid rooms between the four brick and stone walls of his tower, encumbered with hundreds and thousands of books, bound and unbound, were the whole world of Ser Checchi; and the chiming of the church bells, the cries and noises of the street, the twittering of the busy swallows, and the clang of the belfry clocks, had no power to disturb him, as he plodded through a black letter treatise of some extinct ecclesiastical order, or noticed respectfully, but doubtingly, some questionable copy of some of the Fathers of the Church, or penned a learned essay on some disputed point in Florentine history, or discoursed upon the publications of the Giuntina Classics, or the worth of some early quarto from Bernardo Cennini's press.

Custom came rarely, and money came sparsely to the tower of the amorini; too sparsely for all except its master, who lived in the quiet shelter of his bookshelves, and only woke up unwillingly to perceive now and then that there were people around him who needed such tiresome and common things as oil and charcoal, boots and shoes, beans and bread.

To the scholar his own need of such things is always an odious necessity, importunate and disagreeable; and Ser Checchi, like Vespasino and Magliabecchi and Anton Cocchi before him, was a scholar to the inmost fibre of his heart, although only nominally a librarian and a bookseller.

At such rare occasions as he was absent on book-buying errands or antiquarian researches, Beldia stayed in those two sacred chambers of the library to be in readiness for any customers who might come thither; but few customers of any kind climbed the steep stair. She sat at a little ancient desk amongst a sea of books, and watched the boy-clerk Poldo, who was as agile as a squirrel and as mischievous as a monkey, and answered in her grave, sweet voice all such questions and demands as people put to her.

The clientela of the tower was a sparse but a cultured one; it consisted chiefly of aged men, grown gray in meditation, bibliophiles, antiquaries, philologists, professors of abstruse sciences, students of ecclesiastical history, lovers of what was old and obscure and difficult to procure or decipher. From these learned priests and professors, who were friends of her father, she acquired a mass of information of a grave and noble kind, though not of the kind which is popular or usual in a world busied with modern things. She knew as well as her father what volumes treated of this, that, or the other subject, and could find such authorities unerringly amongst the thousands of books tossed all together in a great heap, like the stones on a wayside cairn. 'We will ask the maiden,' said all these rusty scholars one to another, when they wanted any treatise found, or any monograph on a forgotten theme discovered. Beldia could find it, if anybody could. Altogether unknown to herself, the name of Ser Checchi's daughter became spoken of beyond these reverend gentlemen by younger and more imaginative men; a narrow circle still, for it was limited to scholars, and scholars of a certain kind, but these, though few, brought others, less learned, but equally curious about a pretty girl enshrined in musty books like a flower growing among sand and rocks. These younger visitors, lawyers, teachers, professors, architects, and the like, received but a cold welcome from Beldia, and a suggestion that they could as well pursue their studies at the Magliabecchian or Laurentian libraries. Nevertheless, two or three of them had, undaunted by her reception, made her offers of marriage, which she had at once, and without consideration, rejected; not even disturbing the peace of her father by telling him of such follies.

She loved the books and the city, the country and the mountains; and that was all. She had hardly even read of love, for, from the severity of her father's intellectual tastes, most of the poets and all the novelists were banished. She knew that men and women loved, and sometimes were married and sometimes were not; but it all seemed very foolish, and altogether out of her own path. Ser Checchi always told her that Beatrice was only a metaphor, and Laura only a symbol, and it seemed to her that any love which she might ever feel would be also only a metaphor, only a symbol. But the young men who were patronized by Veronica did not suggest to her either of these.

For the moment she had no sentiment save for her father, who, if he did not fully appreciate her value, was most gentle, kind, and reverent to her, as he was to all living and dead things, from the chandler's mastiff who kept guard at the warehouse, to the nuns who came to solicit alms at his door; from the old woman who sold vegetables on the other side of the street, to the beautiful bronze Bacchus which stands in a niche at the corner of his street, to which he took off his hat once a day regularly in memory of the classic past which it symbolized. It was not because he was neglectful or unfeeling that it never occurred to him that the life led by Beldia was a dull and sad one for a woman of her years; he had taught her Latin, and she had free and unrestricted access to all his books: what more could any human soul desire? Moreover, when the heats of July came, he went away reluctantly, for her sake, to their little place in the Casentino; locking up the beloved books with enormous iron keys, which had in other times served to lock in human prisoners in the precincts of the tower. He descended twice a week into the city to visit them, and carried up into the hill with him new purchases which required looking into, or rebacking, or were worthy of study or annotation; but these summer months at Antella were painful to him, though he bore them meekly, and he was never really happy until he was down again in the narrow, dusky street, under the wings of his own angels and amorini. To Beldia the return was not so joyful: she loved the breezy hills, the windswept stretches of heather and gorse, the pomp of the sunset, the spirituality of the sunrise, the tall, straight trunks of the pine-trees with the woodpeckers and the cuckoos flitting between them; the steep, narrow, sandy roads, with the mule-carts of the charcoal-burners winding down them; the divine rural stillness in which the distant bells rang softly as with a blessing.

She loved all these things with that ardour which lovers of the country know so well; and when she came back into the city life, its confinement, and want of light and restricted horizon were painful to her, but she said nothing, and took up her yoke of daily tasks, and bore it bravely; and after all she loved the tower with a fonder passion, a more filial affection, than she felt for any other thing or place.

She rarely went out when in the town for pleasure: she attended Mass at one of the many churches near at hand, and bought what she wanted at the shops of her quarter; sometimes she went to market on such days as her woman was busy ironing the linen which had been washed in the country, or bottling off into flasks the barrels of oil and of wine which had come from there.

Other generations will not know the old Florence market as Beldia and Veronica knew it, under the gloomy and noble shadows of the ancient towers and palaces; a union of colour, form, light, shade, costume, and architecture which was delightful to the eyes and which now is to be no more seen, because greed, and bad taste, and passion for change, and shame of ancient ways, and jealousy of ancient fame, have conspired together and decided to raze its precincts to the ground. The old market, with its amber-hued leathern awnings, its good-humoured populace, its piles of fruits, and herbs, and vegetables, its centre of jest and bargain, its ever-turning public spits, its noisy and joyous animation, gathered underneath the stately walls, the high roofs, the grated casements, was a picture meet for the burin of Callot and the brush of Carpaccio. Now it is no more; the venders are shut up in cases of iron and glass hideous to behold, and the buyers hurry over their purchases, cross and cantankerous, and the old grace and the old mirth and old colours are things dead and gone for ever.

But when Beldia dwelt in the tower of Taddeo they were still existent; and she was wont to take her way, as soon as the sun was up, over the Jeweller's Bridge to the market; always giving a thought backward over the centuries to Cammilla Martelli, who, for her sorrow, was once seen sitting at her lone casement on that bridge by the great Medici, and knew a sultry, brief summer of love and happiness, followed by a long life-time of enforced seclusion and unavailing regret.

And yet Cammilla's had been an enviable fate, she thought; to have known that wondrous magical transformation of circumstance, and to be remembered by the poets and the scholars and the artists, whenever they pass over the paved road between the little quaint, glittering shops; to live in memory thus, associated for ever with the stories of the city —such a destiny seemed to Beldia the most beautiful kind of immortality that anyone could wish or gain.

But her remembrance of Cammilla and of many another lovely legend did not prevent her, when she came to the market stalls, from looking very shrewdly at the feet of the chickens she bought, and at the gills of the fish she purchased, to be sure of their age and freshness, and no one would have been able by specious words to persuade her that stale spinach was fresh, or that eggs from a crate were new-laid. The poetic side of her nature made her say a prayer for the soul of Cammilla; but the practical side of her character made her get due value for every centime she spent. She would give to the poor as though she had Ceres' horn of plenty; but she would not be cheated out of a bronze halfpenny.

Veronica scolded, shrieked, bullied, and wrangled violently for an hour, only to be put off at last with inferior victuals; but Beldia, though she never raised her voice a semitone higher, and never said a harsh word to anyone, was not to be imposed upon, and all the market knew it.

'It is the maiden of Taddeo's tower. She must have her own way,' said the sellers of fish, flesh, and fowl, provoked, and yet admiring.

In these early morning excursions she was dressed like a girl of the people, with thick shoes and a short kirtle; a handkerchief, woollen or silken according to the season, was tied over her shining hair, and a big basket was poised upon her arm. But there was something in her walk, and in the carriage of her head, and in her soft, clear, low speech, which spoke of race and of culture, and opened a free, unmolested passage for her amongst the noisy and rough throng there. Many young men looked at, followed, and would have addressed her, but she daunted them by the absolute unconsciousness which she seemed to have of their existence, and a certain severity of pride which now and then hardened her features, which were attractive, gentle, and fair, not unlike the Madonnas of Lippo Lippi.

'One could paint her with a nimbus, and a little Christ sucking at her breast, and a St. John with a lily standing at her knee,' said one of these persons watching her as she stood for a moment at the flower-stall: he was a teacher at the Belle Arte, and spoke to a friend younger than himself, who was an architect from Lombardy.

'Yes; I see,' said the younger man. 'I would sooner make her a statue of Charity, with a rod of white lilies in her hand, and her foot on a snake, and a star on her brow shedding rays of light; that is my idea of Charity—the Charity which thinks no evil. We have had enough of Charities modelled on nursing mothers. No, I am not disrespectful to Correggio and Holbein, nor even to Bouguereau.'

They were standing by the pillar which is called the Column of Mars, and where it is said that Buondelmonte fell. Beldia had just passed them carrying her basket, and had stopped at the corner of the Strozzi palace to look at the flowers which were there for sale.

'How admirably she walks!' the Lombard added. 'Who is she? A poor girl? A maiden or a matron?'

'Not poor and not married. She is the daughter of the old librarian at the old tower of the Brancaleone which Taddeo Gaddi built,' replied the Florentine.

'I know the tower, I think,' said his companion. 'What kind of books does he sell?'

'Old books, ecclesiastical, historical, philosophical, architectural, which will suit you. He is a droll old fellow, crammed with useless learning; we go there sometimes to see him and his girl: she is often all alone amongst the books, and knows a good deal about them also.'

'She looks like some learned daughter of *docta Bononia*.'

'Despite the market basket and the handkerchief on her head?'

'Yes; she wears the one till it looks like Minerva's

casque, and carries the other as if it contained the books of the Sibyl.'

'She is more a Madonna than a Sibyl, I think.'

'Then let us hope, for her own sake, that she will have the sucking Gesu, not the Sibylline tomes.'

They parted company a few moments later, the Florentine to go to his class at the Accademia, where he was a teacher of perspective; the other, a stranger in the town, strolled towards the river, which was in a flood from recent rainfalls, yellow and brown with earth, and carrying shrubs, and trees, and hay, and straw, and planks, and rocks which it had loosened and whirled down on its way.

Insensibly following a romantic impulse, the Lombard, a man of Brescia, crossed the bridge of the Holy Trinity and bent his steps to that old shady quarter of Oltarno, where the tower of the loves was to be found. It was very little past eight of the clock: a fine, clear, breezy morning after the storms of the night. The deep bell of Santo Spirito was tolling sonorously for some citizen's death.

'It is too early to go and buy a book,' he thought; 'I had better go and breakfast first.'

Nearly opposite to the tower which he wished to observe was a humble eating place, half bakery, half coffee-house, with round, big loaves, and baskets of eggs, and a card which intimated that within might be had a cup of coffee and a white roll for the small price of thirty centimes.

'This collation will not ruin me,' thought the student of Brescia, whose purse was scantily furnished; and he pushed open the door and entered, disturbing a sleek white and gray cat by his entrance.

They served him quickly, for the coffee was already on the fire in a back-kitchen behind the shop ; the air was full of the sweet, appetising smell of newly-baked bread ; the cat came and had a share of the milk. Whilst he ate and drank the Brescian looked at the tower, which was visible a few yards farther down the street, the morning sunshine glistening on its amorini, and its garlands, and its saints.

' A fine old tower, that,' he said to the woman who had served him, a clean, buxom young woman, with red Titian-coloured hair, and a yellow cotton jacket. ' It was built by Taddeo, was it not ?'

She shrugged her shoulders.

' We call it Taddeo's tower, or the tower of the loves, if you like that better. You see all those little loves gambolling above the doorway? It belongs to old Maso Donati, the grain merchant, and Ser Checchi has lived in it all his life, and so did his fathers before him.'

' Ser Checchi ?' repeated the Brescian inquiringly.

' The old man who lives in the books like a worm. The whole place is full of books up to the roof; he could fill the cellars, too, only Nani and Peppino have them for their goods. Ser Checchi is a little cracked, you know. Those over-learned people always are half daft. If you overfill the barrel it will leak somewhere.'

' No doubt. But I am fond of books myself. Will he sell any ?'

' Surely ! Selling them is his trade ; but nobody

ever buys. They go there, the old ones to read and jabber and steal his learning, and the young ones to make court to the signorina, for she is handsome, and some think she will have money; but I know better—che!—the old man is a leaking barrel, I tell you, and his money trickles away with his wits.'

She looked very knowing, and made a gesture as of one who pours water upon the ground, and struck the silver pin in her hair a smart blow, with the air of a person who could tell a great deal if she chose. The Brescian conceived an instantaneous hatred of her.

'Do they buy your bread?' he said with curt significance.

'Che! not they. They make their own. They bake once a week, and so eat well one day in seven, and all the other six eat crusts as hard as bricks.'

'I see,' said her customer, and thought to himself, 'When you want a baker's good word do not eat home-made bread.'

'There is old Ser Checchi!—look!' said the young woman, pointing to a stooping figure, clothed in old-fashioned clothes, which came forth from the doorway underneath the playing loves.

'Going to buy more books, I will warrant!' she said with supreme contempt. 'That is the way his daughter's dower goes, in old musty, fusty, mouldy, mildewed, worm-eaten things which nobody in their senses would ever use to wrap up a pat of butter. And when I asked him once if he could sell me a copy of the Sesto Astrologer's Calendar, which tells you all that is going to happen all through the year, he laughed at me, and said he did not keep such silly rubbish in his place. Silly! the Astrologer of Sesto! Did ever you know such impudence?'

'Rank blasphemy,' replied the Lombard, gazing curiously and reverently at the venerable figure of Ser Checchi as it went down the narrow street in the shadow cast by the tall dark houses.

'But the librarian is away now,' he added. 'If anyone wanted to buy books, or to look over some in stock, would the shop be open?'

'Shop! Che! He has no shop—he has nothing so sensible. There are rooms and rooms, and there are books in all of them, one over another, like the flotsam and jetsam floating and tossing on Arno to-day, and there is Madonna Beldia to tell you all about them as if she were a printed book herself. If there were a shop where the warehouse is, with some glass and gilding and fine-bound books behind it, in red and blue and yellow, as you see them in Tornabuoni Street, I dare say he would sell some and wouldn't be out at elbows, as he is, they say, and at his wits' end how to pay Cirillo's debts. Yes, Cirillo is the son: a fine lad, the only one of them who has any spirit or sense. He has been a soldier, and now he is a painter down in Rome.'

'Art is a poor trade to all but the few who "arrive," as the French say,' answered the Brescian as he rose, paid his three bronze coins, thanked her courteously, and left the place.

With that instinct of secrecy which accompanies the dawn of all amorous fancy, he did not choose that the loquacious and malicious neighbour should see him go to the tower. So he sauntered in a leisurely fashion along the street, lighted a cigarette and smoked it, and went as far as the Piazza of Santo Spirito, where he stood awhile gazing at the massive dome and the graceful campanile; then he turned back and retraced his steps, and before many minutes had passed found himself back again in that most ancient street, where the loves of Luca della Robbia guarded the tower portal. Arrived before the door, he threw away the cigarette, and began to ascend the staircase — Lillo, the big brindled mastiff who belonged to the warehouse, smelling in a distant but not unfriendly manner at him as he went by; he was a stranger, but Lillo let him go by unchallenged.

The staircase was dark as night, being lighted only by small slits in the wall like portholes, through which in other ages the defenders of the place had been able to fire their arquebuses, or pour their hot pitch on their assailants below in the street. On the first floor he found an open door, above which he could read in a dim light the words 'Libreria Ardiglione' written on a placard, and underneath them the inscription which used to be above the entrance of the Marrucillian library: 'Publicæ Maxime Pauperum Utilitatio.' With uncovered head he entered this chamber, and found himself, as the bakeress had told him that he would do, in a sea of books tossed one over another like the petrified waves of a once heaving ocean. That chamber was only occupied by the books, but in a farther room he saw a boy writing at a desk, and at another desk was seated the woman or girl whom he had seen by the Column of Mars.

Then a great diffidence came over him, and

although in Brescia, in Cremona, in Bergamo, he had always been ready to talk and laugh with women, he stood now on the threshold of the inner room hesitating and mute.

Then Beldia saw him and rose.

'Good-morning, sir,' she said to him in her serene, harmonious tones. 'Is there anything, in which I can have the pleasure to serve you?'

She was dressed in a plain gray gown, and had no ornament of any sort, and her hair was as closely wound around her head as its large coils would allow; but standing there amongst the sea of books, she looked to his already captured fancy, as she leaned one arm upon her desk, like the Sibylla Persica of Guercino: she had the Sibyl's serious and yet smiling expression, a look at once of meditation and of expectation, of brightness and of repose.

He gazed at her with such earnestness that he embarrassed her, and, seeing that he did so, he stammered some request for works on architecture.

'That is rather a vague demand,' said Beldia doubtfully. 'Of what kind, of what epoch, of what tongue?'

'Any age you will,' answered her customer incoherently, 'and whether Italian or Latin, it is the same to me.'

Beldia hesitated, feeling that the request was only a feint to excuse his entrance.

'If you could return in the afternoon my father would be here,' she said at last. 'He is more acquainted with such works than I; he is an archæologist, and very learned.'

'I should be honoured to make the acquaintance

of Ser Francesco,' replied the Brescian, recovering his address as he observed her embarrassment. 'But I need—I greatly need—at once a copy of Piranesi: or, at least, I cannot afford to purchase it, but might I be allowed to verify one passage?'

'We have a before-letter copy of Piranesi here,' said Beldia, 'and you are welcome to look through any of the volumes.'

She went to one spot in the crowded shelves where various works of that date were gathered, and pointed out the 'Antichitæ Romanæ' to the stranger, whilst she bade the boy Poldo take the books down and carry them to the table.

'You are too good,' murmured the young man; 'I am ashamed to give so much trouble.'

'It is no trouble,' she answered. 'And my father is always glad if he can be of use to scholars. Ours is a library rather than a shop.'

'And a very hospitable one,' he said gratefully. 'I am an architect from the North, I know no one in your city, and can have no claim upon your literary hospitality. My name is Odisio Fontano,' he added timidly. 'Is it familiar to you?' he asked, as he saw a light as of recognition pass over her face.

'Oh, in the past,' she answered. 'It was a good and great name of Lombardy.'

'That is a very long while ago,' said the young man. 'We have fallen from our high estate, and have been poor people for centuries.'

'That does not alter anything. What was, was; and the Fontano shield hangs, I believe, on the Broletto of Bergamo.'

'Yes, truly, we were lords in Bergamo. But that

is long, long ago, as I said. Now we are very poor.'

'But how did your people change from Bergamo to Brescia?'

'It was in the last century. My great-grandfather married a gentlewoman of Brescia.'

'Indeed!' said Beldia, intimating by her accent that this colloquy had lasted long enough.

It took him a long while to find the plate or the passage which he required, and ever and again he kept looking off divers volumes to where Beldia sat, who was writing diligently, making a copy for her father of some monograph or some annotated paragraph, and was wholly undisturbed by the presence of a stranger.

The sound from the narrow street came muffled to that height, seeming far away as in a dream; Poldo caught flies and yawned, and furtively nibbled nuts, where he sat at his desk, with his back turned to his mistress; the mouldy yet fragrant smell of old books and of old walls filled the chamber; a stray sunbeam came in through the thick, dull glass, and touched the maiden's throat and hair.

The young man sighed, and closed a copy of Marco Recci's designs as the clock tolled eleven.

'Can you not find what you want? Tell me what it is, and perhaps I can help you,' said Beldia, as she ended the last line of her copy.

He coloured and murmured his thanks and excuses.

As he wanted nothing that any books could give him, and his search was wholly fictitious, he could not reply more clearly; he could not say: 'I only wanted to look at you, and see the sunshine play amongst the little curls above your throat.'

'May I return to have the honour of seeing your father?' he asked her, as he rose and replaced the big volume with respect upon its shelf.

'Our library is always open until six,' said Beldia, taking his inquiry literally, 'and my father is always glad to be of use to scholars, as I told you.'

She remained standing, as a hint to him to take his departure. But he still lingered, fascinated by the still, ancient, studious place, and its fair-haired occupant.

'Have you anything to say?' she asked at last, a little impatiently. 'Is there any message which you wish to leave—any work or passage which you wish especially to consult?'

'No, no; nothing,' said the Lombard hurriedly. 'Pardon me, madamigella; I have intruded so long. I will return at three, by your kind permission.'

Then at last he went; and Beldia, returning to her seat, sought out other work to do, and bent her fair head over her inkstand.

The stranger had made little impression upon her; she was so used to see men come and go, and she did not concern herself with them except as scholars. This one had seemed to her a desultory and half-hearted student by the distraught manner in which he had turned over the precious pages of the famous works.

CHAPTER III.

At eleven Ser Checchi returned, and at two o'clock they sat down to their dinner in a little room which, though nominally set aside for eating, was overflowing with books and papers. Their dinner was frugal, but Beldia had been taught by her mother that good cooking means good digestion, and the dishes were savoury and excellent, though few in number; the wine was the sound though simple drink of their own vineyards, and artistic instinct had made her set a few daffodils and late anemones in a vase of Casteldurante pottery four centuries old. The slovenliness and unloveliness and disorder of ordinary Italian ways were alien to her; and the antique silver shone, the old china was bright, and the homespun linen was white and scented with iris and rosemary, upon her table. Ser Checchi did not notice these things, but he derived a vague, unconscious gratification from them, and would have missed them had they been wanting there.

To him his daughter remained always a little girl. He never realized that she was now twenty-three years old, and that her life had not much more pleasure in it than a nun's, except in so far as her intelligence and her perceptions gave her joys and interests, and her power of ruling her house taught her that independence which is to the character what a fresh sea-wind blowing over it is to an expanse of waters.

It was a very simple, regular, retired life which she led in her old tower. She had few friends and no distractions; but she was happy and interested in her many occupations, and whether she sat in winter by the open hearth with its brass dogs, or in summer on her terrace amongst the carnations and mignonettes, her hand was busied with work, and her eyes regaled themselves on a book.

It was what most women of her age would have called a dull life, but she was never dull; there was so much to do, so much to see to, so much to think of, and her rare leisure was never long enough to learn all that she desired to learn from history and art.

Her father was the great occupation of her existence. To forestall all his wishes, to get the best and uttermost that could be got out of their means for him, to spare him all trouble and worry, and to be, as it were, a lamp before his feet in all shadows, was her constant desire and effort. Ser Checchi, manlike, never guessed or measured all the continual thought and care and sacrifice which went to make up the sum of his daily comforts and customs, and kept the atmosphere of his household clear and serene about him.

He loved his daughter with a great and most tender love, but he thought her lot an enviable one, and underrated, because he did not understand, the unselfishness of her devotion to himself. For the rest, gentle and sweet of temper although he was, he held to ancient views concerning parental authority, and had unconsciously something of the old Greek and Roman contempt for the mind and the opinions of women.

She, indeed, could read Latin well, and could quote

great authors without error, and could find chapter and verse in the classics and the Fathers of the Church; and this he knew, because it was his own doing that her studies had taken this bent; still, he would never have consulted her seriously upon any matter of business or learning, and would not have deemed her opinion worth asking on anything beyond a fruit-pudding, a roll of linen, or a sack of fresh coffee-berries.

Therefore of his affairs, and of his possessions, she knew little if anything: all she had to do was to lay out to the utmost of her ability the sum given her for household expenses, rent, taxes, and the wages of Veronica; the boy, Poldo, was in a manner apprenticed, and received nothing but his food, which was no small matter, for his appetite was huge, as the human appetite usually is when it can be indulged at another person's expense.

To the Lombard she seemed like a fair and fine lily growing in a sunless garden-border; but to her father, as to herself, she appeared a maiden exceptionally blest, and safe, and happy, with little money, indeed, but otherwise most favoured.

Many a time Veronica longed to take her master to task for his negligence of his daughter's interest, in not having had her married, or at least betrothed, before her twentieth year, a period which seems in Italy the commencement of old age for every woman. But Ser Checchi, with his dreamy gentleness, inspired a respect which amounted to awe in the breast of his dependents. Out of his sight she despised him as a useless oddity, who did not know his right hand from his left, and who would drink vinegar for wine without perceiving it; but in his presence the rough, coarse, sensual mind of the servant felt the influence which emanates from a high intelligence and a stainless character; she did not dare to blame her employer to his face. She had never, in the twenty years that she had been in his service, seen him seriously angry, except once. It was when Cirillo was about twelve years of age; he had stolen a cake of panforte (a kind of petrified plum-pudding, dear to the appetite of Tuscans) from the cupboard of a neighbour, and then the wrath of the gentle-scholar had been terrible, and had left an ineffaceable impression on the memories of all around him. Since then Cirillo had done many worse things, but Veronica had never forgotten that scene after the theft of the cake. 'From the anger of meek Ser Checchi the saints deliver me!' she said often whilst crossing herself.

'Why will you send all the youths away?' she asked her young mistress once; she had many a silver coin slipped into her hand by these suitors, and favoured them one and all impartially. 'I suppose you will not spend all your life dusting books and copying papers, and tending on Ser Checchi day and night?'

'I dare say I shall,' replied Beldia tranquilly. 'Do you think that I should have to work, and dust, and write, and sew the less for any one of those young men? They all wish to marry me because they know I am useful.'

'But you are beautiful, too, my dear,' said Veronica. 'And the lads see that, and they would make a queen of you.'

'For a week or two, yes. And then they would want their shirts, and their soup, and their cigarettes, and their absinthe; and I should be the slave. I would rather be my father's slave. He is a tender master.'

'Ser Checchi is good. I never said he was not good,' said Veronica crossly. 'But there is such a thing as pleasure, and such a thing as love; and like goes to like, and youth to youth.'

'Oh!' Beldia laughed a little with the supreme derision of ignorance. 'You know I do not think of these follies, 'Nica, and the youngsters you patronize are not likely to inspire them.'

'What do you wait for?' grumbled the old servant. 'Do you think a god will come down from the skies or a knight out of the tapestry?'

'I wait for Ulysses,' said Beldia gaily.

'Anybody over seas? A stranger?' said Veronica sharply, with sudden suspicion: could her young mistress have an affection unknown to her faithful servant?

'Very far over seas,' replied Beldia. 'Over the far, far seas of death.'

'Pish! Some of your rubbishing history men!' said Veronica, with scorn; to her thinking a living lover, who wore a gold watch, chain, and a ruby ring, and who could take his dama to the Pagliano and the Politeama, was worth all the heroes of Greece and of Rome.

To Beldia, whose mind was filled with the heroic figures of the men of old, from the days of Troy to the days of Montemurlo, the young men of her own generation, with their round hats, their foul cigars, their checked trousers, their cropped pates, their bad manners, seemed rather like apes, corrupted in morals and ill-dressed in person, than beings of the same humanity as Odysseus or Caracciolo, Leonidas or Ferruceio.

Her heart had never been touched to even so much as a passing sentiment by any of these suitors of modern days. She loved her father, she loved her brother, she loved the tower of Taddeo, and these three filled up her heart.

Of all outside worlds, the worlds of great passions and great ambitions, of ceaseless movement and breathless excitement, she knew nothing whatever. She saw, indeed, the equipages rolling by along the river's length, with the young and graceful people in them, to whom, surely, she thought, life must be like one long play-hour. But she knew nothing of these, and they never troubled her. Envy was not in her nature, and her days were full of contentment. The only anxiety which she had was the culpable extravagance of her brother and the harmless extravagance of her father. Neither of these male creatures attached the smallest value to money. It was always Beldia on whom the burden devolved of making ends meet in the household. If everything, indeed, had been in her hands, the task would have been easier; but in many matters Ser Checchi kept his own counsel carefully; she was ignorant of all the resources which he possessed and of many things which he did.

Scarcely was their dinner over this afternoon, and she had peeled for him a Bergamot pear, preserved in straw through the winter, than a knock came at the door of the dining-room, and a pleasant, cheerful voice asked through the keyhole:

'May Vestuccio speak a moment with the honoured master?'

Even as the words were being uttered, the door was softly opened, and the speaker advanced into the room.

He was a man of middle age, and of that indefinable class to which belong working men who have made money; he had a candid, kind, and attractive countenance, his eyes were clear and laughing, and his mouth good-natured, with a quiet smile very familiar to it; his glance was quick, too, and not so frank as was his smile.

Across the calm, thoughtful features of Ser Checchi a shadow of troubled impatience passed. He rose hurriedly, leaving the pear untasted, and passed to the door.

'Not here, not here, Vestuccio,' he said quickly. 'Go to my own room; in a moment I will be with you.'

'Your servant, Ser Checchi,' said the new-comer, pausing a moment in the doorway, whilst his eyes rested on the Casteldurante vase with an expression of inquisitive appreciation.

'Good-morning, Signor Aurelio,' said Beldia courteously; and Aurelio Vestuccio bowed his salutation in return with flattered eagerness and his brightest smile.

Ser Checchi, in a hurried manner, unlike his slow and quiet movements, did not return to his seat, but led his visitor away.

'Oh, father! the pear!' cried Beldia, in dismay at such neglect of her finest fruit.

'Eat it yourself, my love,' said Ser Checchi, as he hastily closed the door behind him.

'The master seems troubled,' said Veronica to her mistress, and Beldia looked at her apprehensively and wistfully.

'No, no; he is always pleased to see Ser Aurelio,' she said, with a trace of anxiety in her glance at the closed doorway. 'I dare say Vestuccio has come to let him know that some manuscript or copy he wishes for is beyond his reach, and that vexes him.'

'Some people speak ill of Vestuccio,' said the servant dubiously.

'Some people speak ill of the saints in heaven,' replied Beldia.

'Ugh! He is no saint,' said Veronica. 'But he has a good name on the Piazza, that I grant.'

A good name on the Piazza means a fair repute amongst your fellows. It is derived from the habit which the Italian citizens had in the past, and still have in the present, of congregating in some public square—generally before the communal palace—to make their bargains and discuss the solvency or insolvency of their debtors. A good name on the Piazza will carry a man far and well in his commercial transactions, as a fair breeze carries a sailing boat.

Aurelio Vestuccio had this good name.

'I hope they will not be away long,' said Beldia; 'for that stranger of this forenoon is returning to see my father and talk about architecture. If you hear anyone coming up the stairs, ask him to wait in the book-room.'

Veronica grumbled inaudibly, and began to clear away the dinner dishes, leaving the Casteldurante pot and the spring-tide flowers sole occupants of the table.

At that moment the bell attached to the entrance door, which opened on the staircase, rang gently. There is a great deal of character shown in ringing a bell, and the temper of the ringer is often disclosed in its tintinnabulations.

'You must go: that is the Brescian student, Veronica,' said Beldia.

'I cannot; you know that, signorina,' said the serving woman crossly. 'Who is to do my work? All the washing up and the ironing? Three o'clock now, and the days getting so short there is hardly room to turn round in them.'

'Go and open the door, and show the stranger in,' said Beldia. 'He can amuse himself amongst the books till my father is free.'

Veronica went, grumbling; she was always reduced to obedience when her young mistress spoke with that tone of decision. Beldia went to her own chamber. It was a little narrow place, with a grated window looking only on the red-brick, moss-grown tiles of the houses at the back of the tower; but it was picturesque and home-like, with a timber ceiling, and some pieces of old tapestry on its walls, and a little stair led up from it to the platform where her air-garden was; and swallows had nested under its cornice for more centuries than could be counted on the fingers of each hand; they were at this moment circling round and round above the house roof, arranging for that autumn flight which caused so much regret every year to Beldia. Even the bats, at the approach of winter, would withdraw themselves into their homes in the belfries, and lofts, and old monastic turrets and cloisters round, and no winged creatures would remain there except the sparrows.

This afternoon she could give little thought to the birds or the flowers; she had received a letter from her brother, which she re-read in the solitude of her chamber, whilst her father was closeted with his visitor Vestuccio. It caused her long and painful thought, for it was one with which it seemed to her wholly impossible to comply.

Cirillo asked for money, money, money, as if money could be gathered off the stonecrop growing on the tiles, or the Madonna's herb flourishing in the crevices of the parapet.

'My dearest child,' he wrote to her, 'I want two thousand francs at once. Get them from the old man for me, and post them as soon as you receive this. If I do not get them I shall be dishonoured in the sight of all my friends. You know, my little angel, what a man's honour means.'

'Yes,' thought Beldia sadly; 'it means to take all he wishes for from others, however he may pain or ruin them!'

The letter was long, the same arguments being again and again repeated in it with ingenuity and eloquence, but with that false ring in them all which comes from insincerity in the writer. The perception of this want of candour jarred on his sister, and hurt her as his clever and heartless impositions had often troubled her in their childhood; her finer moral sense becoming conscious of them, whilst her love and affection turned in vain from them, striving resolutely to be blind.

The plea of honour offended her. It was a note he was too found of sounding. She tried with all her might to believe in the necessity which he pleaded; but she could not. It was a necessity, perhaps, but one of coarser mould than the kind alleged. Well as she loved Cirillo, she knew that he constantly tampered with the exigencies of honour, and wore its yoke but lightly.

It was often difficult for her to make the weekly allowance which her father gave suffice for all their needs, and when each Saturday came round, and she discharged her household accounts, inclusive of the woman's wage, there was no margin left. Besides which, she knew that large sums slipped away in the purchase of those multitudinous books which were for ever increasing: and the demands of her brother were numerous and unsparing upon the family purse. He was an artist of promise, but an extravagant one; and he never denied himself any pleasure for so simple a reason as the mere fact that he had not the money to pay for it.

Cirillo never credited that his father was not rich; he thought the librarian old-fashioned, prejudiced, abstemious, eccentric; but he argued that no man would ever throw away such large sums on musty folios and decaying pamphlets, unless there were plenty of money behind the bookshelves; besides, there was always the land in the Casentino. He had never known any particulars of his father's means; but he always supposed him to be well off, and spoke of him to all his Roman comrades as a rich old fellow with queer, miserly ways; so that he never hesitated to worry and importune his sister to obtain whatever funds he wanted, and he wanted much often.

Many women are not good to men; many women are niggardly, suspicious, foolish, jealous, and unkind in their relations with the men belonging to them; but when they are good to such men they are very good, and Beldia was one of those. Her affection, patience, and comprehension were of infinite duration and elasticity. And she understood, what few young women ever do understand, that the measure which was abundant for herself could not possibly content Cirillo. He was one year older than herself, and she had always been accustomed to obey him without criticism or hesitation; what he wished she never doubted must be accomplished.

She had read and re-read this letter, with pain and perplexity, when the voice of Veronica roused her, shouting up the shaft of the ladder-like staircase.

'Signorina! the master says you are to come down into the library and see this strange gentleman; he himself has business with Vestuccio which will take him a half-hour or more. Come down, do you hear?'

Beldia heard, and obeyed, because it was her habit to obey. She went without even casting a glance at herself in the little old silver-framed mirror which had belonged in the Trecento to some lady of the Brancaleone race, and now served herself. Old men or young, good-looking or ill-favoured, they counted nothing to her; they were merely buyers or sellers of books; or else graceless robbers of her father's erudition.

The Brescian student was waiting in the inner back room; he had changed his clothes; he wore the velvet coat and broad-leaved hat common to artists; his crisp auburn hair and soft silken beard were carefully brushed. He had a look of distinction and grace, and an air which would have better suited the times in which the tower of Taddeo had been built, than these in which the modest and dusty library of Ser Checchi was established in it; it seemed to Beldia difficult to believe that he could be only a poor architect seeking his fortunes, and the doubt made her suspicious of, and cold to, him.

Old races have been too often impoverished and vulgarized, all their features are too often obliterated and stamped down into the common, meaningless, banal modern type, but still in Italy at times one meets the knights of Giorgione in Venice, the youths of Massaccio in Florence, the men and women of Sodoma in Siena, the forms and physiognomies of Signorelli in Orvieto, the children and the virgins of Correggio under the vines of Lombardy; still often there stands beneath a stone archway, or leans over a bridge parapet, or comes across a marble pavement, a figure which seems to have stepped down from the heroic pageants emblazoned on the storied walls, or to be the statue of the Discobolus or of the Faun, animated, and breathing once more the sunny air in which they were begotten.

The blood of Lombard nobles ran quick and warm in the veins of this artist, who owned nothing in the world except a little old house under the shadow of the Broletto where he had been born, the only relic left of what had once been a wide and princely heritage; and though he was but a poor wanderer who had to push his own way to fortune with his pencil and compasses, if ever he reached it at all, he had the carriage of a knight and the head of a troubadour.

He now saluted Beldia gravely, apologizing for his too early arrival.

'Nay, you are very punctual. It is my father who is engaged at the hour I named to you,' she answered, not well pleased to be forced to attend to him. 'He will be here, I think, before very long; meantime, what works can I show you?'

He gave some names at random, but they were of authors too recent to be found in the Ardiglione collection; then, though he could ill afford to do so, he purchased some odd volumes of Giuseppe Vasi and some sheets of plans by Baldassare Peruzzi.

He felt ashamed to come here again and trouble this stately maiden for nothing, and again go away with empty hands. He leaned over the counters strewn with old books and old pamplets of all kinds, and did his best to draw her on from architectural subjects into general conversation; but she was reserved by habit and from a secluded life, seldom going farther off her own doorstep than the church close by in the Piazza, and was so accustomed to treat the younger visitors who came thither with formality, that he did not make much progress with

her until he spoke of the tower in which she dwelt. Then her eyes lightened, her lips smiled, her voice became full of feeling. She answered readily as to its architect, its age, its traditions; she told him the history of its building; she grew eloquent over the legends attached to its loves and garlands, and the tale of the plague, which was associated with its shrine of the Madonna. She never tired of talking of her home, and of all it had seen and heard and known, and in him she found an eager listener, ready to share her enthusiasm and veneration for its dark and massive stones. In turn he told her of Brescia and Bergamo, and of his own little house there, once the mere loggia to the great palace owned by the Fontana family. Its arches had been filled in towards the beginning of the eighteenth century, and its columns had then been roofed, and its once stately frescoed beauty changed into a humble dwelling-house such as it was still, and in which his mother now lived, a widow, all alone, pious, gentle, and cheerful, thinking ever of his graceless self in many sleepless nights and useless prayers.

He had succeeded in interesting his companion, when Ser Checchi at last appeared; a shadow on his calm features as of worried moments lately passed, but ready to enter into any subjects, classical or mediæval, which it might please his customer to suggest. It is at once the joy and the peril of scholars, like artists, that their mundane and prosaic interests are immediately laid aside and forgotten, if the impersonal topics which attract them are mooted in their presence. To them the abstract far outweighs and eclipses the practical; and to the scholar's, as to the artist's, mind, the impersonal is so infinitely greater than the personal that the claims of the latter are cast aside for the charms of the former, without a moment's hesitation or contrition. Whatever the business was on which Vestuccio had come to the old librarian, its vexatious recollections were now put aside and forgotten the moment that the new-comer questioned him as to the place of burial of Il Magnifico, a disputed point amongst Tuscan scholars.

They conversed long and cordially, with that satisfaction which comes from mutual tastes and opinions, whilst Beldia listened, working at a piece of sewing which she kept in a drawer under the desk, to fill up her idle moments in the book-room.

She perceived reluctantly, but clearly, the use which many unscrupulous visitors made so frequently of her father; the avidity with which they drove the sharp pickaxe of their minor intelligence into the gold-mine of his long-amassed knowledge, and took thence all they needed to make their paltry storehouse rich.

He, in the single-hearted devotion of the humanist, out of the generous abundance of the enthusiast, delighted to aid, to encourage, to enlighten, to assist all who came to him; was blind to all the petty larcenies by which he was robbed of information and experience, of authority and data, while the gems stolen from his store were set up in the caps of these beardless knaves, without acknowledgment or thanks.

Many an article in newspaper and review was brilliant with the borrowed learning which he had unconsciously supplied to some young scribbler of the public press, and more than one ambitious aspirant to public life had forced himself into notice in high quarters by the antiquarian and philological investigations opened out by the elder scholar, which had been innocently shown and liberally lent to him.

The old man in his book-room, with the sun-rays from the window, or the lamp from the table, shed on his benign and noble countenance, felt like Erasmus or Boethius amongst the pupils of a golden time, as these young men pressed around him, plying him with questions, listening to his suggestions, putting down his dates and judgments with their pencils. He was touched, flattered, mollified, and thought that those of his contemporaries who complained of the rudeness and indifference and cynicism of the younger generation did it wrong.

But Beldia, sitting apart, silent, over her ledgers or her linen, saw what he did not see, overheard what he did not hear, and understood the motives with which these callous and scornful youngsters affected so much deference to age and so much desire of instruction.

There was one amongst them in especial whom she distrusted and detested. He was a young lawyer, by name Pampilio Querci; he was clever, cunning, and of an ambition reaching far beyond the desk and stool of an attorney's office; he had mental power, and had education enough to be able to estimate and admire the vast accumulation of Ser Checchi's learning; and he had skill enough to send his own little bucket of a mind deep down again and again into the profound wells of the librarian's intellect, and to draw up the waters of knowledge, which he knew how to pour forth again thinly and carefully, as if brought from his own especial springs.

Again and again could Beldia recognise her father's erudition, so generously and imprudently displayed, retailed by this young man in the public press, without acknowledgment of or allusion to its giver, in papers signed 'Lex et Lux,' which was the press-name of Pampilio Querci. Once or twice she had pointed out these articles to her father; but he, in whose character there were mingled simplicity and vanity, had waived them aside impatiently.

'If the youngster can find pleasure in these abstruse questions, it is well, it is laudable,' he answered to her; 'let us not check his zeal, my daughter. After all, the fount of learning is open to high and low, to old and young. Let who will drink thereof. God forbid that I should send such away thirsty.'

And Beldia felt with a pang how noble he was, and how foolish; how liberal and how unwise. He set open his jar of honey from Mount Parnassus, and let these flies and wasps come round and upon it, and they sucked their fill, and stung him as their only thanks.

But she could do nothing to make him perceive and believe this, and the antiquarian and philological articles continued to be compiled and printed, signed 'Lex et Lux,' until they attracted the attention of the Minister of Education, who said to the Prefect of Florence that the young writer of them must be a brilliant scholar, and had better be looked after and secured to the interest of the Government with some good official place, lest he should be taken away by the clericals, for whom he seemed to have a leaning, Querci knowing well how to run with the hare and hunt with the hounds.

Beldia, who saw his drift, and guessed the reward he tried to obtain, was impatient of the sight of the lean, small, spruce figure, and the pale, aquiline, demure profile of the young attorney, and begrudged all the hours which her father wasted on him, all the volumes he borrowed for an indefinite time, and often forgot to return, and all the information which he angled for so dexterously and absorbed so ravenously.

Therefore she looked now with prejudice and ill-favour upon the entry of the Brescian architect, seeing in him only another of his younger generation which used and abused her father's good-nature. To allow students to transcribe from and consult manuscripts and folios in the book-room was not the way to sell books and make money by them; this the sober and practical side of her temperament told her, and a volume or a pamphlet was indeed hardly ever sold out of the thousands filling the shelves and cumbering the floors. It pleased Ser Checchi that this should be so, to see any work go away in the hands of a stranger was always painful to him; if it were a rare and valuable work, to sell it was to him like selling a child in bondage. There were hundreds of books in his tower which he had purchased in the days of his youth, and that they should remain there all these years was delightful to him. But they did not fill his purse by remaining there, and the additional purchases which he was continually adding to them drained it.

'Another young man to read, and smile, and listen, and go away laden with borrowed learning, which he will sell to editors and publishers,' thought Beldia, glancing impatiently at the auburn head of the Lombard stranger. But she could not refuse to admit that the newcomer had a different physiognomy to the bloodless face of Pampilio Querci, and he left off his studies to choose some plates of Palladio's plans, which he again paid for, honestly, and at once, without trying to obtain an abatement in their price.

He was of a manlier, finer, bolder type than the undersized young scribes and quill-drivers who came thither to suck the brain of her father. There was something daring, chivalrous, candid, and adventurous in his person and features and manners, before which her suspicions and antipathies melted away despite herself.

He asked frankly if he might return there.

'You have so many volumes of architectural and mechanical drawings,' he added, 'I may find so much here that I have sought for vainly in my native town. But I am well aware that it is most unfair to expect to use a private bookseller's collection as though it were a public library, to be studied in at pleasure.'

Before she could reply, Ser Checchi intervened with his benignant smile and his grave nod of the head.

'That is a very honest and thoughtful scruple,

young sir,' he answered. 'But it is a needless scruple here. I am delighted if you or anyone can find any profit in what I am fortunate enough to have gathered about me. My poor place is wholly at your service at any hour of the day.'

Beldia reddened with vexation. There were already so many of these idlers and thieves, who choked up what little space there was left free in the book-rooms, and wasted her time, and the boy's, and her father's. But at least those frequenters of the place were townsfolk, youths and old men well known from their birth up in their native streets; it seemed natural, it might be only proper, to afford them what advantages were to be secured there; but this was a stranger, a foreigner, a Lombard. There could be no need or obligation to open wide house and heart to him like this.

But Ser Checchi took no heed of her imploring glances, nor of the restraining touch with which she gently pulled the skirt of his long coat. He reiterated his invitation to come and study, and the Brescian accepted it with cordiality and gratitude; and as the latter at last left the library, carrying his Palladian engravings with him, the old man looked after his tall figure approvingly.

'A well-made and well-mannered youth,' he said with satisfaction. 'They grow fine manhood in the north. Child, did you mark how eager he was concerning the Domenican Fathers as printers at Rifredi? Let him come; let him come; if there be anything here which can profit him, he is heartily welcome to it.'

Beldia sighed.

She had heard those generous words spoken so many times, and she had never known any gratitude shown for them from those for whose benefit they were spoken.

'An accomplished man and a modest one,' added Ser Checchi, turning over the volumes used by his visitor; 'I shall be glad to afford him any possible opportunities for study that he may be able to find here. Mind that you make him welcome in my absence, Beldia, and let him search for all the dates and authorities which he may wish to find.'

'Certainly, father,' she answered, a little unwillingly. 'But no one will ever buy books if you allow all your visitors to come and glean all they want here without paying for the privilege.'

'What a speech for my daughter to make!' cried Ser Checchi, displeased and scandalized. 'Let the State be vile enough to put a tax on art and learning, as it does at its libraries and galleries, I will never grudge the free use of my book-shelves to any serious scholar.'

'But they will not buy if they can turn over a hundred volumes for nothing.'

'Perhaps they cannot buy. Perhaps they are honest and earnest lovers of learning who are very scantily supplied with this world's goods. Shall I grudge them a ray from my poor lantern on their path to help their search? Shall I refuse them a crust from my cupboard, when they are honestly hungering for the truth? Fie, fie! for shame, my child! You have not lived amongst the eloquence of the dead to hide such sordid thoughts within your breast? Surely, surely not, Beldia?'

She was silent.

She was too docile to contradict her father, and too generous not to appreciate his generosity; but she knew what all these volumes cost, and she knew what rent and taxes cost, and she knew that the library of the tower was kept open year after year at a dead loss.

She knew, also, enough of commerce to know that trade cannot be carried on successfully on such romantic principles as her father's But he, vaguely sensible of the disagreement implied by her silence, waxed warmer and warmer on the theme.

'Who knows but that some one of these youths may not be on the highway to immortality, though he look to our purblind eyes but a needy idler?' he said vehemently. 'Was not Cervantes poor? was not Tasso deemed a madman? was not Giotto a shepherd on the hills? was not Camoens sold for a slave? Has not Genius been impoverished, and starved, and persecuted in every age of the world? If we help these stumbling feet on to even the lowest rung of the ladder of renown—nay, if we do what is better still, happier still, help to confirm the bias of a youth to the choice of the arts of peace and of light, instead of the pursuits of gain or the lust of war—is it not some little good done for the Muses, as they were used to say, for Humanity as men say now? Ah! my dear, surely, surely, in learning, yet more than in life, what is done to the least of these is as if it were done to Deity itself.'

Beldia's eyes grew soft and suffused as they dwelt on her father's face, which was lighted up with the radiance of a high and impersonal passion. Her heart ached at this noble and guileless enthusiasm. She knew how men traded on it to their own base profit. She knew that it was not genius, but cunning, which came there to glean the gold of his knowledge and kindness; that it was not the ingenious youth of a Platonic Academy which sought his counsels and teachings, but the keen, sharp, narrow wits of modern youngsters pilfering to prosper. She knew how his ideas were stolen, his culture was borrowed, his library shelves were ransacked by the journalists, writers, professors, attorneys, and the like, who came to him to carry off a harvest of quotation and knowledge which they would have been incapable of gleaning for themselves.

She knew this well; it was why she received all younger men so coldly, and only smiled on the aged scholars.

But how was she to say this to him? How damp that good faith, and lower that exaltation which had carried on into old age the beautiful ignorance and confidence of youth?

CHAPTER IV.

SHE turned the subject by an allusion to Vestuccio.

'Did Messer Aurelio vex you to-day, father?' she asked him. 'I thought you looked disturbed at his arrival. Was his business so very urgent that he need have come at dinner-time?'

Her father's face clouded.

'Vestuccio came about a financial matter,' he said evasively. 'He is a careful man. It always vexes me to lay aside study for practical matters. Business is Martha, and study is Mary. I have dwelt with Mary all my days, and walked with her in green and shady places; I am ill fitted for the noise and clatter, however useful and well meant, which her ruder sister makes about her work.'

'Could not I see to this matter, whatever it is, for you?' asked Beldia wistfully.

'Certainly not,' said her father peremptorily. 'Buy your marketings, my love, and your linen, and your sugar and spice, but leave graver business to me. You are Mary and Martha in one person, I know, but that is not a reason for overstepping your duties. Attend to your daisy-roots on the roof, and your pigeons, and sweet herbs, and do not offer me counsel until I ask for it.'

'I did not mean any forwardness or officiousness,' she murmured, distressed and ashamed at his reproof.

'No, no; you meant nothing but what was right,' he said kindly. 'You are only too anxious to spare me trouble, I know. Women should confine themselves to household cares. Now go to your room, or out-of-doors, if you will. I will attend to the library this afternoon, and I am expecting Don Gervasio and Massimo. We are in doubt still if we have read aright that passage in Avicenna. It is very obscure.'

Don Gervasio was a priest, the vicar of a small church near, and Massimo was the baptismal name of an aged teacher of Greek and Arabic, who was the bosom friend of Ser Checchi. With these two cronies he spent the happiest hours of every year, re-reading disputed passages, questioning received readings, searching obscure authorities, and familiarizing themselves with the forgotten authors whose bones were dust.

Beldia retired, as he bade her do; but not to work or to amuse herself. She had all the household needs upon her head and hands, all those daily and small labours which go together to make up the guidance of a house, and upon the discharge of which, well or ill done, depends the comfort or discomfort of that house.

Men rarely understand the labour which this involves, and have neither compassion nor gratitude for the efforts which surround them with creature-comforts and create around them a serene domestic atmosphere. Like other men, Ser Checchi believed that his house ordered itself, and thought of his daughter's life as of one long holiday of perfect and continual ease.

He never dreamed of the constant supervision by which the naturally noisy and careless servant was kept quiet and made careful, the constant attention by which the dusky old chambers were kept fresh and sweet, the constant economy by which the best possible was obtained and the least possible spent, and the constant industry with which linen was repaired, conserves were made, accounts were kept, and stores were husbanded. Beldia knew that the means of her father were not large, and that his habits were costly from liberality of temper, and the absence of mind of a man whose thoughts were with the dead rather than with his butcher, and his baker and his tallow-chandler. Keeping the accounts, indeed, as she did, she saw that the commerce of the library was almost at a standstill—that few buyers ever came thither, and that the purchases of books were a hundred times in excess of the demand for them But as the books of which she saw the entry were all bought cheaply at sales, and those more costly purchases were unexplained to her, the real price paid for such additions remained unknown to her, and the outlay which the library caused was, as far as she knew, to be placed at a low figure. She thought it rather her father's hobby than his trade, and was not as uneasy as she would have been had she known the true price of the beautiful and ancient copies which were being every now and then added to the already overflowing sea of literature which surrounded her. The love of books was such a holy and noble passion, that it seemed to her impossible any harm should ever come out of it.

Yet she could not but perceive that her father was often preoccupied, often troubled, and received visits and letters which caused him perplexities of which he explained nothing to her; he did not even permit her to allude to them. And Vestuccio—she did not understand them, but she was afraid of his relations with Vestuccio.

The prosperous citizen who bore this name had been born of poor parents, rope-makers and sail-menders at a dirty but romantic village nestled under a cliff near a large seaport on the Italian Riviera. He had run about half naked in the sun and sand and surf, and grown strong and healthy on his diet of fish and rye-bread. He had made friends with the skippers of brigs at the port near, and they had given him odds and ends of foreign trifles, which he sold about the streets with such pretty shells and seaweed, or bits of agate and cornelian, as he had picked up along the shore. He was a clever, agile, merry child, with an engaging smile and bright blue eyes; and people bought of him because he asked them so nicely, his white teeth shining, his brown curls blowing, and his tray slung in front of his little bare chest.

Most boys would have either spent the pence thus gained on food and drink, or carried them home to their mothers. He did neither; he saved them up and put them by, and, when he had enough to do so, lent out little sums to his companions, or to the fishermen and mariners, and did it so well that he multiplied his pence very quickly, and yet, strange to say, never made an enemy, and none grudged him his gains.

Little by little the pence and the francs swelled, till they became a goodly sum, and Aurelio, now become a youth of eighteen, opened a little shop in the seaport town—a little den under an arch—where coral and shells and such cheap bits of Oriental finery as he could buy, half damaged, off the quays, were put together in the darkness; and he himself sat or stood, ever smiling, behind the board which served him as a counter.

To buy something of 'Rello, as he was called, became the fashion with the seafaring folks and their sweethearts; and many of the sailors brought him pretty outlandish articles, ivories, and parrots and ostrich feathers, and little jade idols, in exchange for the good tobacco and brandy which he smuggled in for them undetected; and at his little cabin the seafaring men, native and foreign, met the buxom, blowsy women of their hearts, and he could turn an honest penny by helping on such amorous intercourse.

After a few years of this small trading he had realized enough to leave the sea-town, with its disreputable associations, and quietly and sagaciously he established himself in Florence, in a very modest manner, as a seller of curios and foreign trifles; his old comrades, the sailors, still often put him in the way of bargains from the East and West, and he was always cordial and unassuming, and content with a moderate percentage on what he sold.

It was a humble little dusky corner, hardly bigger than a dog-kennel, but in it were sometimes found really good and strange things, and before many more years had passed over his head he was able to move from this obscure dwelling, to a large although unpretending shop in the Piazza della Madonna, over the door of which he had painted in bold lettering, ' Aurelio Vestuccio, Antiquario,' where, in a little office in a back-court, under a plane-tree, he did much business, beside his ostensible traffic in majolica and bronzes and old furniture. His career was made.

'All gained by hard work and honest dealing,' he said, with a glow of pride and self-respect. He had married the daughter of a tallow-chandler with a round little dowry of her own, and had put out her little fortune in his business with the same prudence and sagacity with which, as a child, he had sold shell and seaweed. He had always a pleasant, good-humoured, clean-shaved face, and was always willing to do anyone a good turn. He had become popular and respected in the town; and, from the dilettante who wanted a piece of old stamped leather, to the embarrassed tradesman who wanted a loan of twenty pounds, everyone who required something quickly found out and cheerfully arranged for, went to the little office under the plane-tree, where Aurelio Vestuccio was to be seen from nine till four.

He was a model of what industry and thrift can make of a man by the time he is forty, though all the circumstances of his early life had been against him, and he had had no advantages except his shrewd and cautious mind and his pleasant and politic manner. Many half-naked boys sell shells and seaweed on many shores; but to few of them is it given to be born with a brain as quick as mercury, a clever tongue which can chatter constantly yet reveal nothing, and a heart as hard as a nether millstone. This last possession was the most useful of all his many gifts from nature, but it would have availed nothing without the ever-watching, and ever-bright, intelligence behind it.

Many people have hard hearts, but not many have long heads: he had both, and he had also a most admirable cordiality and simplicity of manner which stood him in good stead. Then, he was known to be a good father and husband; and on Sunday, at noon, might be seen listening to the military music in the Piazza of San Marco, or in the Piazzone of the Cascine, with a tribe of nice-looking and neatly-clad children about him, hostages and warrants of his many civic virtues.

Ser Checchi had known and helped him from the earliest years of his establishment in his first modest little shop; and Vestuccio had ingratiated himself with the old scholar by putting in his way many an old pamphlet or volume which had come under his hand in his various expeditions to far-off villages or castles in the mountains north and south in search of curiosities.

Some seven years before the arrival of the Lombard student in the city, an incident had occurred which had brought the bric-à-brac seller and the librarian in closer commerce and communication.

Ser Checchi, when at Antella, was much given to roaming over the hills and valleys of the Casentino in the summer season in search of old books, such as lie forgotten and neglected in many a sacristy cupboard where the good priest is more learned in village news and wine diseases than in the value of Horæ and Evangeliarium. Though he walked apparently with feebleness, because his shoulders were bowed and his gait was slow, he could cover many a mile without fatigue, with no steed except his ebony-handled stick, and no companion except the white dog Folko, who always went into the country when his master did.

In one of these country rambles he grew thirsty, and paused to ask for a draught of water at the forge of a blacksmith called Io. The forge was high up in the hills, and the anvil and hammer had little work to do, but the smith was also in a small way a landowner and farmer, having inherited part and bought part, of the arable land and of the pine-wood around and about his smithy. Io was a well-known man in the district, by name Iorio Lencioni, and was a familiar acquaintance of Ser Checchi's, whom he now welcomed with delight, and for whom he insisted on opening a flask of old Chianti, which his visitor, sorely to his distress, insisted for his part on mixing with spring water.

It was three o'clock, and the June day was hot. Ser Checchi was tired, for he had strolled more miles than he had counted along the fragrant hillside, where nightingales sang under the bay thickets and the yellow gorse was blossoming and the wild rose.

'You are fatigued, sir; rest for an hour or two,' said the blacksmith, a big, good-tempered, middle-aged man, with his reaping-hook in his hand and his shirt-sleeves rolled up to his shoulder.

'Thanks to you, I will do so,' said Ser Checchi; 'at least, if you will promise me to go back to your field-work, for your corn is over-ripe, and I fear me that there is rain in the air for this evening, and your grain is not half cut.'

'Sit and rest, then, and we will go and finish cutting the corner field,' said Iorio to him; 'and, by the way, Ser Checchi, there is an old chest which you may like to look over—there are papers and suchlike in it. I found it under a heap of old hay in the loft. It has been there, I be bound, as many years as the house is old. We hoped there was something good in it; but there was nothing but an odd lot of books, so we threw them back again, being spited not to have laid our hand heartily on something better. You are welcome to it if there be any paper or book as may please you; they are only a pack of rubbish, I fear—copybooks and ciphering-books and the like; but if you care to look over them the house is yours, and we will get, by your leave, to our reaping.'

Ser Checchi thanked him and looked longingly towards a dusty, worm-eaten old wooden chest of solid nutwood, with a coat-of-arms carved heavily on its lid, and with rusty iron handles.

Old books!—the sound of the word was as sweet to him as the promise of bridal gifts to a maiden, or winter toys to a child by the fireside. They might most probably be of no value, but old volumes were always of interest, were they only records of household expenditure or of clerkly memoranda.

A few minutes later the whole family trooped out through the open doorway to go to finish their reaping, even the small children clinging to the women's skirts and eager to be taken to the field, to lie and sleep amongst the warm wheat whilst the sickles of their elders were at work. Ser Checchi and Folko were left alone in the blacksmith's kitchen, with the sunshine streaming in through the green tracery of the window and the old clock drowsily ticking the minutes in a corner.

Ser Checchi slumbered a little while in the heat and the stillness and the fragrant hill air, the dog outstretched at his feet. Then he shook himself awake, drank a little more of the watered wine, and stooped over the chest, which the smith had considerately drawn close to the window for his easier inspection. There were quantities of yellow documents written in crabbed characters—household and farm books for the most part, belonging to the seventeenth century, records of the credit and debit of the large estate of which the house and lands now owned by Iorio had formed a portion. They were large books, massive, heavy, covering the expenditure of well-nigh a century. Ser Checchi, with fatigue, lifted them up one after the other over the tall sides of the chest. They interested him, like everything which belonged to a past age and had been written by dead hands, but to examine them thoroughly would take days and weeks, and he had many similar ones at home. Beneath all these ancient folios were, however, a few bound volumes lying under numbers of loose pages and deeds, which all appeared to have reference to what had once been the great estate of a great family now extinct.

He took these volumes out and brushed from them tenderly the dust, the dirt, and the seeds of hay with which they were covered. They were all books of the same date, the seventeenth century, to which the ledgers and household books belonged; there were prayer-books, lives of saints, copies of ecclesiastical works, in all some dozen volumes, none of any rarity or especial mark, none of any uncommon binding or unusual typography. But one volume much longer and larger than the others, with a binding of another epoch, caught his instructed eyes where it lay in a corner of the desk, more than half hidden under the loose and dusty hayseed.

His hands trembled as he drew it forth. His sight swam as he opened its pages. His hands shook, his whole person quivered, his eyes were full of longing and light; they were the eyes of a man of twenty years old.

Learned in such things as he was, he knew its antiquity and its value at a glance. To find such a treasure mouldering neglected in a dusty chest in a cottage had been the dream of his whole life. Indignation, amaze, awe, delight, all held him breathless and entranced before the worm-eaten bench on which it lay. Oh, how happy the scribe who had penned it, though long ago his hand had crumbled to ashes!

The sun poured in through the strings of flowering beans which were running up the window, and the gentle air blew the yellow dry leaves to and fro irreverently. He remained on his knees before the manuscript, gazing with a lover's ardour and a devotee's devotion at the marvellous fine regular lines of the penman, the serried ranks of this black letter, in which not a blot, nor a deviation, nor an erasure was visible. Oh, the marvel of it! Look what the handwriting of men had become since the days of printing! Who wrote now what would be clear and beautiful for ever as this was? What would the sprawled, careless, hurried, blotted caligraphy of the present age tell men, as this work told them, of the beauty and holiness of ardour, of perseverance, and of labour, where the hand was but the instrument of the soul?

It was a Codex of the 'Divina Commedia,' dated under the colophon as finished at Ravenna in May, 1320.

There are but few such in the world, and those few are numbered and known to all bibliophiles, like the folios of Shakespeare. To have discovered one other was to a lover and student of books what the discovery of a new world was to navigators of old—an ecstasy, an hononr, a miracle, an intoxication of happiness.

He examined the parchment, the capitals, the writing, the headpiece, the colophon, the binding, which was of leather much eaten and gnawed by mice, with some unpolished cornelians, cut and mounted on silver, on its clasps; he scarcely breathed as he bent over it, whilst the full sun fell warm and golden on to these pages, which had once, like enough, been touched and seen by Dante's self. There could be no question of its age and its authenticity; indeed, the finding of it in such a place was proof enough of these. How many other treasures there are, doubtless, lying unknown in attic and cellar, in granary and wood-house in remote country places, where even the tireless feet of the collector and the dealer never wander, and the wand of the modern Hermes of the book-mart is unknown!

The binding was of a much later date, and the folio had been probably laid away by some scholar, when the blast of trumpet or the smoke of torches had told of the tide of war rolling up towards that calm hillside, and there it had remained in its obscurity ever since, visited only by the mice, who had nibbled its edges and peeled its leather here and there.

For the first time in all his pure and upright life, a great temptation to an act of dishonour, of dishonesty, assailed him as he knelt there before it. No one knew that it was there; no one around him even beholding it would see in it anything more than an old book, quite worthless, only fit, perhaps, to be torn up to kindle a fire or to stop a leak in a cask. Nothing could be simpler, nothing more easy, than to put it in his pocket or take it away under his arm. No one on that hillside would ever know or care. Unless his learning enlightened their ignorance, no one of the people around him would ever dream that this old brown volume, moth-eaten and mice-gnawed, would be worth its weight in gold to the libraries of great cities and great men. There was not a soul near, not even in sight; all the family were out in the fields; there was not even a child asleep in the cradle, nor a dog, save his own by the threshold. He had only to walk out of the open doorway along the grass paths of the hillside towards his own home, and carry the precious manuscript with him.

Never was any temptation made more easy and more alluring to an innocent soul!

He bent over the Codex, his hands pressed around it lovingly as a woman's hands round the body of her child; his was no cold appetite of a dryasdust, but a passion infinitely tender, and yearning, and even romantic; beside all that old books said to him as a scholar, they awoke his affections and his imaginations; to hold thus, what likely enough

Dante once had held, thrilled him to his utmost soul; he could never see a volume which had weathered centuries, a manuscript which had been written in other ages, without a strong emotion as of tears.

He would have given half the few years remaining to him to have had this one in his own possession, safe locked under his own keys; and to so possess it he had nothing to do but to put it under his arm and walk quietly away down the hillside; no one would ever have known. '

It was so intense a temptation that the dew stood on his temples, and the blue veins swelled in his throat, as he knelt there, his hands about the old dark rusty cover of it. There it had lain so long, and no eyes but his could have recognised it for what it was. It was his own by all right of affinity, all title of sympathy. What was it to those who owned it?

He stayed there gazing on it so long that his limbs grew cramped and stagnated, and he lost all sense of nerve and pulse whilst the sun sank down out of sight behind the mountain afar off in the west.

The sound of voices laughing and talking and singing came to his ear as the reapers approached from the fields. Then he arose slowly, for his knees were stiff and bruised by the bricks on which he had so long knelt.

He took the volume in his hand, and crossed the kitchen, and met the peasants at the threshold.

'My friend! my friend!' he said to the blacksmith. 'Here is a treasure I have found for you in that which you thought was a mere heap of rubbish.

This volume is worth its weight in gold, if it be truly that which I think. To-morrow we will go together into the city and have it fully appraised.'

Iorio drew near with startled round eyes, alight with joy and covetousness, and the women with him pressed close also in excitement and wonder, expecting to see some vessels of gold and silver or some jewelled pyx or cross.

'An old book! a leather book!' said the smith's wife with derision and disappointment. 'You are joking, Ser Checchi! You are so fond of books that your head gets turned about them. Any rubbish bewitches you.'

'You mistake,' said Ser Checchi almost harshly, for his temptation to say otherwise was almost greater than his strength. 'Take my word on a matter of which you are yourself utterly ignorant. This book is so old, and of such a nature, that it is extremely valuable. Keep it carefully all the night, and to-morrow I will take you to those in the town who will confirm what I say. You will learn from them precisely its worth. Only, good man,' he added, as he clasped the volume in both hands and gazed at it with swimming, reverent eyes, 'if that value be what I can pay you, you will let me become the purchaser of it at its due price, will you not?'

The smith, brawny, bare-legged, bare-armed, sunburnt till he was almost black, stared sheepishly at the volume, which to him looked worth no more than, nay, not half as much as, a clod of good brown earth. The other men, with the women and children, were all gaping with wide-open mouths, and nudging one another, and whispering that it was commonly said that the good Ser Checchi was in his dotage on certain matters.

'You will find what I say is true,' said the old man abruptly; 'and—and—you will give me the preference over other buyers, if the price come within my means?'

'About what might be the price?' asked Iorio in a shamefaced, awed tone, the avarice of the Tuscan peasant beginning to stir in him at the idea of a possible gain.

'That I would rather not say, since I intend to be, if possible, a buyer,' replied Ser Checchi a little austerely, for what he had done had cost him a sharp effort, and he suffered at the idea of this precious treasure-trove going away from his own hands, even for this one short summer night.

'Keep it as the apple of your eye,' he said to the smith, and reluctantly relinquished it to the dirty rough hand outstretched to take it.

'Lord! It's been in that chest, I will be bound, for hundreds and hundreds of years,' said the smith, staring confusedly down on this dingy, mouse-nibbled, leathern folio, of which such wonders were told him.

'I will meet you at the foot of the hill at day-break,' said Ser Checchi, hastily averting his eyes from the sight of the volume in those ignorant and impious hands.

Then he turned his back on them and went down the steep grass path under the olive boughs, through the sheaves of wheat.

'"Lead us not into temptation,"' he thought. 'Who has not need to say that?'

All the night he could not sleep for the memory of the manuscript confided to the stupid care of a peasant ignorant and contemptuous of its value, and it made him restless and ashamed to feel how nearly, how closely, the temptation to secrecy had assailed him.

'We are wretched creatures, and can find fair sophisms to cover all our evil-doing,' he thought sadly as he lay wide awake looking at the clouds sweeping slowly past his moonlit casement, and hearing the prolonged and harmonious call of the scops owl through the shadows.

In the morning he kept his word, and went down with the blacksmith into the city, Iorio wholly incredulous, but carrying with him, wrapped in a bit of cotton stuff which his wife had given him, the dingy volume which in his soul he utterly depised.

After long and careful examination the book was pronounced by those most competent to judge on such matters to be undoubtedly one of the very earliest copies of the great poem extant, worth many thousand francs in private sale, likely to be sold for its weight in gold in an auction-room.

The smith was stupefied. That a common old book, all nibbled and dog-eared as it looked, should be likely to realize such a vast sum of money seemed to turn the very world topsy-turvy to him.

'Sure the wisest men are the biggest fools,' he said to his wife, who had come with him to see that he should not be cheated. 'An old black book all in gnawed leather! Could any soul in his senses care for it?'

'Well, they do, and it's no business of yours to

put them out of grace with it,' said his helpmeet. 'Take time by the forelock, and the cat when she jumps.'

'But Ser Checchi might have kept it to himself, and we been none the wiser!'

'Ay, ay,' said his wife. 'The good man always was three parts daft, or he'd have kept his tongue behind his teeth.'

'Iorio,' said Ser Checchi at that moment, 'you see what I said is true. You have heard from sound judges the value of your volume. Now, what will you do with it? Will you offer it to the State, or will you let me have it, or will you wait your chance to meet with some great fancier and collector of these things?'

He spoke quietly, but his hands shook as they had done when he had first touched the precious manuscript, and his eyes dwelt longingly on it where it lay wrapped in the piece of flowered cotton.

'Why, Ser Checchi, sure the volume is half yours already, for you found it,' began Iorio, who was a simple and amiable man, but he was checked suddenly by his wife, who said quickly:

'Of course, sir, we would sooner sell it to you than to any mortal creature, so crazy fond of these things as you are, and no offence meant; but we are very poor people, as your honour knows, and with nine children and times so bad and taxes what they are, we cannot follow just the first wish of our hearts, sir, and the book these gentlemen seem to say is worth ten times its weight in gold and more.'

'Nay, nay—not so much as that,' murmured Iorio.

Ser Checchi was very pale. He saw that the folio was slipping from his hands. His stanch rectitude forced him to admit the truth of what the woman had said.

'You may realize a fancy price by it, certainly,' he answered; 'but to make one of those sensational prices you must wait the propitious season, and find the willing purchaser. If you like to sell it to me for the small sum which the public libraries here would give you, I will buy it at that. If you prefer to take your chance, you must wait till you find your rich amateur. But amateurs do not come up in your hills. You will have to trust to some dealer to find you one, and you may trust unwisely.'

Iorio opened his mouth to speak, but his wife spoke before him.

'Quite so, sir, we can see that,' she said, taking up the volume in its flowered wrapper. 'But a waiting race is always a safe race to ride. We will wait about this rare book. It lay long years enough in the old walnut chest, and it can go back there, and no harm done. I will clean up the red stones on it a bit, and we will ponder well what is best to be done. I saw Vestuccio just now, and he spoke of our sending it to Paris. But there's time enough for Paris, say I.'

'You have shown it to Vestuccio?' asked Ser Checchi, with anxious lines on his brow, his eyes resting longingly on the treasure where it lay in the woman's stout arms.

' He had heard of it somehow already,' replied the smith with some confusion, 'and asked to be allowed to look at it. " Ser Checchi would give you a barrowload of gold plate for it," says he; but you know, sir, he always has a merry way. One never knows if he be in joke or in earnest.'

'I have no gold plate to give, nor silver,' said Ser Checchi sadly. 'Truly, to those who honour the things of the spirit the volume were worth more than many tons' weight of either.'

He murmured the last words rather to himself than to the man and woman. His heart was heavy. He had dealt by them with all candour, loyalty, and honour. He had hoped that they would show some sensibility of what he had done. He offered the fair library price; it seemed to him hard that they would not give it him for that, when but for him they would never have known that it was theirs at all.

'Good-day,' he said to them with a swelling heart, and turned away. He was proud, and he was, like all sensitive people, quickly rebuffed.

Their colloquy had taken place in the piazza of San Lorenzo, in front of the warehouse where there are sold terra-cotta images, and flower-pots, and lemon-vases. The cart waited for the smith and his wife, with the patient horse in the dusty shafts dropping his nose over his bag of chaff and shaking his worsted tassels. Ser Checchi went on towards the Canto di' Nelli with slow steps and head hung down. He longed inexpressibly for the Dante, with that love of the bibliophile which has in it all the tenderness of a lover, all the eagerness of a child, all the devotion of a slave, all the hunger of a miser. He had found it, he had aroused it from its slumber beneath the dust of centuries, and restored it to the light of earth, and yet he could have no share in it. A peasant who could not tell what its initial letters meant, could bear it away from him held in her stout stubborn arms, and covered with her unlovely cotton-chintz. He did not repent him of his honesty, because he was an integrally honest man. But he felt, what honest men feel sadly, often, that honesty costs very dear.

'It's cruel to take it from him, when he loves the senseless old parcel so, God knows why,' whispered Iorio, with an uneasy sense that there must be something uncanny in the volume of which he knew nothing.

'Do not you be soft,' said his wife; 'softness never earned a penny yet.'

But the smith did not assent. He was a good-hearted man, though his means were small and his cupidity was excited by the idea of these vast sums circling in the air above this strange, darksome old volume. He overtook Ser Checchi with a few quick strides, while his wife vainly screamed to him from the seat to which she had climbed in the cart.

'Ser Checchi,' he whispered, 'if it be really that your heart is set on this book, why, it would be a shame that you should not have it, if you will pay the price the dealers here would give. You pay that, sir, and you shall have it. No, do not say any more now. My woman is looking after us; the women are always unreasoning and niggard. I would give it to you, sir,' he added, ' give it you and right welcome, for nothing ; but a man with a wife and children is always a man bound ; he cannot help himself when he is bid to do dirty things.'

Then he left the old librarian's side as quickly as he had overtaken him, and got up into his cart.

'You have never promised him anything?' said the woman with suspicious anger.

'Set your mind easy,' said Iorio curtly. 'You've made me as close and as nasty as yourself. I never did a thing I was right-down ashamed of before to-day, but to-day I have.'

Ser Checchi's heart had given a great leap of joy, and the dusty stones of the crowded Canto di' Nelli seemed to him precious gems glowing with colour and light: the sky was blue between the walls; roses and carnations were glowing in bunches on the corner of the lane, the bells of the great church were clanging and vibrating excellently, the whole morning seemed full of light and gladness to him. He would be the owner of the manuscript of 1320.

To pay for it, indeed, would cause some difficulty, but that question he put aside for the moment. Paid for it should be, and within the week; but like a lover, like a child, he did not stay to count the cost which might attend the fulfilment of his infinite desire. As he went through the streets strangers turned to look at the old man with his bowed shoulders on which his silvery hair floated, for on his face there was a radiance as of earliest youth. The joys of the spirit illumine the countenance as a light shining through a shell.

'Good-morrow, Ser Checchi,' said a pleasant voice at his elbow, as Vestuccio, with his good-natured smile and deferential salutation, paused beside him somewhat later by the Croce al Trebbia.

'Good-day to you,' answered Ser Checchi

dreamily, his thoughts always with the manuscript Dante, and far from the throngs about him.

'Might I have a word with you, Ser?' asked the younger man with hesitation.

'Certainly,' said the elder, a vague disquietude stirring in him; the smith had said that the dealer had seen the folio.

'We are near my little place, if you would honour me by stepping in and sitting down; the sun is very warm to-day,' said Vestuccio.

His 'little place,' where he had lately opened business, was the shop in the Piazza della Madonna degli Aldobrandini; modest and unassuming, with 'Aurelio Vestuccio, Antiquario' painted above its door, and the artistic medley of a bric-à-brac dealer's odds and ends shown in its larger window; bronzes, carvings, jars, vases, marbles, woodwork, mosaics, and brasses, most of them clever imitations of what they pretended to be, filling up the rooms, which opened one out of another. Ser Checchi passed within its doors. He liked Vestuccio, who had such a civil, pleasant, intelligent manner, and who had more than once put in his way rare books which the dealer had fallen in with, and of which, as he said, he would have known nothing of the value but for the lessons received from the librarian.

'Walk in here, sir,' said Vestuccio now, opening an inner door into a small den only big enough to hold a desk and two stools, with some shelves filled by ledgers.

He shut the door, although there was no one in hearing.

The little office looked on a yard in which his

workmen were used to pack up sold goods, furbish up old rubbish, fit plain old furniture with metal brass handles and locks, and render more attractive and picturesque all objects which required such embellishment. It was now noonday; and there was no one in the yard; the only living thing there was a gray striped cat, asleep on a rusty and rickety kneeling-chair.

'You want to speak to me?' asked Ser Checchi uneasily, his mind ever following the Dante where it was jogging along, wrapped in the flowered print and nursed on the fat woman's knees.

'The smith of Giogoli brought me a manuscript,' began Vestuccio.

'Ah!' said Ser Checchi, with a little gasping sigh of inquiry and uneasiness. He understood that the book was going away from him, that some rich purchaser had been found.

'He told me of your goodness in acquainting him with its date and value,' continued Vestuccio. 'Is it really worth so much? You know, Ser, I am very ignorant of manuscripts and their like.'

'Its worth is incalculable,' said Ser Checchi, with courageous integrity, though the admission tore at his heart-strings; 'that is, if it be sold to foreigners. Our libraries have no money. Did Iorio speak to you of selling it to me?'

'He did,' answered Vestuccio. 'He is grateful, and feels that you have no little right to command its purchase. What would he have known of its very existence even, had it not been for you? I ventured to inquire if you wished to buy it, because I have a client, a German dealer, who would be anxious to get it, before it could be offered to our own Government or to the foreign libraries. But, of course, if you intend to buy it yourself, your prior claim would never be disputed by me.'

'I wish to buy it; I mean to buy it,' said Ser Checchi, with incautious haste.

Vestuccio's merry blue eyes smiled, as a grown person's eyes may smile at the silliness of a child; but he answered seriously, and with great respect of tone:

'That is enough, sir; for my part, I shall tell the man from Hamburg that the volume is already disposed of, and will never come into the market at all.'

'Yes, yes,' said Ser Checchi hurriedly. 'Quite so. If Iorio will cede it at the price he would obtain in Italy, I will purchase it.'

'Ready money?' murmured Vestuccio, with a vague apology in his tone for his mention of the two words.

Ser Checchi hesitated. He was the most candid of all men and transparent as an alabaster vase. He knew that he could not pay ready money for the book; that to pay for it at all would require thought, negotiation, sacrifice, time. He had drooped his head on his chest, his delicate pale hand played nervously with a sheet of blotting-paper on the office desk before him. Vestuccio, to whom all his neighbours' affairs were as well known as the brass nails which he had driven into a leathern chair, or the new gilding with which he revived the glory of a mediæval nimbus, watched him with a gentle and compassionate amusement. He knew that Ser Checchi could no more put his hand at the moment on a thousand francs than he could have taken hold of the moon or the sun in the heavens.

He saw the trouble and the perplexity of mind which his two words had caused, and he left the old man for a few minutes to his own meditations, while he himself went out into the yard to drive the cat away over the wall. When he came back Ser Checchi was still nervously folding the blotting-paper to and fro, a shadow cast on his mobile features. Ready money! Ready money should and must be found.

'The truth is, Ser Checchi,' said the dealer, coming in, and removing the square smoking-cap he wore—'the truth is, that this good fellow of Giogoli knows the wish which you have for this volume. It was a thousand pities you let him know it; a thousand pities you did not keep the worth of the manuscript dark——'

'What! Oh, hush! how can you?' said the bookseller, lifting his head in pained indignation.

Vestuccio smiled and waved his hand.

'Well, well, sir, pardon me; I know that honour and generosity rule your life. It was noble, very noble, but you throw pearls before swine, you know. However, what is done is done. This smith knows now; and, having the knowledge, he will take the money too. We cannot blame him. Of course your conscience ruled you. Mine rules me, and loses me many a hundred-franc note in the year. It is terrible—yes, it is terrible in this knavish world to be an honest man.'

Ser Checchi made an impatient and slightly haughty movement.

'It is an elementary virtue!' he said, with a sarcastic intonation. 'It is known even amongst savages.'

Vestuccio perceived that he had taken a wrong tack; that to congratulate a man of integrity upon his integrity is an affront not easily condoned.

Ser Checchi rose and took his hat.

'I thought you said that you had business with me. I see I mistook. Good-day, Vestuccio.'

'Stay a moment, sir,' said the dealer obsequiously. 'Pray do not go in anger. I am a blunt, unpolished fellow, but my heart is sound—my heart is sound. The truth is, sir, knowing how you wished for this Dante folio, I ventured to hope that if you cannot find it quite convenient to pay for it down on the nail, you would let me have the pleasure of doing so for you, and you could then repay me when you pleased at your leisure. I owe you much, Ser Checchi; many a rare bit of knowledge and many a date and secret of art have I, a poor, ignorant, common fellow, learned from you and been your debtor for, in my commerce.'

The elder man was silent. A faint flush came on his cheeks and forehead: the proud and delicate spirit in him winced and shrank at the idea that his necessities, however slight, were known to others.

'You mean well, and I thank you, my good Aurelio,' he said a little distantly. 'But I have not asked your help.'

'Help! I would never give it such a name,' cried Vestuccio. 'It would be a favour which you would do me, for I owe you much, and though I am a rough man, I am not a thankless one. I know how you wish for this old book, which is, by all right of treasure-trove, yours, and the fellow who owns it has placed the sale of it in my hands. I suppose you are sure of its authenticity?'

Ser Checchi smiled with the pity of culture for ignorance.

'It is a Codex which the poet himself may have had written!'

'Well, well, sir; I take your word for it, you are a learned man,' said Vestuccio, who desired to depreciate or appear sceptical of its value.

With that he lifted the lid of the desk, and took out, from the hollow underneath, the Dante, and with a careless touch opened it, and turned the yellow parchment pages, whilst the sunlight slanting in from the window shone on the regular lines of its black-letter columns.

Ser Checchi thrilled from head to foot like a man who beholds a beloved mistress.

'Iorio has sold it to you!' he exclaimed involuntarily. 'He promised me—he promised me—the preference.'

Vestuccio smiled.

'The good fellow has a wife; and the gray mare is the better horse. He left it with me because he wished you to have it. The woman would have allowed him no peace if it had remained with them.'

Ser Checchi leaned over the desk, touching the manuscript caressingly with his long slender fingers; the colour came and went on his face; he felt as if he had been degraded and soiled by Vestuccio's praise of his action and by his own sense of how sharp a struggle it had cost him. And the sight of the Dante on the dealer's desk brought home to him the sense of how certainly, if it did not become his own then and there, it would soon pass forever out of his vision and grasp.

Vestuccio watched him smilingly—an indulgent smile as of a man looking down on a whimsical and half-witted child; after a pause he said gently:

'See now, Ser Checchi, your heart is set on this thing, and for sure, as I say, it is yours already by all the right of treasure-trove. I will buy it of the smith, and you shall buy it of me at your perfect convenience. You will sign me a little paper, just for form's sake, to set your mind at ease because you are so proud and solitary: and you can take the Dante home with you and put it under your pillow if you like to-night, if it will make you sleep the better. Leave me to deal with Iorio. I know those bumpkins; they are as sharp as needles, though they look such simple souls. Take the Codex, as you call it, sir; you and I shall never quarrel.'

'No, no; I could not be so deeply beholden to you or to anyone,' said Ser Checchi, as he closed the volume and laid it inside the desk. 'You mean well, that I am sure, but I should not be at peace a moment if I took it on those terms. I do not do business so.'

'Then the book must go to the Hamburg people,' said Vestuccio, with a sigh, as he turned the key on his safe. 'Think twice of what I have said, sir; it is no obligation; you will just sign to pay me at three months, six, twelve—at any date you please—and the Dante will belong to you, the one man in Europe who is worthy of it!'

'But why should you do this service to me?' asked Ser Checchi, with a flash of insight lightening the placid, even tenor of his trust in human nature.

'It is no service,' said Vestuccio, 'and, to prevent your feeling that it is one, we will put it in as regular a business form as you may please that it shall take. I wish you to have the book, sir: first of all because justice is justice, and should be done when it can; and secondly because you have been a good friend to me, and I am glad if I can do you ever so slight a benefit. Take the volume home with you, honoured sir, and we will write out the memorandum some other day.'

Ser Checchi knew the ways of commerce, although so little trade came nigh his tower, and he ought to have remembered what had been his experiences all his life, that he who leaves a signature behind him gives the costliest of hostages to fortune.

But the manuscript folio allured him irresistibly; even shut away beneath the lid of the desk, like a dead friend beneath a coffin lid, it seemed to draw him towards it with a subtle and magnetic power, and when he left the shop of Aurelio Vestuccio that day, he carried the Codex of the 'Commedia' with him; and in the desk, in its stead, was lying a small oblong piece of stamped paper bearing his clear, fine handwriting upon it, and at which Vestuccio looked with a satisfied smile.

'Chi va piano va sano,' murmured that shrewd

tradesman to himself; heaven had sent fools into the world to be the support of clever men, as little fish are made to be the food of big ones.

He watched the figure of Ser Checchi passing through the artistic lumber of his yard with benevolent compassion, and saw the gates close on him with that triumphant sense of cruel success which moves the trapper in the woods when he sees the gentle beast for whom the trap is set walk guilelessly within its meshes.

And he turned his admirable mind on the morrow to the successful and secret persuasion of the smith of Giogoli that there had been a mistake about the value of the old vellum book; but that nothing must be said about that to Ser Checchi, whose brain was softening and growing childish.

CHAPTER V.

SER CHECCHI displayed the Codex to his daughter with pride and joy, and found in her all the sympathy with his pleasure which a cultured intelligence and a warm heart could give. But he offered no explanation of how it had come into his possession, beyond saying that he had discovered it amongst some musty and worthless volumes, which Iorio the blacksmith had turned out of an old chest; and Beldia, who was but sixteen at that time, was too respectful to ask more than he chose to explain, and too loyal to inquire from others any details which he did not himself proffer to her. She was not curious; and she was even then so accustomed to have entire liberty in all household matters, but to be wholly excluded from the affairs of her father's business, that it never seemed to her rather odd or ominous that the cost of the early Dante was concealed from her.

Vestuccio had his own reasons for not speaking of the matter: and Iorio had been so rated by his wife for not waiting for some princely purchaser, that the subject was a sore one to him. But it was the beginning of serious financial transactions between Ser Checchi and the dealer in the Piazza della Madonna; and sometimes when he unlocked the drawer in which the precious volume lay, even though he loved it so dearly, the elder man almost found it in his soul to wish that he had never stopped for that fatal draught of watered wine on the hillside of Giogoli. There were moments of exquisite happiness, when he displayed his treasure to scholars by whom it could be appreciated, and it was a source of profound joy to him always to have a contemporary Dante Codex for his very own; but at times he realized that he had entered into bondage through and for it.

To get money by merely writing your name is so easy that its ease has been the ruin of tens of thousands; and Vestuccio beyond all others knew how to render it so easy, that a man of absent mind, of scholarly extravagance, and of dreamful indolence, like Ser Checchi, never perceived what it might ultimately cost him to possess himself of monastic manuscripts and precious palimpsests by the mere

DANTE'S HOUSE.

stroke of a pen in his fine, small, clear, clerkly handwriting.

He did not even know how many times he had written ' Francesco Ardiglione ' upon those stamped sheets of paper, which the dealer put away with as apparent a carelessness as though he were merely going to light his pipe with them.

The bibliophile, like the artist, and the poet, and the lover, will do anything wise or unwise, good or bad, to reach the object of his desires. Sometimes Beldia thought with a pang of what a source of happiness his literary passion would have been to him had he been a rich man. Alas! rich men usually look upon their libraries as mere show places to assist their pomp, or as mere inherited wealth, to be quickly sent to the hammer. Perception is so seldom united with possessions; the wisdom of the soul is so rarely given with the power of the purse!

Beldia was the most dutiful of daughters; and the infinite respect which she entertained for him never permitted her to blame what he did, even in her own thoughts; but he did not care all the same to meet the questioning gravity of her eyes when he had been making unwise purchases, so that little by little he had grown to conceal from her any unusually costly book or manuscript, and the various straits to which he was sometimes put to pay for them. For Ser Checchi would no more have bought a book on credit than a fond mother would get into debt for her child's christening robe. It would have been difficult to do so, for most rare volumes were found at auction rooms, or in antiquaries' shops, or in remote presbyteries and church-closets, where immediate payment was the *sine quâ non* of purchase. But when he could have bought on credit he would not; credit would have seemed to him to soil the pure grave faces of the beloved books and manuscripts, which he would touch with such a reverent, caressing gesture of the hand, as you will see in a sculptor when he passes his fingers softly down some marble curve of arm or hip or breast.

'It will sell for ten times its value, my dear,' he would invariably say when she observed it; but as buyers of such costly goods hardly ever came to the tower, and as, whenever they did so, he invariably shrank from losing his favourite volumes, and to that end either hid them, or named some preposterous and prohibitive price, she knew by experience that what their worth would or would not realize mattered very little to her father, except in so far as his pride as a bibliophile was flattered by the possession.

'If he were a rich man collecting a library to enjoy it, there could be no healthier or happier pursuit,' she thought; 'but when it is his trade, when he should only buy and sell, and do both wisely, his adoration of his books is fatal.'

All the filial veneration of her soul could not blind her clear and keen intelligence to the fact that the commerce of books, as Ser Checchi conducted it, could only be more ruinous than to pursue no trade at all.

'He is as dilettante as if he were a duke!' said Cirillo angrily once. He, for his part, would have made a bonfire of all the books with the utmost pleasure.

Beldia would not admit the truth of it, but in her heart she felt that it was only too true. All the delicate research, the fastidious judgment, and the severe taste of her father would have made the joy and the renown of an amateur collector, but in a librarian were but so many costly impediments. Ser Checchi knew this himself, and it made his conscience twinge and tremble at times; but he thrust the consciousness aside. He was ruled by his master passion, and when he saw an old copy, of undoubted age and value, or any manuscript of some great dead hand, his whole gentle and unassuming person was transformed; he became indifferent to everything, except the means by which he might become the owner of such a treasure, and he had even developed a clever and ingenious, though childlike, cunning, in concealing the temptations of this sort which he met with in his daily saunterings through the street. Once he had discovered several pages of autograph verse of Politziano's in a chandler's shop, enwrapping some butter, and this discovery had served him for excuse and warrant ever since. True, his honesty had compelled him to acquaint the butterman with the value of his wrapping-paper before offering money for it, but the butterman had been incredulous, and had said with a pitying, benignant smile that it was only robaccia (rubbish), so that he had taken his Politziano home for the price of the butter itself, and this lucky chance had served as an example, and as an incentive to purchases, ever since. Many things, however, cost him much more than a pound of butter; and for some of his manuscripts and folios he had paid as heavily as though he had been a curator for the Luxembourg or for the Bodleian.

'They will be a fine dower for Beldia,' he told his conscience. But at that thought his heart contracted and his bowels yearned; for to become a dower for her they would have, of necessity, to be sold. And the thought of selling them was torture to him. He would have liked to think that his coffin would be filled with them, and that he would lie in his tomb with his folios on his breast, as knights have their shields on theirs.

From the time of the purchase of the Dante, Vestuccio had become the chief adviser and assistant in financial matters of the librarian, by whom money matters had always been esteemed the most vulgar and debasing of all mundane concerns.

Ser Checchi, though too trustful and compliant, was no fool, however, and at times there came over him with uneasiness the perception that he was trusting too much and leaving too much to his good friend of the Piazza della Madonna. Nor did he desire that his daughter should know how thoroughly Vestuccio had ingratiated himself with him, and wound himself into his confidence.

Ser Checchi, like all scholars and people who love impersonal meditation, was reluctant to be roused out of his studies and pursuits, and forced into contact with the vulgar and commonplace interests of daily and practical life. The eminently practical mind of Vestuccio quickly found out this tendency, and knew how to turn it and humour it to serve his own purpose. While the old philosopher floated in an empyrean of fine thought, or pursued some philological or historical question, which for him seemed of as vast import as the conquest of Asia seemed to Alexander, he was very glad to find a quick-witted, pleasant-tempered, and unobtrusive person who spared him much trouble and attended to many things in his name.

'The Signorina Beldia does not like me, though she is so good to my little ones,' said Vestuccio regretfully more than once.

And Ser Checchi answered more than once:

'Tut, tut! what does a young woman's fancy matter, my good fellow, to you? My daughter is always very slow to give her liking, except to animals and children.'

'If she does not approve of men, who shall say that she has not right on her side?' answered the dealer with his good-humoured smile, and added more seriously: 'The signorina is certainly fitter for babes and saints than for our clumsy and rough company. They all call her Madonna Beldia, and for certain such a woman as she is puts most of us to shame.'

Being shrewd and full of tact, he did not try to force his good qualities on her attention, but contented himself with greeting her respectfully whenever he met her, and kept carefully away from her knowledge the transactions which he and her father had together. Something of them, however, she dimly suspected, and the mere suspicion made her uneasy. Aurelio Vestuccio had a good name on the Piazza, and had a pleasant countenance and manner; but Folko growled when he approached, and Folko's mistress felt the same instinct of distrust and apprehension as the dog. She liked his little girls, nevertheless, and the children were never so happy as when they could climb the steep stone stair of the tower, and mount the ladder which led on to the roof amongst the flowering plants and the pigeons.

They were pretty little girls, with long fair hair and dancing blue eyes, like what their father's had been when he had sold his shells and seaweed at their age; they were known as Gemma and Dina, and they were often seen tying up the pinks, drying the rose-leaves for pot-pourri, feeding the birds, or otherwise aiding, or imagining that they aided, Ser Checchi's daughter. Every Christmas their father sent them with a bouquet and some dried fruit to her, and every Easter they brought her a basket of eggs and lemons in acknowledgment of, and return for, the many kindnesses she showed to them, and the courage with which she had nursed them in their sickness.

'Always be pretty behaved, my treasures,' said Vestuccio to them.

Pretty behaviour had stood himself in such good stead, and had paid him a hundred per cent. on it. Vestuccio could never understand why people were rough and rude, and coarse and repellent, and told the truth and swore at their neighbours. It was so much simpler and nicer to behave well, and speak as if the world were a pot of cream and a bowl of sugar.

You could put what poison you liked in the cream, and you could disguise so many things with the sugar.

Beldia was used to seeing Vestuccio come and go about her father's chambers. She gave no thought to his frequent visits, but she did not like him any better than she liked the advocate Querci. She knew, however, that her father esteemed him and employed him, and therefore she endeavoured to restrain her own prejudices, and at the end of each year made pretty little presents for his children, of whom he had many, as behoved a good citizen.

'The signorina is an angel,' said Vestuccio more than once, and said so with genuine tears in his eyes when she saved the life of his eldest little girl by her judicious and courageous nursing during diphtheria, when the child's mother was helpless and useless from fright, and lay on the floor in hysterics all day long.

But he did not for that reason cease to accumulate Ser Checchi's signatures within his desk.

He would have said that the one thing had nothing to do with the other. Feelings and accounts are as far apart from each other as the rose in your button-hole from the boots on your feet.

He one day gave orders to his foreman never to sell anything to a certain person; the certain person could not pay. The foreman, foolish and new to the business, bluntly told the impecunious client that it was of no use to come to the shop; he would be given nothing. Vestuccio, on learning this coarse and unpardonable blunder, was as violently angry as so good-tempered a man could be.

'This is how you should get rid of people without offending them,' he said to the foreman, and planted a tall, high-backed chair in the middle of the warehouse, and bowed to it with many smiles, softly rubbing his hands together. 'Represent to yourself that this chair is a well-born, well-bred person, without credit, whom we know well—and know will never pay in twenty years' time, and has nothing to render it worth our having the law upon him. Now behold me receive him when he wishes to purchase.'

And he walked in front of the chair, courteously bending his supple backbone.

'Most illustrious Sir Chair,' he said unctuously, 'my very soul is rent, my pain is inexpressible, but, alas! that article which you desire is sold already; and this, and this, and this also—all, alas! that you see around you. I will telegraph to the purchaser to try and obtain a release of these objects for your most eminent self; for there is no monarch or minister in Europe whom I would serve with such joy as I would serve you. Your taste is so perfect. You appreciate so exquisitely. It is delightful to feel that a beautiful object passes to your hands. I will telegraph instantly, but if the buyer will not release them, alas! what can I do? I would lose twenty per cent. to know the joy of selling to you, dear Sir Chair, but they are already promised, more than promised—sold! And, alas! one's commercial word is one's bond!'

Then he rubbed his hands and made three graceful bows, and walked backwards from the chair, smiling and sighing.

'There, idiot!' he said, turning to the foreman with a frown, 'that is how you should rid yourself of a bad customer without making an enemy of him. You will never give him a centime's worth, but he will believe that you would trust him with millions. Never make a foe, even of an insolvent debtor!'

The foreman, a stupid young man, unworthy of the school in which it was his happiness to dwell, shrugged his shoulders.

'Life is too short for all that farce,' he said sheepishly, replacing the high-backed chair amongst its fellows.

His master eyed him with compassionate contempt.

'Life is long, my friend,' he answered, 'to those who know how to play the farce—long and sweet. Sweet!' he repeated, smacking his lips with unction. 'And, besides, one should never give pain unnecessarily—not even to a debtor who cannot pay.'

The foreman looked at his employer and grinned: the grin was disrespectful, but Aurelio Vestuccio did not resent it. He smiled broadly and brightly himself, the same smile with which—when a little lad on the seashore—he had sold shells which were cracked and rotting star-fish.

Life was sweet to him, whatever it might be to his clients and customers, and everything in it was sweet to him, from that straight, tall, ebony chair which he had had made a few hours before—with 1547 carved on its back, and the worm-holes drilled along its legs—to the round sums lent out at compound interest, which multiplied themselves like ants and rabbits.

Any bystander overhearing him talk of Ser Checchi, as they sat at a little round marble table in some coffee-house, would have heard only such tender and reverent praises, such fine phrases of respect and esteem, as would have warmed his heart to hear; he only sighed over the old librarian's too credulous virtue.

'Business cannot be done as our dear Ser Checchi does it,' he observed to Pampilio Querci one day when they met at the Birraria Cornelio.

'He believes everyone is as pure of mouth and of hand as himself,' answered the young lawyer.

'He is as trustful as a lamb,' said the dealer.

'He is a saint and a sage, and thinks men's breasts are made of glass,' said the man of law.

'His own is so,' replied the other, and added warmly and solemnly as he drained his glass, 'Woe be to those who wrong him!'

'Woe be on them indeed!' said the lawyer, finishing his vermuth.

So they spoke together, understanding one another.

Rude, rough Northern men would have said bluntly to each other:

'This client is a goose—let us pluck him.'

Vestuccio and Querci wrapped up the same meaning in admirable and admiring sentences, which deceived no one, indeed, but soothed and pleased themselves, and preserved their self-respect in their own sight and that of each other.

Vestuccio and Querci never trusted each other an inch, and they always kept up an elaborate comedy for each other's benefit. To each of them the world was a stage, on which, as on the stage of the Greeks, the masks and the stilts mattered more than the words. Each of these worthies knew that he did not for a moment deceive the other; yet to play the comedy pleased both, gratified their consciousness of wit and wisdom, and gave the agreeable sense of security which is given by a domino and mask.

Cicero's countrymen have still the same sense of propriety and politeness which characterized his gentle and polished utterance of *vixerunt* when his enemies lay dying with throats bleeding like slaughtered pigs.

CHAPTER VI.

OF her father's learning and nobility of character Beldia was passionately reverent and proud; but to certain weaknesses in him she could not be wholly blind. When the new-comer from the north timidly hinted to her his perception that she had little pleasure in seeing him return frequently to the library, she answered him with honesty and candour.

'It is true,' she replied, 'that I cannot fail to perceive that my father trusts too much and gives too much; and many young men make him talk that they may carry off the riches of intellect and learning. For truly, sir,' she added proudly, 'the mere crumbs from my father's stores would be more rich than the fullest granaries of many.'

'I understand,' said the Brescian; 'I know now what it is that you think. But God is my witness that I had none such evil designs. I honour your father, and gain wisdom from all he says, indeed;

but I assure you I have not the faintest thought of making use of what he tells me in my own interests, except in the sense that all must benefit who hear a learned scholar.'

Beldia felt that she might have been ungenerous and unjust.

'I beg your pardon for harbouring such a doubt,' she said more gently. 'Young men do too often make my father a stepping-stone to their own honour; and when they have mounted where they wished, forget the means by which they rose.'

'I fear that ingratitude is too common in human nature,' said the Lombard, 'and from whosoever gives much, much is taken, and thanklessly. Ser Checchi should go on his ways and not attend to importunity.'

'My father is most generous,' said Beldia, 'with the food of the mind as well as the nourishment of the body.'

'May it be rendered to him!' the Brescian answered; but it was rather the utterance of a desire than of a belief, for he had seen enough of the world to know that such liberality as Francesco Ardiglione's ruins the man who practises it more than all selfish indulgence would ever do.

He had the quick apprehension of the artistic temperament, and he could well imagine the difficulties and conflicting duties by which she was beset in her endeavour to approve her father in all he did, yet fill up the vacuum which he left in their finances. She had a serene and clear intelligence, fit for Athene's self; but Athene herself could not have filled up a bottomless vase.

He divined something of the anxieties and ineffectual efforts of the scholar's daughter, and it stimulated the admiration which he felt for her, and gave his respect for her the softer and warmer glow of pity. From the day when she had candidly confessed to him her suspicions of his motives such doubts had been dissipated; and she and he had become gradually companions and friends.

He was wholly unlike the young men whom she had seen come to the tower, who were only of two classes: the wild, dissipated comrades of Cirillo, or the young doctrinaires and journalists who frequented the library. He was of a higher type than either; the blood of a once martial and generous race ran in his veins; and though he was poor and humble in position, he had the temper and the instincts of a gentleman, and belonged to a different order to the finical and varnished gentlemanhood of Pampilio Querci and his fellows.

There were a candour, simplicity, and kindliness about him which endeared him quickly to old people and to young; and he made himself at home in the tower of Taddeo without the slightest presumption or intrusiveness. It soon became quite natural in her sight that he should accompany her father in his evening rambles through the by-streets; assist in dusting and arranging the interminable volumes which were piled one on another on the floors; and even venture upstairs on the roof at sunset to see what he could do in trimming and watering the herbs and flowers.

Little by little he had become a comrade and a companion to her, without ever seeming to presume on the privileges. Ser Checchi found in him a listener after his own heart, and Beldia, though she was by nature reserved and slow to give her regard to strangers, found much that was attractive and akin to her in this frank-eyed and gentle-mannered scholar from the north.

She was a woman who had thought little of men as lovers; like many women who have been accustomed to male companionship and intellectual commerce, her life was too full and too various to leave her leisure for the amorous fancies which lead the lighter brains of the unoccupied and more frivolous so many a useless dance after the marsh-lights of imaginary passions. When men had asked her hand, as they had done some few times, she had thanked them gravely for the token of their esteem, and declined to leave her father, or entertain any suit, however favoured by him.

But she did not think that because a man watered her carnations, or classified the pamphlets of the book-rooms, he must of necessity fall at her feet on the morrow; and the intercourse between her and the Lombard artist, when the ice of her reserve had once been broken, was frank and friendly, as it might have been between two youths of similar tastes and studies. Only, in his own heart, he speedily began to sigh for warmer things, freer speech.

Ser Checchi, indeed, had taken him on trust, and had made him welcome to his house, as Erasmus or as Boethius might have done, simply on the strength of mutual tastes and studies, and in the confidence engendered by mutual simplicity and candour. But, from being welcome as a reader of old books in a library, to being welcome as a suitor to a woman's hand from her family, there is a wide difference, of which Odisio was keenly sensible.

' How my mother would admire and welcome her!' he thought, when he saw her diligently bending over the catalogues and ledgers, so content and tranquil in what would have been to any other woman of her age an existence dull and laborious. It was not his mother's fault that he had not wherewithal to offer Ser Checchi's daughter a more cheerful and a happier life.

His mother had given him a fine education, and had denied herself of all luxuries to enable him to study and to travel. It was his own fault, and no one else's, that he had let the best years of his youth drift away in a Bohemian's wandering, and his talents and knowledge rust unused. With far fewer opportunities, and far less intelligence than he had been blessed with, men had made themselves a place and a name before their thirtieth year. He had enjoyed his liberty, and now he paid its cost. And often, as he walked back at night to his temporary lodging, he bitterly lamented the carelessness with which he had let so many years go by without making for himself such a place in life as would have enabled him to become Beldia's suitor. He had all the humility and timidity which accompany a genuine passion; and, though she was only the daughter of the bookseller of the tower in San Jacopo, she was to him as a queen clothed in raiment of light.

He was poor; he had only had seventy francs in his

purse when he had entered the city, and of that he had spent thirty in the purchase of the plates of Palladio, and the other designs and volumes. He had to work for his bread, but this did not affright him; he was a man of courage and energy, and his wants were few; the need of money hurt him most when he could not aid others. He was generous by temper, and came of what had been a lavish and magnificent race in other days.

When he could make enough to live simply himself and send some little presents to his mother, of fine coffee or wine, or fruits, or a little piece of old lace, he was quite content. The future could take care of itself, he had always thought; he had no one dependent on him.

But when he looked back over the years which had fled since he had left the Paduan University, and realized that, had he chosen, he might have so employed them as to have had a fixed home and a fair income to offer to Belda Ardiglione, he was wroth with himself for the want of stability and of application which had left him thus penniless in the flower of his age.

He was like one of those errant students of the Middle Ages, who roamed over Europe with nothing but a staff and a satchel, welcome everywhere to scholars for sake of their facile wit and well-stored brain. But the times in which he was born were no longer those in which this picturesque, wandering, aimless life was judged wise and praiseworthy; and there were no longer monastery doors open to such students, no ducal courts like those of the Can Grande and Lionello d'Este, where fine Latin and a love of the Humanities were passport enough to board and lodging. Had he knocked now at any great man's gates with no warrant but his portfolio of designs and his classical knowledge, he would have been consigned to the police or handed quickly over to the mercies of a mendicant society. Although he had fallen on evil, niggardly, and suspicious days, he had, however, always found life pleasant and easy, until now that he had seen the serene-eyed maiden of the tower of Taddeo. Since then it seemed to him that at his years he ought to have secured some sounder basis for subsistence, some surer means whereby to be able to maintain himself and others. What could he look like to her and to her father—except a careless ne'er-do-well and vagabond?

They might see that he had talent, and believe that he had honour, but he was a man who, at thirty years old, had neither place nor income.

It was now warm June weather; not the season in which strangers willingly stay in the city, and he, Lombard-born, was used to spend his summers where winds were cool, on high chestnut-wooded hills, within sight of snow-clad mountains. Yet he now remained in his attic by the fountain of San Jacopo, finding excuse enough in his architectural studies, and even being so fortunate as to obtain momentary employment in making mechanical drawings for an architect in the town, who chanced to be a friend of that Milanese artist under whom he had studied seven years earlier.

Odisio had a grace and candour in his manner which attracted people, and, in his work, an exactitude and zeal which confirmed the sympathy his manner aroused. He had practical ability, as well as imagination and invention. Something of the fire and of the emotion were in him in his attitude towards his art, which made the men of the Middle Ages call the builder in stone *magister in vive lapide*. These feelings had indeed no field for practical expression, but they were evident in the depth and ardour of his gaze, as he looked on great architecture or great sculpture, in the freedom and fancy of his sketches of imaginary buildings, and in the torture which he suffered when he saw the mighty walls and noble arches of a past age going down under the dust of the leveller's pickaxes and the shovels of the destroyers, as may be seen in this age over all Italy.

His reverence for the past formed a common bond between him and Ser Checchi; and the latter said approvingly that it was a good sight to see a young man so unlike his own generation and so full of respect for those who had gone before him.

The spirit of the past had entered into him in his studious boyhood, passed amongst the old streets and ancient palaces of Brescia and Bergamo, and some regret also for that time when his forefathers had hung up their shields amongst the knights and lords upon the frescoed walls of the Broletto.

'What a ninny!' said Pampilio Querci, as, going one morning to his office, he saw the Lombard gazing for many moments in rapt admiration of Giotto's Campanile, with the soft and manifold hues on its marbles, like those of the pigeons which flew around it, and the morning light shed on it so clear, so cool, so luminous, that the building seemed scarcely more touched and made by the hand of man than were the clouds which floated in the sapphire sky.

Pampilio Querci admired nothing except the smoke of the dirty tramway car in which he went out to Sesto or Campi on feast days to shoot songbirds in the hedges; and the stuccoed box which he was pleased to call a house, where he slept every night amongst iron rails, pollarded acacias, a brannew jute factory, and an acre or two of hoarding covered with posters and lithographed advertisements of new soaps and cheap furniture. When the young attorney went to sleep amongst those surroundings, he felt indeed that his head was pillowed on progress.

'You look at the bell-tower? It is most inconveniently placed, it sorely impedes traffic,' he said with polite disdain to the Brescian as he passed beside him.

The Brescian glanced down on him with a wondering disdain of another kind.

'Look? Ay, indeed!' he cried; 'the American who took his hat off to it the other day was worthier of it than the Florentines who brush by it without a benediction.'

'You are an enthusiast,' said Querci, with the tips of his thin curled lips, and a little frigid, cynical, pitying smile.

'Thank Heaven! yes, when I see what is worthy of enthusiasm.'

'Ah,' said the young lawyer with bland contempt; 'the American might take his hat off here to the campanile. In his own country he would soon change it into a grain-elevator!'

Then he gave a little twirl of his slim cane and of his small moustache, and went on to his office, where he sat down amongst his law books and law papers, and wrote a clever archæological article for a learned society, based on matter which he had gleaned from the too eloquent tongue of Ser Checchi.

The Brescian looked after him with boundless scorn.

'How would his wind last on the slope of Monte Genneroso?' he thought grimly; 'or swimming from shore to shore on the Garda waters?'

He felt that he should extremely like to have the spruce, slender, self-satisfied lawyer out with him in rough weather on one of those snow-filled passes or wind-swept lakes, on which he himself was as much at home as a chamois on the one or a trout in the other. He had often seen Querci at the tower, and knew, although he had never heard her say so, that Beldia disliked him; and he had a shrewd instinct also that he had a rival in the pert attorney, and felt, with a furious impotence to retrace his steps, that he might, had he chosen, have already occupied a higher position than the lawyer owned.

His face grew hot with shame when he thought that, if he even disclosed to her the admiration with which he regarded her, he would only appear to her and to her father as a mercenary seeker of a home and of a dower. Ser Checchi seemed a man altogether beyond and above his own hand-to-mouth existence, and Beldia also herself daunted him and kept him at a distance.

She was kind, but kindness was her nature. She was gentle, but that also was natural to her. She smiled at him, but she smiled in the same way when she chided the boy Poldo for going upstairs with dusty boots, or caressed the woolly white curls of her dog, or mixed a glass of syrup and water for the old priest, Don Gervasio.

The serenity and seriousness of her manner, so unlike the excitability of Italian women, and that dignity which he had noted in her on the first day that he had seen her in the market-place, intensified his admiration of her, but repressed all expression of it. Her mind and heart and time appeared so entirely and so well filled that it would have seemed to him the most preposterous presumption to think that there could be any place in them for him, or for any ordinary human passions.

'You have lived under the wings of the amorini until you scarcely belong to the earth,' he said to her one evening when she stood on the flat roof of the tower amongst her herbs and flowers, whilst the sky above was all in a roseate glow, warm and fair as the roses of May.

Beldia, who had her watering-pot in her hand and her garden-scissors at her girdle, laughed a little as she stooped over her carnations.

'No one was ever more earthly,' she made answer. 'Surely you must have seen—I am the busiest of housewives. I have hardly ever a moment to look up yonder. And yet all the whole world should pause to adore *that*.'

She straightened her back and looked upward as she spoke at that vault of azure light, flushed with clouds like rose-leaves, which was above their heads, above the whole city, the mountains, the plain, the river, in a glory of transfigured radiance, in which the stars and a crescent moon of silver were shining.

She raised her left hand above her head, pointing to the zenith. On her face shone reflected the luminance from the skies; on that high place, with the sound of the streets far below them, and nothing near except the belfries dark against the light, and the black wings of whirling swallows and circling bats, she might have been Beatrice or Laura, and the world been young beneath her feet.

She forgot the stranger beside her. She was lost in the beauty at which she gazed. Church bells were chiming, deep and low, from the towers and spires near. No other sound reached them there. The soft crimson of the zenith glowed richer and warmer as the azure darkened, and the planets grew larger, and more stars shone out from the tremulous blue.

And the Lombard thought:

'What could be the miserable, egotistical love of a man to a woman who feels the whole heart of nature throb in unison with hers as she does?'

It seemed to him that she was as far away from him as the crescent moon which shone amidst the rose and gold of the horizon.

Yet she wore a rough linen apron tied over her

cotton gown, and had a common watering-can in her hand, and had been a moment before solely intent on tying up her carnations and brushing the ants off her picotees.

She stood, long gazing up at that evening splendour stretched above the city, and the valley, and the amethyst ring of the mountains. She had forgotten that she was not alone. A pigeon, coming home to roost, flew down on her shoulder, and pecked with loving familiarity at her ear.

It startled her, and brought her thoughts to earth.

As she turned to caress the bird, she saw the gaze of Odisio Fontano fixed upon her as hers had been upon the skies.

The warmth from the heavens made his face seem full of light, and his eyes revealed what his lips never ventured to speak. With an embarrassment wholly novel to her, she put down the pigeon from her shoulder and began to water her plants again, whilst the cadence of the bells rocked drowsily through the air, and the roseate vault of the evening bent like a benediction over the city.

CHAPTER VII.

THE following day Ser Checchi was busied in his book-room. The accumulation of dust has few terrors for scholars, and the derangement and disturbance of the books have manifold terrors for them. Nevertheless, having drops of Frisian blood in him, through his maternal ancestress, he loved cleanliness, and as he abhorred to see his volumes touched, even by Beldia, he was wont at times to clean his shelves himself from cobweb and that fine powder-like sand which was blown up from the street and the bed of the river.

This morning he was thus engaged, standing on a pair of library-steps, and using a hand-brush made of cocks' feathers. He was at the same time partially rearranging the contents of the shelves, and was so engrossed in his occupation that he did not hear Odisio enter, and the respectful salutation of the new-comer took him by surprise.

'Sit down, sit down,' he said cordially; 'you will pardon me if I continue my work. No, you cannot help me. I thank you for the offer, but it is a thing which I prefer to do, though it is troublesome. I know where to lay my hand on every volume and pamphlet when I arrange them myself, and I cannot blame others if they be ill-arranged.'

'But I wanted to speak to you,' said his visitor shyly, standing irresolute beside the ladder instead of going at once to the tables to resume his studies, as it was his habit to do.

'Well, speak on; I can hear whilst I finish my job,' said Ser Checchi indifferently.

His mind was but little in what he was saying, for he had just come upon a 'Father of the Church,' stained and gnawed by mice, and the sight distressed him sorely.

'What use is it to have cats and women in a house?' he murmured, as he turned over the desecrated pages, forgetful that neither his cats nor his women were allowed to do what they chose in those rooms.

The younger man continued to stand at the foot of the steps, holding his soft felt hat in his hands. He was embarrassed and constrained; he had come to do what was difficult and distressing to him, and he would have been glad of any remark from Ser Checchi which should have made it less abrupt and painful to begin the subject on which he came thither. But Ser Checchi said nothing; he stood turning over the palimpsest regretfully, wholly engrossed by the sight of the sacrilegious inroads of the mice. Odisio saw that he must break rudely into the confession which he came prepared to make, or leave it unconfessed.

'Ser Checchi, you have been very kind to me,' said the younger man, in a low voice. 'I do not wish to abuse or disgrace your kindness. So I go whilst I still have done neither.'

'What?' asked Ser Checchi, pausing in his work with his feather-brush poised in the air. It always cost him an effort to leave the lucid air of impersonal thought for the vexed and hazy atmosphere of human fancies and actions. 'What do you mean to imply? Have I accused you of any wrongdoing?'

Was it possible, he wondered, that the temptation to steal some of his manuscripts, or purloin some of his annotations upon them, was so strong that the Brescian feared to succumb to its influence if he stayed?

'No,' replied Odisio, with hesitation, 'I do not

think that you remember or perceive. Ser Checchi, I do not like to leave with any misunderstanding between us. You have opened your doors and your books so hospitably to a stranger, that I had better be honest with you. If I remain near her I cannot answer for my own self-control. I may say to your daughter what would offend and distress you.'

The old man did not answer. He looked astonished and perplexed, but not displeased.

'My daughter—Beldia?' he said aloud at last. How strange and sad it was that a fine scholar and diligent student like this Lombard should be led away from the pursuit of learning by any amorous fancy!

The younger man watched him with a beating heart. He was strongly attached to the librarian, and he was afraid that his own confession, and the discussion which might arise from it, would make an irrevocable difference between them.

But he spoke the truth manfully.

'Yes,' he answered, 'Madamigella Beldia. Who could be with her as you have allowed me to be and not see in her the flower of womanhood, one beside whom all other women are as nought? I cannot —I dare not—say to her what I feel; therefore I go.'

Ser Checchi stared at him, still astonished, and unable to persuade himself of the truth.

'I thought you came for the sake of *these!*' he said sadly, and with severity of reproach, as he included all the hundreds of volumes, bound and unbound, which were around them in the circle of his lifted feather-brush.

'I care for them, indeed, but not as I care for her,' murmured Odisio.

Ser Checchi gave a gesture of reproach and of scorn.

He turned round to the shelves again, and resumed his labour of love, flicking the dust off the tops and sides of the books, and now and then moving some stray volume back to its proper place, or putting together some loose pamphlets which had got into disorder.

There was no sound in the room, into which the sunshine came mellowed through the yellow time-dimmed casements behind their iron bars.

It seemed to him so sorrowful, so shameful, that no one except himself loved learning as it should be loved, as so far beyond, as so far above, all human frailties and attachments.

'I have offended and disappointed you?' Odisio said timidly, after a long silence.

'No, no,' said the elder man gently, but with a certain tone of chagrin and regret. 'You are young. It was to be expected. Youth is always drawn to youth, and filled with folly.'

'Folly!' said Odisio, with irrepressible indignation. 'Methinks higher wisdom there cannot be than to appreciate the perfections of a woman so noble and so pure!'

Ser Checchi smiled faintly as one who looked down upon a child at play.

'You are an enthusiast,' he said, with a little irony. 'My daughter is a good and industrious maiden, but nothing more wonderful than that. Thank Heaven, such are not rare! If it be true that you regard her with tenderness, I know not why you should so fear and hesitate to say so. Neither she nor I can claim to be great or gentle people. She has had many suitors—but she favours them little. She is wedded to her duties here. I cannot tell whether she would favour you any more than those whom she has dismissed; but I see no reason why you should not try your fate.'

Odisio heard with mingled bewilderment and joy and pain. He was ashamed of himself and of his poverty. Ser Checchi was so unworldly, that it was evident the things of the world had no place in his calculations. But the younger man could not forget or ignore the miserable nudity of his own circumstances, the cruel fact that he in reality possessed nothing except the clothes in his trunk, the instruments and portfolios of his art, and such scanty pittance as he could earn by daily work.

'Ser Checchi,' he said with visible emotion, 'I have been a foolish, graceless idler; I have thrown away my opportunities and the intelligence Nature gave me; I have no position, no home, no fixed income, no fixed stipend even to depend on. I have no right to speak as a suitor to any woman, however poor; much less to one as favoured as your daughter.'

Ser Checchi sighed impatiently, and his pale cheek grew hot.

'My daughter——' he began abruptly, and then paused. 'My daughter,' he added, in another tone, 'has an extravagant brother, and a father who has never been wise in financial matters. Cease to think of her as a maiden well dowered. She might once have been so. Now she never can be so. It matters not why, but she will never be so now. If she care for you, and you for her, I would not oppose the betrothal. But I would make one condition. You must have some assured position, or have gained some small capital, before I could sanction your marriage. I should not be exacting, but she would have to be guaranteed from want.'

He spoke with deep feeling and some pained embarrassment.

Odisio heard with an immense and unutterable amazement ousting for the moment every other sentiment from his mind. That he could be a welcome suitor to Beldia's father seemed to him such a miraculous happiness that he was bewildered and stunned. He could not even find consecutive words to express his gratitude, and he did not even perceive how strange it was that a man so reserved as Francesco Ardiglione should thus confess his necessities, or one so apparently well situated be conscious of his own inability to keep his favourite child from poverty. All the younger man was sensible of was that a future suddenly opened out before him like the very gates of heaven.

'But, but——' he stammered, 'would it be possible, could I comply with your conditions, that Madamigella Beldia ever would deign to think of me? Surely, oh, surely not!'

Ser Checchi dusted some books with a few impatient movements.

'That is for you to judge,' he said. 'You are a personable man, and should not be too modest. I have no idea of my daughter's opinion of you : but

I should not think it unfavourable. You have my leave to try and please her. But remember—she is poor, poor, poor.'

He said the words with so strong an emphasis and with so strange a manner, and such obvious agitation, that a wild fancy struck the Lombard for a moment: was Ser Checchi one of those harmless monomaniacs who call themselves penniless when their secret drawers and hidden boxes are full of gold and silver?

Was it possible to believe that a man who knew that he must leave his daughter portionless would keep unsold a ' Divina Commedia ' worth a hundred thousand francs?

But this thought was secondary to him, and almost unimportant, beside the marvellous rapture of the fact that the old man authorized him to gain the heart and hand of Beldia, if he could.

He could scarcely believe his senses. The sombre walls of the book-room swam before him in a circle of light. He saw the thin, pale hand of Ser Checchi and the moving feather-duster in a dazzle of dancing sun-rays. Then, in a rush of exquisite joy and gratitude, while the tears gushed to his eyes, he stayed that ivory-like hand in its wandering amongst the volumes, and, bending very low, touched it with his lips.

The elder man drew it quickly away, not unkindly, but with embarrassment, as of one before a homage undeserved.

'I am not worthy; I am not worthy,' he said, with a tinge of red coming on his pale, fine features.

CHAPTER VIII.

THE morrow was the Feast of St. John, the time-honoured popular feast of Florence. In other times it used to be a day of rare pageantry, civic, military, and ecclesiastical. In these times it is shorn of its splendours, which are transferred to the democratic celebration of the statute.

The heart of the Florentine populace, however, is still closely attached to St. John's Day; and from break of dawn, when the great bells boom and swell over the sleeping city, to midnight, when the fires die one by one on the cupolas and domes and belfries, the population is astir in joyous and harmless agitation.

Beldia was wont to see what she could see of the illuminations from the tower platform, and avoid the press and noise and trouble of the crowds.

From her terraced roof she could watch the fireworks blaze upon the Carrara bridge, and the rockets slide along the cords above the river, and the great belfry of the Palazzo Vecchio glitter with its many stars of light, while the communal banner streamed upon the wind. Below her stretched the moonlit and firelit river, the black masses of the gathered crowds, the palaces, the bridges, the quays, and far away the deep woods of the Cascine, and the hills, lit here and there with bonfires. She liked better to sit there in quietude by her father's side, amongst her herbs and plants, in the intense silence of night, to which no echo even from the rejoicing city below could reach them, than to descend into the crowded streets, to be jostled and hustled and pushed from side to side under the illumined dome of the cathedral or the sparkling of the baptistery.

'Will you not come down into the streets?' asked Odisio of her on that evening. 'There is music in many places, and the illuminations are fine. I would take care that no harm should come to you or to your father.'

She thanked him, but declined.

'I am not afraid in any way. Our crowds are always good-natured and orderly. But I dislike all noise, and up here it is more mysterious, more romantic, more beautiful. One can believe that one is still in the Renaissance. One sees the lights and the fires, the sky and the water, the grand cupolas and towers and spires; and one does not see the modern ugliness which, when one is in the streets, spoils the illusion of it all.'

'As you will,' said Odisio. 'May I stay here with you?'

'Certainly.'

Ser Checchi had come up to the room, as it had been his habit to do ever since he had been a little boy in the years when the century had been young. It was one of the things unchanged, wholly unchanged, since his childhood. Down below there were changes; the people were no more the merry and picturesque throngs of his youth, and the populace no more went with devout unanimity to the noonday Mass in the duomo; but, as he looked down from his tower platform on St. John's Night, nothing seemed altered in the city lying below.

The fireworks, the illuminations, the river alive with light, the spires and domes outlined with fire, the hills studded with bonfires, the quays and bridges black with multitudes—all these were the same as they had been in the days of his childhood, and the scene was precisely the same which stretched below, radiant in moonlight and lamplight, and with the same summer skies and the same shadowy landscape around it.

Ser Checchi felt as if he were a young child once more, in his little nankeen vest and breeches, with his ruffled shirt open at his throat, and his light hair curling on his shoulders.

Ah, what good times those had been! How simple and honest and cheerful and full of goodwill all life had been when his good father—sacred be his dust!—had brought him up the wooden ladder-like stair on his shoulders, and had set him by the battlemented parapet to watch the night! There was the same kind of flowers growing then as now in their pots and boxes; the same kind of pigeons roosted then as now in their green wooden dovecot; and the same fires lighted water, and bridge, and dome, and palace. At such moments Ser Checchi almost wished that he had read less, and that he had lived more.

'How like you look to my grandmother!' he said to Beldia this evening.

Perhaps it was only his imagination, but it seemed to him as if Beldia grew more like her great-grand-dame every year. She had the same calm carriage, and the same serene, kind smile, the same clear skin that no sun could tan or redden, the same grave fair brows, like those of a Madonna of Dürer or a maiden of Mieris.

As he looked at her on this festal night, as the light from the brilliant skies shone on her eyes and breast, Ser Checchi thought for the first time that it was natural that young men should find her fair, and dream of her as a companion for their lives.

'And it would be well if she had someone besides myself to care for her,' he thought, with a pang. 'I have been too selfish and too careless by far.'

The sun had sunk down behind the Carrara mountains some half-hour before, but the skies were still radiant when the fireworks began, and the blending of moonlight and lamplight and sunset reflection made a beautiful glory on the river and the shores.

Up above, on the tower-roof, Beldia and her father and Odisio watched it all; the dog also, with his forelegs resting on the parapet, and his excitement finding vent in sharp, quick, smothered barks like minute-guns. Folko had seen many an illumination thus during his ten years of life, but the sight never failed to agitate and puzzle him exceedingly, as though it were something which he had never beheld before.

It was a balmy and brilliant night: the air was clear, though warm; the scent of the carnations and lemon verbena was sweet under the dew; the bats flew above their heads, startled by the fires leaping and sparkling below, and the rushing and roaring of the pyrotechnic showers. The spectacle was soon over, the last girandola shot up from the centre of the bridge, and the last reflection faded off the water; alone the illuminated cupolas and towers across the river remained ablaze, and the old iron cressets, filled with lighted oil, which were hung round beneath the battlements of Taddeo's tower, answered them as they had done with every midsummer throughout six centuries.

The night of St. John was over for another year.

Ser Checchi turned away from the parapet, and went noiselessly through the flowers, down the wooden stair, leaving the Lombard alone with his daughter; for the woman-servant had already hurried away to her kitchen to see that her saucepans for the supper were not burning or cooling.

Folko remained with his forepaws upon the stone ledge, his eyes gazing intently down on to the crowded streets below, and Beldia stayed also, lost in thought as she gazed at the flowing river, rippling like molten silver underneath the stars. She, too, had seen the illuminations of St. John's Night for as many years as she could remember.

Odisio stood beside her silently, his heart beating in tumult.

He understood that her father had left them on purpose thus alone. But he seemed to himself much too wretched, penniless, and friendless a wanderer to dare to offer her his empty hand.

At last, as she turned slowly and reluctantly away from gazing on the beauty of the night, he dared to speak, his throat contracting as though his own voice choked him.

'Madamigella Beldia,' he said with great timidity, 'I told your father yesterday that I must go away, because I am a miserable idler with no home or fortune. But he gave me leave to tell you—to tell you—what I think you must know well. You are the only woman who lives on earth for me.'

She did not answer; she looked away from him, drawing one of the red carnations through her fingers; the moonlight fell on her white gown and her bent head.

'If you could pardon me—give me any hope?' he murmured, gathering courage, 'I would try to make some money, some place, worthy of you. Would it be ever possible?'

'I could not leave my father,' she answered in a low, soft voice, which thrilled him to the soul.

Folko came and thrust his nose in friendly fashion against their hands, which in that moment touched and clasped each other.

CHAPTER IX.

'THAT she should go and promise herself to a foreigner, a Lombard, a Brescian!' said Veronica with indignation to the boy Poldo. 'When she could have had Pampilio Querci, who will die a town councillor, or any good, sound-moneyed man who comes about her, and would have kept her in silk gowns and velvet mantles all her years! Ay, I know the Lombard is a fine-built man and a soft-spoken and goodly to look at; but good looks make no bread, and gentle words butter no parsnips, and he says himself he is as poor as a church rat! What use is that? There will be waiting, waiting, waiting, and what does that mean? That a woman's bloom goes like the bloom off the grapes which you shut up in a closet to keep for Christmas. The grapes are the same grapes as they were when you put them away, but when you send them up on your dish they are wrinkled and faded, and the flavour is gone. This is what waiting does for women. The signorina is bonnier than most, and will be well-looking when she is fifty; but, all the same, it will do her no good to wait till this stranger has got the wherewithal to keep her. Querci is already as round as an egg, and is a youngster who will die Syndic of the city likely enough. Besides, there are other reasons——'

She stopped short, for though grumbling and garrulous, and sensible to the charm of the attorney's five-franc pieces, she was a loyal soul, and knew that she had no right to discuss her master's and mistress's circumstances with a young lad like Poldo.

All that was known to her or to the neighbours was that the stranger from the North was affianced to the daughter of Ser Checchi—vaguely known, no date, nor any kind of detail being added to the bare fact. Much gossip was made about it—set on foot by the baker's wife, who had a piqued and jealous fancy for the handsome Lombard herself; and when anyone ventured to speak directly of it to Ser Checchi, he replied in a reserved tone, that his consent had been given conditionally, but that there was no reason to believe that the marriage would take place for years.

'There are many reasons to believe that it will never take place at all,' said Vestuccio to himself with a smile, whilst with a beaming countenance he bowed before Ser Checchi, and said aloud, 'Long life and all joy and honour to the betrothed young people, sir! Surely an angel is in your dwelling, if anywhere on earth.'

'My daughter has been well brought up, and resembles her mother and grandmother,' replied Ser Checchi stiffly and distantly.

Beldia received her neighbours' felicitations with her usual serenity of manner.

'There is nothing fixed,' she answered to their importunate inquiries. 'Of course I shall never leave my father whilst he needs me.'

It was no one's business what had been decided on between her father and her betrothed. She shrank from comment and curiosity with the sensitiveness of a refined and reserved nature.

Odisio was too happy to heed or weigh any material questions. Ser Checchi had indeed said to him:

'You know my conditions. You must show me that you can maintain her before I can give her to you. Look for nothing from me,' he added more harshly. 'I am ill off—ill off—and my son would drain the purse of Plutus dry.'

But this was enough to fill the heart of the younger man with rejoicing. He had her promise to wait for him; it seemed to him that it would inspire the dullest clod into genius and ambition, and give to a block of stone the impulse of vitality and effort. He wrote to his mother the tenderest

and gayest letter he had ever penned ; and to his old
master in Milan he sent a pressing entreaty to find
him work, no matter how hard, but lucrative. His
idle, careless, whimsical life of accident and adventure
was at an end: he was sensible of powers and
learning in him beyond the common possession of
ordinary men, and he saw the future in radiant
colours like the fires of the girandola on that ever-
blessed night of St. John.

As he walked through the streets with his elastic
tread and his erect and martial carriage, a smile in
his eyes and a song on his lips, his rivals looked
after him with scowling glances, and Pampilio
Querci muttered an oath as his own small thin
shadow fell across the sunny path.

'Never mind,' said Vestuccio consolingly to him.
'Let the poor fools dream on as they like. Their
plans will never come to anything, you may be
sure.'

Meantime those midsummer days and eves were
full of sweetness to Beldia. She had not thought
the earth could hold so much happiness. The old
tower-roof in the starry evenings, with its odours of
thyme and sweet peas, seemed to her like the enchanted garden of Angelica. Her suitor loved to
converse of the future; but to her the present was
fully enough. She did not care to look forward;
these quiet morning hours, which brought him to
his studies in the book-room, this balmy evening
time, when all the labours of the day were over, and
they were free to go up and sit against the old stone
battlements, and watch the stars in their courses,
were all she coveted. Odisio's mother had written

with tenderness and gladness; and his master had also answered in kindest strain, promising his influence and efforts; only Cirillo had replied not a word to the tidings sent him. They supposed that he had been absent from Rome when the news had been written; they never knew much of his movements.

'It does not matter whether he is well or ill-pleased,' said her father angrily, when such silence pained her. 'He is not your master nor mine, and we have no need to consult his wishes.'

One night, when it was late, and no one but Beldia was awake in the tower, there came a loud knocking at the iron-barred door below, and Folko barked loudly. Everyone in the place was asleep. Beldia alone leaned against the parapet of the roof, whither she had gone half an hour before to watch the tall form of the Lombard pass down the narrow street. Being wakeful, and allured by the sublimity of the night, she had remained there looking, now up at Saturn and Jupiter in the heavens, and now down on the gliding Arno water and the blackness of the bridge arches.

At the loud rapping below she leaned over the machicolations and called loudly:

'Who is there?'

Far above as she was, her voice reached the street below faintly in the perfect stillness of the night.

'It is I, Cirillo!' called her brother angrily, from beneath the arch of the door.

Taking her lantern in her hand, she called the dog and hurried down the dark shaft of the stairway. It was long and steep, but she knew those winding steps by heart and ran down them with quick, sure feet. She set her lantern on the stone floor when she reached the bottom, and began to pull aside the rusty and massive bolts, and turn in its lock the huge key, which had been made by a cunning locksmith in the thirteenth century.

Slowly the great door yielded to her effort, and she dragged it open, little by little, to the summer night without. Her brother came in roughly, scarcely returning her embrace.

'Who could suppose you were all abed at this hour?' he said impatiently. 'The train is only just in from Rome.'

'My father is always early to bed and early to rise, as you know,' she said, in surprise at his negligent and ill-tempered greeting. 'Please come upstairs as quietly as you can, not to wake him. Your room is always ready, and I will call up Veronica and soon get you some supper.'

With muttered words of dissatisfaction Cirillo climbed the stairs after her, pushing back, ill-humouredly, the well-meant caresses of Folko.

'Bring me some wine,' he said, when he reached the chamber in which their meals were served; 'I want no food. Do not call up the woman. I only came to speak to you. The devil fetch me! How good-looking you have grown!'

Beldia looked at him in trouble and astonishment. He was flushed, dusty, dishevelled; he had a sullen and coarse expression, and the natural beauty of his face was inflamed and swollen.

'Are you not well?' she said with hesitation, as she lighted a lamp and placed it on the table.

'Get the wine, the best wine you have: or, better still, some brandy,' he replied, as he cast himself heavily into his father's great arm-chair.

Greatly disquieted, she went and took a flask of seven-year-old Chianti wine from a cupboard and set it before him.

'I will bring you cold meats and bread in a moment, if you wish,' she said; 'or I will fry some eggs and bacon.'

'I want no food,' said her brother ungraciously; and he poured himself out a big beaker of the wine and drained it. 'Have you no brandy?' he asked.

'No; father never buys it.'

Cirillo drank again and again, then leaned his elbows on the table, and his chin on his hands, and looked up at her.

'What cursed trash did you write me, that you are betrothed to a Lombard without a penny?'

Her face flushed with anger.

'I am promised to a man whom I love.'

Cirillo laughed unkindly.

'Women do not marry men they love. They marry men who help their families. I mean you to wed with Pampilio Querci, and with no one else, my fair one.'

'I do not ask you what I shall do,' said Beldia quietly. 'It is enough that my father and I are of one mind.'

'Who cares for your mind or your heart? You have a handsome person, and that you will give where I tell you.'

'You had better go to your chamber. We can speak of these matters in the morning.'

'I will speak of them now,' said Cirillo, taking another draught of wine. 'Things are in a bad way with me. I have no luck. I have played and lost. I have fought the city guards, and there is a hue and cry out against me, and I want to get to the coast and out of the country.'

Beldia listened, with her face growing white and set.

'My father,' she said faintly, looking towards the door of the room, as though she saw her father's form there.

'Oh, I do not want to see him, that you may be sure,' said her brother, with a fierce, short laugh. 'You must give me all the money you have, and I will go to sleep in this chair for a few hours, and then take the earliest train to Livorno; there is one at five in the morning, I think. How much money can you get together?'

'I have no money,' she replied. 'I have a few francs left of the house-allowance for the week. You know that I have nothing of my own.',

'And you would marry a penniless scholar? you fool! Querci would give you money if you asked him——'

'That is a shameful thing to say, Cirillo.'

'A fig for your fancies! Do you suppose a woman like you cannot get money if she wants it? Many men have come and gone here who would have asked nothing better than to open their purses to you. But you were always a stiff-necked jade.'

'For shame, Cirillo!'

He looked cunningly at her out of his swimming and sleepy eyes.

'You are in love with your Lombard?'

She said nothing, but a wave of colour passed over her face and she turned away her head. It hurt her inexpressibly to have this coarse, rude touch laid on her tenderest and most sacred feelings.

Cirillo laughed aloud.

'Very well, my saint. Then if you do not bring me out your pearls, I shall go and knock up this Messer Odisio and tell him that I forbid the banns.'

'My pearls?'

The pearls had been her mother's, and they constituted those vezzi or dowry-jewels without which no Florentine maiden can be decently betrothed or wedded. These necklaces vary in value from the rare virgin pearls, large as cherries, of the young princess, to the seed pearls, small as grains of rice, of the girl of the populace or of the peasantry. Those of Beldia were of medium excellence: three strings of them, worth, on the whole, some three thousand francs. Cirillo knew their value to a centime, for they had often been in his hands.

'I could not give you my pearls,' she said, stupefied. 'You must be mad to ask it. Father would never consent.'

'No doubt he will never consent. If we were fools enough to ask him!' said Cirillo, with an ironical laugh in her face. 'But you will go and get them, Madonna mine, or I will go and find your betrothed and tell him you are to wed with Pampilio Querci.'

'You may tell him what you like. He will not believe it.'

'I intend you to marry Querci.'

'You may intend what you please. I shall not do it.'

'We shall see. But first get me the pearls. I must be out of the country as fast as I can, for—I may as well tell you the whole. There was a quarrel, and the guards drew their swords, and I shot one, and I believe he is dead. The affair may be troublesome. The pater would not care to see the carabineers come in here after me. Yet that will be so if I be found at daybreak in Florence.'

Beldia said nothing. The callous carelessness of the confession froze her blood. It was worse than the crime itself to be thus indifferent in its narration.

'Oh, my father! my dear father!' she murmured, with sobs strangling her breath. 'Such a long and pure and honourable life—disgraced by you, disgraced by his own son!'

She was not a woman who ever gave way to emotion, but this horror overwhelmed her; she turned her face to the wall, and her frame shook with the force of her weeping. She had been so happy such a little while before, dreaming her dreams under the starry skies.

'The old idiot is disgraced by himself,' said Cirillo savagely. 'He has his signatures out by the dozen. Querci could square all that; you must marry Querci. But for the moment get me your pearls. I can sell them to the Jew goldsmiths in Livorno, very well. If you had sent me money when I wrote to you last, I should not now be in this plight. It is all your fault. The men set on me because, when I lost, I had no money to pay, and I defended myself, and there was noise and fuss, and the guards came, and I shot one, I tell you. It was all your fault. How can a man live without money?'

'He lives by the work of his hands or his brain,' said Beldia, thinking of Odisio, and in the trouble and confusion of mind scarcely noticing what her brother had said of their father's signatures.

Cirillo swore a bad oath.

'I do not choose to do either,' he said sullenly. 'Whilst I am young I mean to enjoy. When one is old one can labour. Does my father work, that you honour him so? All his substance goes in his one craze for old books. It were a harmless luxury in a rich old man, but in a tradesman it is a crime, a bigger crime than mine. But come, go and get me the pearls. I want to sleep while I can, and you will give me something to eat at four, and then I will get out of the house before anyone wakes. Even the charcoal-men must not see me.'

Beldia did not speak; the sobs in her throat were stilled by a great effort, but she was bewildered and full of horror. Her longing impulse was to send for Odisio—he was so manly, so courageous, so loyal; her heart yearned for the comfort and support of his presence; she had that entire confidence in him which is the joy and strength of love. But for his sake she did not dare to summon him. Her brother was already set against him; the two men might quarrel—if they met would almost surely do so, and Cirillo might use his revolver on him as he had done on the guard in Rome. 'No,' she said to herself; 'no, Odisio should not be brought into danger by her. Sooner would she suffer anything than run that risk.'

'Listen to me,' she said, striving to steady her voice and combat all weakness of emotion. 'There is no testimony that your tale is true. You have a strong imagination when you need money. What guarantee have I that if I beggar myself at your request, you will really leave this town and really cease to trouble those I love?'

'None at all,' said her brother jeeringly. 'I do not offer you vows and proofs. You will bring me out your pearls, because, if you do not, I shall shake my father out of his sleep and get what I want, and I shall then go and find out your Brescian and pick a quarrel with him. There are plenty of knives in Florence. Come, Madonna mine. Do not provoke me. Patience is not one of my many virtues.'

She was clear and firm in resolve when emergency arose, and through the confusion of her mind before the confession and demands of her brother these two necessities were beyond all imperative: her father must not know of Cirillo's visit, and her betrothed must not be brought into any peril from it. Blood soon runs high, she knew, and blows are given which often carry death with them, almost before a word is said. She had not dwelt in a populous riverain quarter without knowing how hot and bitter men's unbridled passions can become.

No; even in the painful stupor of her thoughts, she resolved that Odisio and Cirillo must not meet, nor must her father hear of his son's ill-doing.

CHAPTER X.

WHEN the first rosy warmth of the daybreak came over the Apennines and smote the gray turrets of the tower, arousing the pigeons from their wooden cotes, and sending the bats to roost in the belfry of Santo Spirito, Beldia sat alone in her own chamber, and her brother was gone. She had not undressed, nor had she slept a moment in the past night : she sat still and sorely troubled, the empty case, in which the pearls had been, kept lying on her lap.

Their loss oppressed her with the weight of a deadly calamity. It was not because they were jewels, or because she cared to wear them, but they had been her mother's, and she had always felt a kind of benediction in their cool, soft touch. And how could she account to her father for their disappearance? How could she reconcile him to the sight of her on saints' days and on Sundays, without that three-stringed collar to which he was so used, and which seemed a very part and parcel of her own white throat?

She sat motionless, with the old leather box lying useless on her knees.

Cirillo had tossed it aside as clumsy and cumbersome, and had folded the pearls up in a sheet of paper and slipped them into his waistcoat pocket.

She sat and gazed at it as the cold roseate light of the earliest morning came through the narrow casement.

She had first worn them at her first communion. Her father himself had clasped them about her throat, and had said : 'Be your mother's spirit with you ever.'

And now they were gone, the poor pure, pretty things, to be weighed in the oily hands of dealers, and might lie on the naked breasts of coarse, indecent women! The tears fell from her eyes slowly one by one, and rolled down on to the old black empty jewel-case.

She could not keep a secret from her father. Although she had long been in the habit of keeping to herself all things which would have annoyed or troubled him, in order to leave him to that intellectual quiet which he prized and needed, she had never hidden anything of importance from him, nor answered any question of his untruly or disingenuously.

She resolved that she would tell him that she had given her pearls to Cirillo to sell; but that she would spare him, if she could, the knowledge of his son's offence against the law.

And when she met him in the forenoon she did tell him this much; and it seemed to her that her father took the news in a strange manner.

'You will not have even those, then?' he muttered in a sad and muffled voice. 'Why, oh, why did you strip yourself for that leech, that knave, that hound? What use is it to give Cirillo aught? He is like the thirsty sea-sand, which ever drinks and never has enough.'

He did not ask her how she had known of her brother's demands, or how the pearls had been transmitted to him. He asked no questions; he was only pained and oppressed.

'Even your mother's necklace! Even that!' he repeated. It afflicted him keenly, but he did not show any anger, as she had feared that he would do, nor did he even blame her.

'What right have I to find fault?' she heard him murmur to himself. Had he heard of his son's advent, like that of a thief in the night, and did he purposely avoid interrogation and explanation? She almost fancied that he did so, and that he knew of Cirillo's secret visit: for he sent for a skilful locksmith of the Fondaccio, and had the locks altered of those drawers and chests in which the Dante and the most precious of his manuscripts were lying.

To Odisio she said nothing. She could not bring herself to speak of her brother's evil conduct to one who through poverty and temptation had always kept his head so high, his hands so clean, his honour so unsullied.

The days went on their quiet course, and the summer came, and the city grew empty. Even the little tradesfolk in turn shut up their shutters and went out into the country hills or down to the seashore. The lemon-sellers wandered through vacant streets, and the barrows of melons and plums were rolled underneath deserted houses, and there seemed no living creatures left except the poor thirsty, muzzled dogs, and the hot, tired cab-horses, and the flowers which hung their drooping heads at all the corners of the palaces, and found no buyers, and died of heat and thirst unpitied.

At this season of the year they were always used to go up to Antella, taking Veronica and Folko with them, and leaving the care of the pigeons and plants to the cobbler who lived below, and who fulfilled his trust conscientiously, and was proud and elate when, on her return, Beldia praised the healthy appearance of his charges.

The fifteenth of July had never come and gone without Ser Checchi saying, often with regret :

' It grows too hot for the city : pack your clothes, and we will take the diligence to-morrow or next day.'

And Beldia was so used to the annual exodus that by this date all her arrangements were always already made, and there was nothing to do but to hand over the pigeons' food and the gardening tools to the cobbler for the rest of the summer.

' My father will be sure to ask you to come with us to Antella,' she had said more than once to Odisio.

But the fifteenth of July came and went, and there had been no mention of moving to the country.

It became increasingly difficult, too, to obtain from him the money necessary for the agricultural outlay. On Tuscan lands the owner must purchase cattle, tools, seeds, and all such necessaries, and if the year be a bad one must maintain his peasantry as well. This especial year had been unusually bad ; the rains had been too long withheld, and then had come out of season ; the corn had been ravaged by storms, the vines were sickly, the show of olives was meagre, the foot-and-mouth disease had visited the district ; and her father, who was always wont to take these caprices of nature with perfect philosophy, was now irritated and depressed by such losses and troubles to a degree wholly unlike himself. Yet they were no more than are constantly to be encountered and prepared for by those who have anything to do with land and its cultivation; and the year, though not likely to be a fruitful one, was not more disastrous than a similar one ten years earlier, when she had seen her father's serene and gentle humour scarcely stirred even by a passing regret.

She waited a little while this day, hesitating to worry him with those coarse, cruel needs; and then, as her father was about to return to his studies, she said timidly:

'Ruggiero was here at noon.'

Ruggiero was the contadino at their little country place of Antella.

'Well?' asked Ser Checchi, pausing with some annoyance, his thumb and forefinger between the pages of the volume which he was longing to peruse. 'What of that, my dear?'

'The red cow is dead.'

'Another cow! Cows are always dying. They are melancholy beasts.'

'She drank at the river, and she swallowed a small fish, and it stuck across her gullet and killed her.'

'He must get another,' said Ser Checchi, opening his volume with some annoyance.

'But the yield of the corn is so poor. There are only fifty staie.'

'They are producing new wheat by artificial fertilization, but I am not sure that what is so produced will answer so well as the natural plant,' replied her father. 'Do you not think the most wonderful secret of all in nature is how that germ lies hidden in the grain and sprouts when restored to earth? Those ears of wheat from the Pharaohs' sepulchres which germinate after two thousand years—explain it scientifically how you will, the miracle and the mystery of it still remain the same. Man is dumfounded before it. I once saw an Etruscan tomb opened away yonder by Volterra. There were some small kernels of wheat in a stone cippus. I planted them in a fresh-turned furrow, and they grew and multiplied! That I saw with my own eyes. And in due time I ate bread from the harvest of those grains. They had lain there in the dark, in the bowels of the rock, for hundreds upon hundreds of years; they had been put there in the stone cippus before the birth of Cæsar, before the rise of Rome; yet life was still in them, dormant life, which awoke when they once again felt the moist, warm soil open to receive them—felt the dew, and the mould, and the showers. What is impossible in any resurrection after that? How should the human mind follow or grasp the living spirit which was at work within the dry husk?'

She opened her lips to speak, but closed them again without speaking. His thoughts were happily far away with the impersonal; she had not the heart to call him back to the sordid circumstances of the moment—to the poor harvest, to the dead cow, to the straitened purse.

On the morrow, Beldia, as she gave him his coffee, ventured to say:

'It is very warm. Are we not going to Antella this year?'

'No,' said Ser Checchi harshly, looking away from her as he spoke. 'We shall not go this year.'

Beldia controlled her disappointment with difficulty from any outward expression. She occupied herself with pouring water on the coffee grains and cutting slices of bread for the boy Poldo's breakfast. She longed intensely to ask who would enjoy the summer beauty of her olive orchards and her pine woods, but she restrained the impulse, and kept respectful silence.

He pushed away his cup of excellent coffee half-drunk, and sighed. He was a man of tender heart, and it hurt him to deny or deprive anyone of anything; and he knew that, to Beldia, to pass the hot months in the freedom and freshness of the hills was a source of infinite rejoicing and benefit, and she had gone to the Casentino with every summer of her life.

'We cannot afford it,' he added, in a tone of apology.

'It costs less than living in the town,' said Beldia, in surprise, 'and the city heats weaken you, father; all the doctors say so.'

'I am not weak,' said her father hastily. 'We cannot go to Antella; I have let—I have lent—the house.'

'And never told me!' she cried involuntarily, with an unspoken reproach in the exclamation.

'Am I bound to ask your permission for my action?' said the old man, with a severity and haste wholly unlike himself, and a flush on his face.

'No,' said Beldia meekly. 'But I thought, I hoped, I had your confidence. I have always tried to merit it.'

'I never said that you did not merit it,' replied her father. 'But it is tiresome to be obliged to explain.'

He was ashamed of his own silence and insincerity to her, and it made him irritable and sullen, with that ill-temper which is the result of suffering and contrition.

He beat impatiently on the table with his spoon, and looked away from his daughter's inquiring eyes, which he felt ever and again turned upon him.

With a violent effort at self-control, she did not even ask to whom he had let, or lent, their country retreat.

'I shall know in time,' she said to herself; 'ill news always travels apace. All the gossips of the quarter will be screaming it out to each other soon enough.'

The words of her brother, which had passed by her scarcely noticed in the excitement of his visit, came back on her memory; he had spoken of their father's signatures. Was it possible that he, so prudent, so modest, so careful, so self-denying, so all-wise, as she deemed him, could be in debt? That his means were narrowed of late she knew, but she had attributed it to Cirillo's extravagance, never to any possible act or fault of their parent. All that her father did was in her sight blameless, admirable, never to be doubted.

He took his hat and stick and went out early,

saying something of a business engagement. Beldia had already done her market and household work; she went, as was her wont in her father's absence, to the library, to be in readiness if any customer or inquirer might come thither.

Odisio was at his own labours in the architect's office where he was temporarily engaged; he could never come to the tower until after six o'clock on week-days. She sat long alone, for the boy Poldo was out on an errand, and Veronica busy in her kitchen and scullery, and it was not the hour at which the few frequenters of the library were used to present themselves.

She had taken her work with her, and seated herself near the high-barred window; the books in their multitudes strewn around her, and the volumes and pamphlets, which her father would not allow to be disturbed, lying on the ground. Nine o'clock struck, and then ten; the boy Poldo returned, and went to his desk, where, sitting all day with his head buried in his shoulders, he occupied himself unwillingly with the copying work allotted to him. It was very warm weather, and even the thick stone walls of Taddeo's tower could not keep out the strong, heavy heats of mid July.

'Aren't we going at all to the country, madamigella?' Poldo asked wistfully once, whilst his forefinger pursued the erratic path of a blue-bottle across his written page.

'I am afraid not this year,' said Beldia; and his respect for his mistress was so great, that he did not dare ask why or wherefore. Only the chagrin of his heart spent itself in a loud groan, and found further vent in fiercely striking at the fly with his flat wooden ruler.

'Finish your copying, Poldo, against my father comes back,' said his mistress.

The boy applied himself to his uncongenial task with unwilling compliance, and there was no sound in the book-room except the scratching of his metal pen and the buzzing of the escaped blue-bottle.

Now and then a cry came faintly from the street below of 'Cenc-i-e!' (bring out your rags), 'Ov-a-freschi!' (new-laid eggs), or 'Co-co-me-ro!' (water-melons), but by eleven o'clock even these ceased. The vendors had gone indoors, or sought some shady corner under a wall or a church porch, out of the blazing, cloudless noontide heat.

The lower door of the tower was always left open in the hope that the open portals would invite passers-by to enter and ascend the stairs, and the door of the library also stood open, with a bell hung on to it by a chain, which tinkled when anyone touched the chain. On the silence of the forenoon now the tinkle of this bell was heard, and a footstep sounded on the stone-floor of the entrance.

Beldia looked up, expecting to see her father, and half rose to welcome him and take his sun umbrella. She saw instead a little sandy-haired, thin man, with shabby clothes, who had a sheaf of papers under his arm.

Without taking off his hat he said to her:

'Is the Signor Ardiglione in? No? Who are you then? I will leave this paper with you.'

The boy Poldo turned round in his seat with a scared inquisitive gaze. Beldia approached the visitor, and said, with her habitual dignity and grace :

'I am Signor Ardiglione's daughter. I can take any message for him !'

The rude thin man fumbled in his breast-pocket, and drew out an old-fashioned ink-horn and a new-fashioned metal pen. He scribbled at the foot of the document which he had brought, muttering half aloud as he did so :

' In the absence of—umph, umph !— this day of grace sixteenth July—umph — humph — speaking with his daughter—your name ? What is your name ?'

' Beldia Maria Beatrice.'

' Beldia Maria Beatrice,' murmured the little scribe, finishing his writing and restoring the ink-horn to his pocket; then he handed the paper to her and bustled out of the room.

She stood looking blankly down upon the document, with its ominous preamble, ' In the name of His Majesty,' etc., etc. She had not known who the man was, because he was a newcomer in the neighbourhood; but she knew the look of a law-paper, and she perceived that this was one; a precetto, or sentence to pay money, under threat of distraint from that division of the tribunal which judges the affairs of the quarter of Santo Spirito.

For a precetto to be sent thus, it must have been preceded by citation, interrogation, and announcement of sentence. How was it that she had known nothing of any of these ?

The boy Poldo had left off his copying, and was staring at her blankly.

'The master is in trouble?' he asked stupidly, but good-naturedly. 'They have said so a good while in the street.'

'No, no; you should not think such things of your employer,' said his young mistress, casting the document into a drawer and turning the key on it. 'It is some mere matter of business—a summons for some contravention, I suppose.'

Poldo looked incredulous.

'The people round here all say that he is in debt, head and ears over; and that he has been called up at the Pretura, everybody knows, except you, madamigella.'

'My good lad,' said Beldia with severity, 'never speak of your master, I order you, nor let others speak of him; only be sure that he is the best and wisest man of all men living.'

Poldo turned round to his writing, and, unseen by her, put his tongue in his cheek and winked at the big gray cat of the house.

He was much attached to Beldia, but for his master he had no liking, and he thought the learned scholar a poor fool.

'Throwing away all his means on old paper and musty books, when he might drink *vin santa* and eat lamb and kid three times a day!' thought the young Florentine.

With a great effort over herself and her overwhelming anxiety, Beldia had taken the key out of the drawer and had shut away the fatal document without looking on more than those topmost words which told her what its character and meaning were.

She would not allow herself to intrude on her father's secrets in his absence. But the uncertainty and the anxiety were torture to her.

A precetto, which is in reality a power to seize goods within five days given to a creditor by the tribunal, could mean nothing but trouble; and all the signs which she had seen in her father of late years—of preoccupation, of care, of economy—came back upon her mind with painful distinctness in cruel confirmation of that she feared. She could not go on working, though she made a pretence of doing so to screen her agitation from the boy Poldo, whose sharp, little black eyes she felt ever and again upon her, as though they were gimlets, piercing her very soul.

He was a good-natured boy, and not unfaithful; but he was curious, and had a vulgar tongue when it was allowed to wag at its will.

It grieved her that he should have seen the advent of the officer of the tribunal. She knew that he would talk of nothing else when he should run out for his hour of liberty and play at disc-throwing with other lads in the Santo Spirito square, or loll on the water-steps of the Arno, by the Santa Trinita bridge.

Her lips opened on an impulse to ask him to say nothing, but she did not speak, for she knew that to ask such a thing was useless, and that though he would promise silence readily, it would be beyond him to keep his promise.

Time went on, and the church clocks boomed out the meridian hour.

As its last stroke sounded Ser Checchi entered:

he looked jaded and dusty and hot, and very pale, paler even than was usual with him.

Beldia's heart ached at the thought that she must give him the dreaded document.

She brought him his loose linen library coat, and his slippers and a glass of water, with some slices of fresh lemon cut into it. Then she let him sit and rest a few moments whilst she sent Poldo out on an errand which would occupy him some little time.

He drank thirstily, and remained reclining in the osier chair which she had placed for him : the light fell across his face, and she was struck by the worn, aged look which it wore.

It hurt her to the quick to tell him of the hated paper which had come for him in his absence ; and yet she dared not withhold the knowledge of it from him, lest worse should ensue. She went and unlocked the drawer and brought it to him.

'Dear father,' she said softly, 'this came when you were away. I have not looked at it, but I see it is the kind of paper which brings trouble with it. Will you not let me know what sorrow hangs over you ?'

He snatched the document from her with the roughest movement which she had ever seen in him ; the blue veins on his temples swelled and throbbed ; he held it at arm's-length and stared at it.

'He has broken faith with me,' he said hoarsely. 'He promised by all the saints to wait——'

Then he crumpled the act up in his hands, so that his daughter should not see what was written on it, and thrust it into his coat-pocket, and muttered some unintelligible words of which she could make no sense.

'May I not know?' she said piteously. 'Oh, father, do not mistrust me; do not conceal anything from me—nor from Odisio! He loves you—he would aid you.'

'I want no aid,' said the old man sternly; 'and did you conceal nothing when you gave your pearls to your worthless brother? Go to, go to! I do not call strangers or women to my councils.'

They were the harshest words which he had ever spoken to her, and the most unjust.

She measured his trouble by their injustice.

She did not press him further then, but went away to her own chamber, leaving the doors wide open, that she might hear at his slightest call.

He told her nothing all day. He was at home throughout the afternoon, and two or three of his old customers and friends came thither, and she could hear him discussing and conversing with them as usual. But for the agitation and consternation which the sight of the document had caused him, she could have believed that it was a summons of no importance. She tried to hope that it was so; he was so wise, so frugal, so philosophic, she could not believe that he could have fallen into the common, stupid, vulgar difficulties which dog the steps of prodigals and spendthrifts. No one had ever been in business so exact as he, or so careful and moderate as he in private life.

At supper also Ser Checchi said nothing of the document which had been left that morning, but he ate little and took a little more wine than was his wont, for he was usually over-abstemious in all things. He hurried over the meal under pretext of much business, and, after it, Beldia was left to suppress her torturing anxiety as best she could.

She was thankful when she heard the quick, light step of Odisio that evening on the stairs which led to the roof. She had ascended thither at sunset, partly from the habit of watering her plants at that hour, and partly from a heated sense of disquietude and restlessness and thirsty longing for the air.

She told her betrothed of what had so tormented her, looking eagerly in his face to read there if he had any knowledge of her father's liabilities.

Odisio's face grew overcast; he did not answer her immediately with his usual candour.

'Do you know anything? Have you heard any rumour?' she asked him with earnest entreaty; and he turned from her and walked a few paces up and down the platform before he replied to her questioning eyes and anxious words.

'I think,' he said at last, 'that is, I fear, that Ser Checchi has some dilemmas which he does not confide to us. It is, I believe, thought that he has money troubles; and I fear he has trusted some dealers and money-lenders too much.'

'Vestuccio?' asked Beldia eagerly.

'I have heard no names,' replied Odisio. 'But it may very well be that Vestuccio is one of them, or, indeed, the prime mover in it all. The little I have seen of him gives me the impression that he is a cunning man. He was a poor lad sixteen years ago, and now he has money and houses and land, as well as his acknowledged and unacknowledged trades.'

Beldia sighed wearily.

'I never liked Vestuccio myself; but I think—oh, I do think—he is truly attached to my father.'

Odisio smiled sadly.

'My dear and innocent one, Cicero said long ago that the heart into which the love of gold has entered is shut to every other feeling; and it is as true now as it was in his time. Messer Aurelio, believe me, is attached to no one except to himself.'

Beldia sighed again.

'But it would injure him, surely, to injure anyone so good and so much respected as my father?'

'My love, nothing injures anyone by which they gain. Men like Vestuccio do not care greatly about a pure reputation; they chiefly care about making high percentage and buying cheap to sell dear.'

Beldia was silent; her reason told her that he was right.

'We are not to go to the country,' she said, while her eyes filled with tears.

'Indeed? That looks bad. What cause does your father allege?'

'That he has let, or lent, the house.'

'To Vestuccio, perhaps?'

'Perhaps. I never thought of that. I so longed to be with you at Antella.'

'My dearest, I am happy enough here.'

Beldia said nothing; she employed herself watering her flowers from the cans which he filled at the spout on the roof. The fresh air, the evening shadows, the solace and support of her suitor's presence calmed her apprehensions and soothed her nerves; yet she was profoundly troubled by his echo of her own apprehensions.

'If I am to bring him, as a dower, only debt and anxiety, he had better never have seen my face,' she thought, as she stooped over her carnations.

As if he divined her thoughts, he kissed her hand as he resigned to it the handle of the water-can.

'Come weal, and come woe, my dear, we shall be happy in each other's love; and whatever a man who is poor can do to save and serve another I will do for Ser Checchi.'

'I am sure that you will,' she said gratefully. 'But it is not difficulty and trouble that I wish to bring you as my dower. What will your mother say?'

'My mother will say that I cannot ask a fairer fate than leave to win and work for an angel,' said Odisio with a tender smile. 'And we may distress ourselves needlessly. Your father is, although a scholar, a man of business; and in business there are often momentary embarrassments which a little time and management can tide over; if it were anything exceedingly grave, I do not think he would keep you ignorant of it. At all events, to-morrow I will make inquiries and tell you the result.'

At that moment there came a rush and patter of several feet up the wooden stair leading to the roof, and Folko, with two little girls clinging to him, scrambled up on to the platform, and rushed to his mistress.

The children were Gemma and Dina, the children of Vestuccio.

'Oh, Beldia,' cried the elder, her fair hair blowing in the wind and her hands full of fern fronds and field gladiolas, 'we have just come from Antella; and I brought you these because you are not going there ever any more, you know; and we shall be there all the summer, and we shall ride the donkey and eat the plums and the pears. Father said we were not to tell you—but I would come and tell you, because you may come and stay with us if you like, and we will take Folko for good and all, and be very kind to him; won't we, Folko?' and Gemma, voluble and important, eager in her mingling of pity and patronage, of fondness and condescension, pressed her corn and her flowers on Beldia with one hand, and with the other clutched caressingly the dog's white curls.

'Not the dog, no; he is mine!' said Beldia quickly; and involuntarily she thrust the little girl, and the flowers, and the ferns away from her, and drew close to her the white form of her four-footed friend. 'You see!' she murmured, in a low, startled whisper to Odisio.

The children stared at her in astonishment; they had not meant to be unkind; they were subdued and frightened at the way in which their offer had been received, and they knew that their father and mother had bidden them not speak a syllable of Antella. They began to whimper, dropping their rural treasures on the floor. They were afraid of Odisio and Beldia, standing tall and stern above them.

'We thought you would be glad for us to let you come up there,' they whined between their sobs; 'and we would be so good to Folko, because you are going to be so poor you won't be able to give him anything to eat. He would be happier with us than with you.'

'Get you gone,' said Odisio sternly, laying his hands on their shoulders. 'You are two pert, silly, impertinent babies. Learn to hold your tongues as your parents bade you. Folko will live and die where he is, and Madamigella Beldia will not ask your permission to go where she pleases. Be off with you!'

He pushed them not gently towards the first step of the wooden stair, and crestfallen and disappointed they withdrew, leaving a litter of broken fronds and red flowers on the stones behind them.

When they were out of sight and earshot, he came back to Beldia, and taking her hands in his breast:

'I fear—I fear—the worst,' he said, in answer to the mute appeal of her eyes. 'Little pitchers have long ears, and these children know that their parents have taken Antella. Let us only hope that it is some temporary arrangement which Ser Checchi has deemed it prudent to make.'

'Were it only that, he would have told me,' she replied. 'It is Cirillo who has brought him to this pass.'

'May I speak to him and entreat him to confide in me?'

'It would be of no use. It might offend him. My father is obstinate, and would not readily admit that he had mismanaged his affairs. We do not even know that he has mismanaged them. Misfortunes come in flocks, like swallows.'

Odisio did not attempt to alter her loyalty and unwillingness to see the truth.

'I may need her divine indulgence some day myself,' he thought.

But he was troubled more greatly than he liked to show to her.

Rumours had reached him in the neighbourhood which spoke of her father's liabilities as numerous, and the reserve in which the elder man had wrapped himself up made it difficult and dangerous to attempt to force his confidence.

'If he would sell his choicer manuscripts, especially the Dante?' he suggested.

Beldia shook her head with a sigh.

' He will never do that. They are the treasures of his soul.'

' Heaven send that the law do not take them from him !'. thought Odisio, but he did not say so.

What use was it to add to her anxieties? She was powerless—as powerless as though she were bound by cords to the flagstaff on the roof.

She stooped for the fern leaves and gladiolas which the children of Vestuccio had left behind them on the stones.

' They came from Antella,' she said, kissing them with great emotion.

Perhaps, she thought, they were all that she would ever see again of those breezy and fragrant fields, where she had wandered with light childish feet, and dreamed so many dreams of girlhood.

CHAPTER XI.

THE days went by, and Ser Checchi said nothing of his affairs either to her or to Odisio.

He was still more serious than was his wont, and passed many hours out of the house, ostensibly on business; but they could not tell from his demeanour or conversation that anything was wrong with him.

His old friends and visitors were more loquacious. Especially did the old ecclesiastic, Don Gervasio, shake his head, and say to her when he found her alone:

'Things are awry, sadly awry; your good father has too much bad paper out—they do say even Antella is no longer your own; he is always in notaries' offices, and whoever goes thither rues it.'

But they knew nothing for certain or in detail; they had, like her, only vague fears and imperfect suggestions to go upon; and like herself they dared not intrude their anxieties on the only person who could have satisfied them. Ser Checchi, despite his gentleness and hospitality, had always kept his friends and companions in a little awe of him.

His manner was so much more composed and serene than the impassioned gesticulations of his fellow-citizens, that its dignity imposed upon them, and there was something about him which made all men feel that he was not lightly to be meddled with or interrogated.

Even his son, who jeered and mocked at him behind his back, had never cared to meet the calm, limpid, grave gaze of his large eyes.

Of Cirillo, and of her pearls also, Beldia meanwhile heard nothing; had it not been for the witness of the empty jewel-case, she would have thought that the events of his nocturnal visit had been a dream. 'I will write from Livorno,' he had said, as he had slipped the necklace into the inside pocket of his coat; but no letter whatsoever had come from him from anywhere.

The heat was now great, and she who had never spent the leonine month in the city since her infancy, felt the oppression and drowsiness of the long, dull, scorching days, and the nights in which scarce a leaf stirred or the faintest breeze arose. The smoke of the furnaces and gasworks, by which the banks of the Arno have been defiled, hung over the river from the San Miniato hill on the east to the avenues of poplars in the west, whilst the green water glistened with the last rays of sunset or sunrise, or the effulgence of full moon.

To her apprehensive terrors and fretting disquietude the burden of the canicular heat added a feverish oppression which was very hard to bear; and even midnight scarcely seemed other than, at this season, a less bright, but not less burning day. To increase her sorrow also, the office at which Odisio worked was closed for two months; and he and she both knew that, to fulfil the conditions prescribed by her father, he must leave the city and seek labour and its gains elsewhere.

'Oh! why have we not one thousandth part of all that the gamblers in the clubs and the idlers in the carriages throw away every evening?' said the young man passionately one night. 'To think that

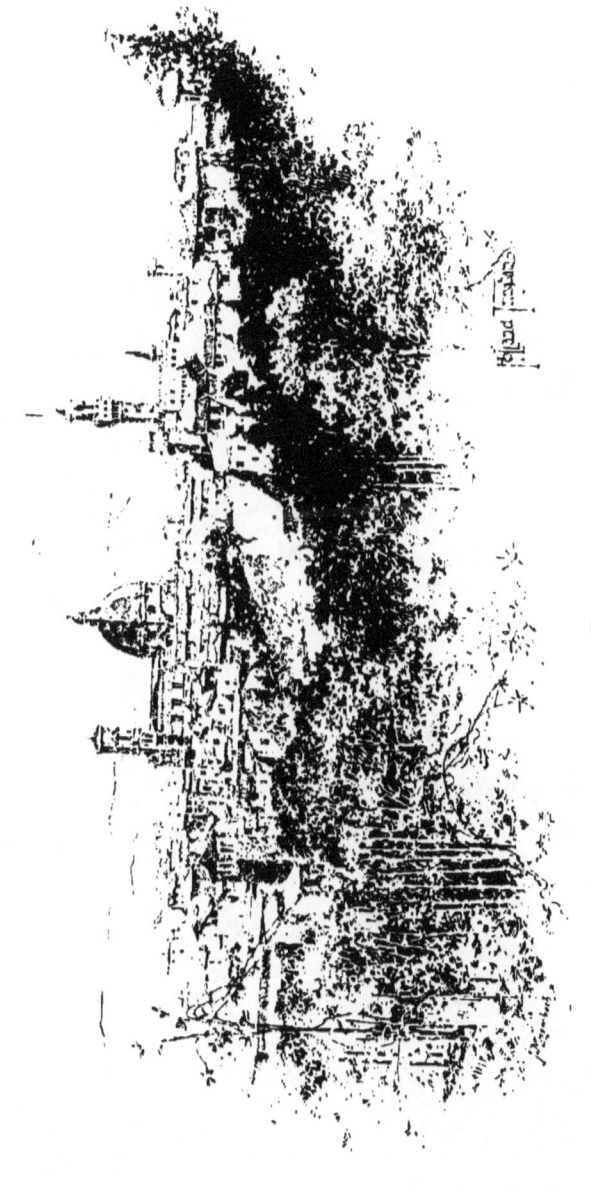

FLORENCE.

we must be parted for want of a little of that wealth which fools and knaves roll in, as crocodiles roll in the yellow sand!'

'We shall not be the happier for envying others,' said Beldia gently. 'Never, never did I wish for anything more than what I had until the last few weeks. Father always had enough for all real wants, and of riches I never thought for a moment.'

'Nor I,' answered Odisio. 'Nor would I wish for them now. But what I fain would have is enough to never leave your side, and to be able to banish all trouble from your father's house. He has forbidden me to think of you, until I can show him that I can maintain you fairly well. I cannot blame him. It is a just and fair demand. But oh, my love, the weariness, the cruelty of waiting!'

'I feel it too,' said Beldia softly, with a sigh which pierced Odisio's heart.

They would have so greatly enjoyed this summer, had they spent it together on the fragrant hills and wind-swept woods of Antella: other summers might be granted them by a kindly fate, but this one summer was for ever lost, unenjoyed, and life is too short for such an irrevocable loss not to be mourned as sadly as the loss of dead Adonais.

When he went down the tower stairs and homeward that night, Odisio found lying in his attic a letter which had come by the evening's post. When he had read it, and one from his mother which was enclosed in it, the news contained in them startled him greatly, and caused him grave and anxious thought: the communication was from his late master in Milan, and contained the offer to him of an appointment as architect and surveyor in Brazil. A Piedmontese banker who had gone out there in his youth, and had made there a vast fortune, desired to build himself a palace in Rio Janeiro, and an entire new quarter also in the city on a scale of great magnificence and elegance. He had invited the Milan artist, who had been a friend of his in youth, to go out and undertake the work, which he wished should, as far as the exigencies of climate permitted, recall the architecture of Lombard Italy.

'But I am too old to seek a new world,' wrote the old architect; 'I wish to lay my bones in the green valley by Biella where I was born, and if I went on board ship to go Westward I should, I am sure, beg to be put on shore again before she could weigh anchor. You have heard of that poor Neapolitan contadino who saved up his little all for ten years to emigrate, and when he had reached La Plata was seized with such homesickness that he worked his passage back at once, and died of joy on seeing the Italian coast on the horizon. So would it be with me. I am too old and too homely to bear transplanting. But you are young, strong, adventurous, new climes and new friends will amuse you, and in a few years' time you will make money enough to return, if you wish, and a reputation too, if you choose. I have proposed you in my place to Don Ercole Vassilva, and this day I received by telegraph his willing consent to employ anyone whom I recommend. He makes only one condition, that you shall go out almost immediately. The monetary conditions are written on the sheet enclosed with this. You will find them generous, and as you will be at no expense whatever whilst there, you can put by a great deal. I have spoken of it to your mother, who, though she would suffer much at having you go so far away, yet sees that it is too good a chance to lose. But she thinks there may be reasons of sentiment why you will be especially loath to leave this country now. Of course you yourself alone can decide this. Be so good, however, as to telegraph me your decision in one way or another within twenty-four hours from your receipt of this letter; it is a golden opportunity, and you are growing too old to be much longer a mere idle student. It is time that your name were cut on some good work in stone.'

Odisio was overwhelmed by the intelligence; he felt as if a mountain had fallen on him and crushed him under it. Before he had known Beldia the proposal might have filled him with rapture: the novelty and excitement promised by it might have been delightful to his spirit of adventure, and he would have seen in it an opening to fame and fortune. But now the thought of wrenching himself from the side of the woman he loved, at a time when she was in sore trouble and difficulty, made the idea of acceptance terrible to him. It would enable him, indeed, to fulfil the condition which her father had laid down to him, but at what a cost of probation and separation! The memory of the wide rolling ocean which would sever them made his heart grow sick.

A few months earlier he might have accepted such a proposal with the ardour of a man young and full of courage, and of curiosity before the unknown, although more probably he would have rejected it even then in favour of liberty and the pleasures of a wandering and careless life. But now the strings of his heart tightened with an intense yearning over his country, his mother, and the woman whom he loved, while at the same time he felt that for the sake of others he ought in duty to utilize this great and fortuitous occasion.

'It is for Beldia to decide,' he said to himself, as he put the letter of his master in his coat pocket and went to the tower of Taddeo, on the following evening, when some designer's work which he had obtained during the closing of the surveyor's office was finished.

Before he went up on to the roof to find Beldia, he first sought her father, and told him of his temptation and his indecision.

In Italy he might spend all the years of his life, as so many clever artists do, without recognition or employment. Alone, however, he might, unreproached, have chosen sooner the poverty, obscurity, and idleness which he had so long preferred; but since these would now for ever sever him from his betrothed, he was tempted to accept a temporary exile for the sake of ultimate happiness and union.

'Do what is best for your future; do not think of me,' wrote his mother: and he felt that Beldia would say the same. Many, even most, women are monsters of selfishness; but when a woman is capable of unselfishness, she crushes her own wishes into dust, and binds her own passions to follow her meekly, as St. Margaret bound the dragon.

He laid the letter from Milan before Ser Checchi, who read it carefully in silence twice over, and sat in silence for some moments, when the younger man had ceased to speak of all his hopes and fears, his doubts and hesitations. At length he said gravely:

'I would bid you go, if you ask my advice. If you love my daughter, you will return with means to pass your life beside her in peace, and to pursue your aims and your art without sordid and harassing anxieties checking you at every step. Go. This is one of those golden occasions which fortune occasionally opens out to a man, and of which he never forgives the refusal. If you reject it, you will regret the rejection all your life. Yes : I admit that I have some troubles. I told you that my daughter was poor. The times are unkind to men who have not the faculty of business. I have it not. I have always loved the impersonal. I live in an age in which to do so is more costly than any crime. But there is no immediate pressure on me, no peril of the kind of which you think. And were there any, what could you do? You are a student; you have to work for your own bread. You would only be the pained witness of sorrows which you could not alleviate. Go and make your own career; Beldia will wait for you. She is constancy incarnated.'

The counsel was sound, the decision was wise; but they fell like stones on the heart of Odisio. He would so willingly have her farther say, ' Nay, I need you ; stay beside us.'

With a slow step and a sad spirit, he mounted the wooden stairs of the tower which so often had seemed to him as a silver ladder to the stars, as a golden pathway to celestial joys. Beldia was as usual at that hour tending her herbs and plants, a rough homespun apron tied over her gown, her watering-can in her hand. She was pouring a shower of rain-water over the thirsty geraniums and pinks; her face was colourless from the great heats, and her actions were more languid than usual: the sultry, heavy, windless air of August in the city robbed her of her customary energy and force; it oppresses alike man and woman, child and animal, humanity and nature; only the swallows, and the bats, and the clouds of evening moths are untouched by it, and whirl and dance and float and circle with unflagging gaiety and unslackened speed.

He went up to her, and without any words of preamble put the letter of the Milan architect in her hand:

'You rule my life,' he said simply. 'Judge for me. What you wish I will do.'

She took the letter and read it through, sitting on the stone coping of the parapet, with the swallows and bats whirling above her head under that pale-green and clear faint gold of the sunset's reflections.

The dangers of absence, the perils of ocean, were a hundredfold more terrible to one who had never left her native city than they can ever seem to the travelled woman of the world. Imagination and ignorance combined to swell their proportions, and to Beldia a long voyage assumed the aspect that it wore to the women who hung in horror over the charts which served to show the mysterious zones whither their lovers, and brothers, and sons had gone with Cristofero Colombo, or with Marco Polo.

She had lived and studied so much with the classic and mediæval writers of her father's bookshelves, that she thought as they did, feared as they did, measured the world as they did. But she resisted her terrors.

'You must go,' she said firmly. Her lips were colourless, and her breath was sharply drawn and uneven.

'Are you so willing that I should leave you?' said Odisio, with reproach and chagrin.

'Ah, no, God knows!' she answered quickly. 'But I would not for worlds stand between you and a fair occasion—between you and your future welfare.'

'If I go, it is only to make that certain provision for you which your father has imposed as his condition that I shall obtain.'

'I know, I know,' said Beldia softly. 'It is for me that you seek an assured provision. But, once there, you may forget, you may change, I may cease to have any great place in your memory; you will grow more endeared to your ambition and your art; and to those you will never alter; it is of those which I would have you think first, it is this which this offer will most surely serve.'

'But at what a price! Sooner would I be the lowliest draughtsman in the meanest builder's office, than I would buy the fame of great Taddeo who put these stones together by a year's loss of you! As for change,' he added in impassioned tones, 'full well you know, my love, that I shall no more change to you than will the moon cease from her course about the earth. You have no right to say such things, not even in pretence to try me. I am not shallow or fickle or untrue. The first day I saw you by the market-place—you were standing looking down upon the flowers at the palace corner—I saw in you all I had dreamed of, all I had desired, and I said in my soul, " By the grace of God she shall be mine, or never shall any woman enter in my life." '

The tears rushed to her eyes and the colour to her face.

'I know, I know! I never doubted you, dear,' she said, with deep emotion. 'But I would not bring trouble upon you, and things are not as I thought they were when first we met: for my father is poor—very poor.'

'So am I.'

'Yes. But you are young and he is old. You must not overshadow your fate with ours.'

'I will work for you both.'

'You have your mother to support.'

'Nay; she maintains herself. I am free to do what I will. If you bid me go, I go; if you bid me stay, I stay.'

Beldia leaned her head upon her hands, and covered her face from his gaze.

Above, the evening clouds floated in pomp and splendour; the golden light quivered in the water below; the night-moths drifted heavily above the heads of the late carnations; the bats circled from steeple to belfry, from flagstaff to weather-vane; the deep toll of the Santo Spirito church chimed the hour. In that sweetness and stillness and solitude the cruelty of such a choice seemed to her greater than it would have done in the glare and business of the noon. She cared nothing for money; she cared nothing for success; she cared only for the humble, peaceful, simple ways of life, fragrant with innocence and imagination and learning, as a garden path which runs through shrubs of gray lavender and bushes of odorous southernwood.

She only wished for such a home as she had hitherto had; for such a homely and lowly happiness as had been that of women of her class in the days of old; such a life as had led the mother of Albrecht Dürer, or the elder daughter of Galileo. For herself, she would have asked nothing better of fate than to dwell where she was until death took her; with Odisio earning his daily bread beside her in honesty and dignity all their days.

But she believed that he had rare talents and fine learning, and that it was in him to make his name known by men. She knew that harder and darker, as every week rolled on, would grow the wants and the woes of her own family. Had she a right to chain him here by her side, only to suffer with her, only to witness what he would be powerless to alleviate—only to share what might lie on him like a stone, crush down his vital powers, and his buoyant aspirations, under the dead weight of a wearing poverty?

She knew how men quickly lose hope and grace beneath the burden of poverty; she knew how all the vigour and zest of manhood are crushed into a withering atrophy, by continual struggle beneath the pressure of debt. She knew it; and she would not, for the sake of her and hers, bind him to such a fate. She lifted her face and looked at him by the warm, shadowy light of the summer evening.

'Go, dear, go,' she said once more. 'I love you too well to keep you here.'

Then she rose, and of her own will, for the first time, she kissed him.

A week later he sailed for the south-western coast.

CHAPTER XII.

THE Borgo San Jacopo was startled one forenoon, soon after the departure of Odisio, by the passage through it of three figures, familiar indeed, but terrible to its sight as the incarnated shapes of an inexorable fate. Often and often were these three figures beheld in this poor quarter of Oltrarno, and where they passed the sun seemed blotted out, the maidens and the children ceased to laugh, the hard-working householders held their breath: they were the modern substitutes for the Parcæ.

The usher, as the sheriff's officer or process-server is termed in Italy, was a small, thin, ferret-faced man with sandy hair and a sharp voice, by name Luigi Fanno, and by nickname Gigi; the custode, or bailiff, who was called Giuseppe Dessi, and was known as Beppe, was short and fat, and red and jovial, making plenty of money out of his wretched trade, and as quick to take a bribe as a swallow to catch gnats. This admirable pair were accompanied by the clerk of the tribunal of the section, a youth of twenty, dark, dirty, pert, and rude, with paste rings on filthy fingers, and a tone intended to awe all hapless debtors into the belief that he held the scales of fate in his unwashed paw. These three persons, with a sheaf of papers, an inkhorn and a Dogberry and Pistol swagger, pushed their way down the narrow street, past the bronze Bacchus, scowling at a little dog, which, in open defiance of law, was skipping and jumping about in play with a bit of string, having no medal on its throat to show that it discharged the tax demanded for its existence.

'Mem.: Little curly dog, brown and white, seen playing on doorstep of No. 12,' the usher wrote down in his note-book, as a matter of contravention to be duly notified to the city-guards, and punished when he should have leisure for minor matters. Then he went onward with his satellites, all three dirty, ill-smelling, and ugly to look at, as they jarred on the radiant sunshine, the masses of flowers, the bright fruits on the barrows, and the laughing faces of the people, which grew grave as they passed. At last, they approached the huge arched door of the tower of Taddeo, and began to mount the stairs; it was not more than ten minutes earlier that Beldia had come down those stairs, and set forth on an errand for her father to his notary Reggiano, whose office was far-off by the Porta Pinta.

'Good-morning, gentlemen,' said the charcoal-seller in the entrance: obsequiously removing his grimy hat, whilst honester Lillo barked, straining at the rope which tied him to his barrel. There is a general subserviency and servility to all minions of the law throughout Italy, bred in the bone and blood of the people by many centuries of tyranny, political, ecclesiastical, and financial.

'Good-morning, gentlemen,' echoed the cobbler and the tailor and the cabinet-maker in the mezzanino, all with a thrill of fear; for times were bad, and any one of them knew that it might be his turn any day to receive undesired visits from these guardians of finance and order.

'Ser Checchi in?' asked the bailiff Beppe Dessi, with his ample paunch thrust out. He was a man who loved to talk when no speech was needed: the bailiff in this country is an amateur, created into an official *pro tempo*, being any householder or citizen whom the sheriff's officer may like to select for the enjoyment of this function and the receipt of the daily dole of money the law awards to him, out of the pocket of the debtor, however empty that pocket may be.

'Yes, gentlemen, yes,' said the cobbler hurriedly, as he bent over his old boot and crossed himself with his awl in his hand, and muttered, 'The Lord save him, poor creature! saved of mortal man he cannot be.'

The trio tramped on noisily up the dark stone shaft of the stair under the lamp which always burned there all the day, while the barking of Folko above responded to the barking of Lillo below.

When they reached the doorway of the library, they took off their felt hats, and wiped their foreheads, and put their hats on again, and said to one another that it was much harder work getting up here than to climb up to the lantern of the Duomo, and bid a good morrow to a milkman who, by their bidding, had joined them there to be the witness which the law exacts.

Then they pushed the door open pompously, making the bell ring with a violent clatter, and walked into the first book-room, Gigi Fanno leading, by virtue of his superior office.

Ser Checchi was as usual seated in his large leathern chair, turning over some manuscript; the boy Poldo was dusting in the inner room; Veronica, above in her kitchen, was making a great clangour with her copper pans and brass pipkins; Beldia was absent on her errand.

The old man started, as the shadows of unbidden visitors appeared between him and the sunlight of the open doorway.

He knew what their approach indicated. They never appeared together thus but on one mission alone.

He did not rise, he did not greet them; he sat looking at them in silence, very pale, very grave.

Gigi Fanno advanced into the middle of the room, and opened one of the long stamped papers which he had brought with him.

He began to read aloud the usual formula: 'Ardiglione, Francesco, of the late Piero, domiciled in the dwelling-place known as the tower of the Brancaleone, but belonging to the most respected Tomaso Saetta, is now at the demand of—hum —hum—hum——' But before he could read more than this Ser Checchi stayed him with a gesture.

'I understand,' he said calmly, 'you are come to levy execution on my goods?'

'Precisely,' said the usher, offended at the interruption to his majestic eloquency, while Beppe Dessi added volubly:

'Unless you are prepared to pay principal, interest, and costs down on the nail this morning;' and the milkman laughed a little nervously, and the young clerk spat on the clean floor, and winked at Poldo, who was standing on the threshold of the inner room, with his round eyes wide open and his mouth still more widely agape.

'I cannot meet your demand,' said Ser Checchi firmly, though his ivory white hands trembled as they held the edge of the table. Then he turned his head to the boy Poldo. 'You may go downstairs,' he said to him; but the usher interposed.

'Pardon me, let the good youth remain; he may be needed as an additional witness.'

The presence or absence of the boy was wholly indifferent to him, but he liked to make a debtor feel that a man who owed money could not be master any more in his own house.

Poldo stayed, curious and breathless, leaning against the doorpost, and thinking what a fine thing it was to be a tribunal clerk, with fine glass rings on your fingers, and nobody to order you to wash your hands.

The men wasted no more words on the insolvent and, in their eyes, contemptible graybeard leaning back in his old leathern chair, and they began their business; the first spot to which they betook themselves was the carved oak box in which the Dante was hidden, enshrined under lock and key.

'Not that, 'not that!' cried the old man, as he involuntarily threw himself between his treasure and the coarse, clutching hands of Gigi Fanno and of Dessi, as he would have thrown himself between his daughter and a violating touch. 'Take the rest first,' muttered Ser Checchi faintly to his tormentors.

The usher swore a filthy oath.

'We are masters here, my old fellow,' he answered. 'Beppe says aright. We do not pick and choose at your bidding. We take all as the law hath a right to take it. Give me the key, quick, or I call the carabineers to force you. I suppose you have some specie or drafts hidden here?'

Ser Checchi did not reply. His face was livid, the blue veins stood out like cords. He heard the lad Poldo laugh; the young clerk laughed in answer.

'It is a Codice; you do not understand,' said the librarian with a cruel tremor in all his spare slight form.

'You have no power of objection or selection,' said Gigi Fanno contemptuously; 'all your goods are forfeit to the law. Quick! give me the key of the box.'

'Come, out with the key,' said Beppe Dessi pompously. 'We are the masters here, good man. A debtor is a cipher in his own house.'

Ser Checchi, without a word, took a small antique key off his watch-chain, and gave it to them.

The usher took no more notice of him than if he had not moved or spoken, but seized the key, pushed him rudely aside, and pulled the great folio out of its hiding-place in the oak brass-bound box, where Ser Checchi had laid it as tenderly as though it were the embalmed body of a king.

'Vellum, eh?' said Gigi Fanno, whilst he wetted his thumb and forefinger, and turned its leaves over one by one with a contemptuous gesture, as he licked his thumb afresh and dog-eared one of the beautiful fairly-written pages.

'Look for an old manuscript of the "Divina Commedia," which lies locked up in an oak box: it does not look like manuscript, but that is what they say it is; it is rotten old rubbish, but a gentleman has a fancy for it whom I know,' Aurelio Vestuccio had whispered the night before, slipping a hundred-franc note in the usher's ready palm: they had been friends for years. Explanation is not needed between kindred spirits and bright intelligences. Many had been the object, curious or valuable, which the man of law had thus been able to seize at a low valuation, and pass on to the auction room where Messer Aurelio knew so well how to have any precious thing knocked down, for little, to his confederates or representatives. Good-fellowship is a most useful factor in business.

'Worth five shillings, eh? Or five pence?' said Beppe Dessi, leaning over the noble folio with a grin, and rubbing the cabuchon carnelians with his cotton handkerchief.

'Put ten francs,' said the usher to the boy who wrote. 'It's big and will sell by weight; they boil up these old parchments, and make new writing papers out of them, all nice and clean.'

He did not want his associates to know the value which Ser Aurelio had attached to the musty folio.

Ser Checchi stood near, the veins in his pale brow swollen like blue cords; his breast heaving, his hands clenched; he suffered as a high priest who beholds his golden gods shattered, and his altar vessels defiled.

'Old "Divina Commedia"—leather—value ten francs,' wrote the young clerk at the table. 'What comes next?'

Ser Checchi's eyes flamed under their hollow brows, with difficulty he restrained himself from violence, and, with a gesture of infinite tenderness and reverence, he lifted the volume up from where they had cast it, dusted it with his handkerchief, as though to wipe off from it their polluting touch, and laid it back in its little chest.

The two men and the boy gave a loud guffaw of derision, and went on with their work: it was too much trouble to enumerate the volumes and the rolls of manuscript and the unbound books one by one; they contented themselves with writing them down by the score and the hundred, as Lot 1, Lot 2, Lot 3, dragging down the pamphlets and manuscripts from the well-ordered shelves, until all the contents of the book-shelves were thus entered on the sheets of stamped paper on which the youth wrote.

They dawdled over their work, they smoked, they cracked jokes, they spat on the floor, they splashed the ink and the sand about on the table, they tossed the volumes to one another as if they were brickbats; they took no more heed of the master of them than if he had been a log of wood.

He had dropped into his chair again, and watched them silently, his nails dug into the palms of his hands in the effort which he made to restrain himself from very violence or opposition. All the order, chronological and archæological, in which the volumes had been with such loving exactitude arranged by him, was destroyed at a stroke, as the men threw them roughly on the floor, piled them together in bundles, and tied them up with string— architecture with ecclesiastical history, archæology with astrology, Benedetto of Imola with Boccaccio, the Fathers of the Church with the Songsters of the Renaissance, Poliziano with St. Gregory, a Giolito Ariosto with the 'Nuova Antologia,' treasures from the Medicean printing press with essays of Emile Lavellye, old chap-books of the Ciompi time with pamphlets of Bonghi's and of Sella's, classics of Bernardo Cennini with the modern Cennini publications—all pell-mell, as they happened to come to their hand from the heaps into which they had thrown them.

When they had finished their labours, they dragged the Dante towards them once more, pulled it out of its box malignantly, and bound it in a packet with some newspapers, then threw it with a loud bang on the top of the parcels of the books, which strewed the ground knee-high, and filled the whole intervening space from wall to wall.

Then the usher called to Ser Checchi;

'Show us the other rooms. We shall lock up these.'

And he took out the keys from the locks.

Ser Checchi then arose; his hands were trembling, and his lips were ashen pale; but he controlled his emotion with a mighty effort, and spoke with courtesy and mildness.

'Gentlemen, you have done what you deemed right, no doubt, and no more than the law allows you; but you have undone all the labours of my life, and I perceive that of books you have no knowledge whatever. If you must, to appease my creditors, sell these volumes, I would not oppose a just sale, but there should be previously judgment of them by those competent in such matters. Volumes full of learning and of antiquity must not be dealt with as though they were the common rubbish of a railway bookstall. There are here specimens of the earliest typographers of the city, which possess claims on all scholars which you cannot comprehend, and would bring high prices from all humanists. These volumes are my all. They are some of them unique, and many of them rare; all—all—all of some value. And you rob me of the last thing I have, when you propose to barter them as mere waste paper. Nay, you rob not me alone, but all true scholars. There are works here of priceless import to all educated men.'

He spoke firmly, though in a faint, low voice, leaning his hand upon the table to hold himself erect. Gigi Fanno listened, jingling the keys impatiently; Beppe Dessi as he drained a flask of wine; the young clerk with his pen behind his ear and a grin upon his mouth. When he had ceased they moved towards the door.

'Go out, sir,' said Fanno roughly to him. 'We lock up the room, as you know.'

That was the only answer they gave to him.

'Lock up my books! Lock me away from my books!'

'Lock you out, certainly,' said Dessi, with a jovial laugh. 'They are yours no longer, good Ser Checchi, and I am responsible for them to your creditors and the tribunal.'

Ser Checchi looked at him, and from him to the ferret-face of the usher, and to the broad, grinning countenance of the clerk. He saw no mercy, no pity, no respect, in any one of them. He was in their eyes only an insolvent debtor, and a madman likewise—a poor aged fool, old and daft, like Lear.

He understood that he was this, and no more than this, in their eyes, and that help from them he would get none.

He turned from the door, and seated himself in his own large leathern chair.

'I remain amongst what hath long been my own, if it be mine no more. Go you and do what you deem your duty. You will find naught missing when you return.'

The men ceased to laugh, and stood irresolute about the doorway of the room. There was that in his tone which awed them.

He had raised the Dante from the floor and undone its cords, and laid it on his knee.

No fallen monarch, seated amidst the ashes of

his burned palace, could have had more dignity than he, as he sat thus, mute and still amongst the havoc of his books.

CHAPTER XIII.

'WILL you trust him?' whispered Gigi Fanno to Beppe Dessi.

Dessi pursed up his mouth dubiously.

'Eh?—well—yes. He can't eat them, and he can't drink them, and if he make away with one of them we can clap him in gaol. Yes; we will chance it. I can come every day, and 'tis but for fifteen days, all told.'

'Well, it is your right that you waive, and your risk that you run, not mine. So be it,' said Fanno, and the three men went out, and down the staircase, to refresh their bodies with fried meats and artichokes at an eating-house near, intending to return in the afternoon to continue their good work.

But at the threshold of the great entrance-door they met Beldia returning from her errand to the notary, and her purchase of such plain, poor food as she could now afford to buy. She recognised them in terror.

'You came hither in my absence?'

'To seize his books in execution of the sentence promulgated by the most worshipful the Pretore of the section of Santo Spirito——' began the usher.

But Beldia stopped him with a cry of horror.

'His books! Even his books are not sacred?

Oh, it is monstrous, it is infamous! Are you Christian men? Have you human hearts in your breasts? Take his books from him!—and in my absence?'

'The law does not wait for the absence or presence of anybody,' answered Gigi Fanno with importance.

'Not even for yours, madamigella!' added Dessi with a leer. 'But we are coming back in the afternoon to finish the inventory, and if you like to be with us, I for one shall be mighty pleased, for a handsome woman——'

'What inventory?' asked Beldia.

'We are not bound to give explanations,' said the usher impatiently. 'Nevertheless, since perhaps you can persuade your father to recognise the straits in which he puts himself, I will read you the terms of the Precetto.'

He took out of his pocket a copy of the document which he had left with Ser Checchi.

'At the demand of,' etc., etc., etc., he began, reading aloud the preamble in pompous, stentorian tones, bringing about them the idlers in the street, and the grinning children who were playing near with a wooden disc.

'Enough, enough, I understand,' she said hurriedly. 'The names are the names of others, but the real mover herein is Vestuccio.'

'Signor Vestuccio? Ser' Rello!' repeated the man in apparently scandalized amazement. 'There is not the very smallest shadow of right to bring that most worthy and excellent citizen into this matter. His claims do not appear here. He desires in his own matter to use the uttermost leniency and patience.'

'He hides his wickedness behind the masks of others.'

'Oh, signorina, pardon me, that is a shameful charge!' said Gigi Fanno, putting back the document into his coat pocket. 'Much may be excused to your distress, but calumnious inventions are always punishable by the law. Of that I warn you, and I can tell you farther that there is not in the whole city a citizen so intelligent, so upright, and so admirable in all his relations as is Signor Vestuccio.'

'Your old man upstairs is only fit for a madhouse,' said Beppe Dessi in his turn. 'But we have strained a point to do him a kindness. We have left him amongst his books; though, had we done our duty, we should have brought the keys away and shut him on the wrong side of the door.'

Impatient of more delay, Gigi Fanno elbowed her off the doorstep, and, cocking his hat on one side of his head, he went away to his fry and his artichokes.

'Never mind, my pretty; I'll show you a way to get over it,' whispered Dessi, thrusting his red round face close to hers. She drew back with such undisguised disgust and repulsion that even his slow and coarse mind could not mistake them.

'Damn your pride, my penniless madam!' he muttered as he joined his colleague. 'You'll come cringing to us on your bare bones before we've done with you.'

She went upstairs to her father, and sat on the

stone floor at his feet, and embraced his knees silently in a passion of sympathy, to which she could give no adequate expression.

He said nothing. He held the Dante folio in his hands, and gazed down on it with a vacant look in his fine luminous eyes, always until now so radiantly lighted with the lambent flame of high intelligence.

'Father,' she said timidly after awhile, and with great deference and tenderness, 'pray do not shut me out of your confidence. I am not a child, nor am I a woman of voluble tongue, that you should fear to trust me. I see these terrible papers from the tribunal come every week: I know what they must mean, although I have not read any one of them. There are rumours that Antella is sold, and I know nothing. Yet I hear that the books even may soon be sold, and that they are already seized. I ask you, is it true? Give me at least the right to deny these calumnies in your name, or tell me the truth, and spare me the indignity of hearing it from the mouths of gossips, and being compelled to confess to them that I am an exile from my father's heart, and less acquainted with his position than the very sweepers in the streets. Time and again, in your absence, those law-papers have been brought to me, and I could have read them and learned all their meaning, whether you willed it or no; but I did not do so. I deserve some pity and some trust.'

She spoke with great emotion, but with great dignity and simplicity. The tone of her words, rather than the words themselves, carried conviction of their justice to her father's mind, and filled him with repentance and relenting.

Slow tears rose to his eyes and fell down his pale cheeks. He stretched his hand out to her, and drew her to his chair.

'You have deserved all good from me, and you get but ill,' he said in a broken voice. 'I will tell you of my misery if it will make it to you, who will be forced to share it, less bitter. I have been a blind, weak, credulous fool. I am ruined. And—and— yea, the cup is draining to the dregs!—the books must go!'

Then, for the first time in his life he leaned his forehead on his hands and wept.

CHAPTER XIV.

IN the early afternoon the trio of the tribunal returned, and pursued their work. They were more rough, more rude, more hasty, and more sullen, for they had in the interval drunk a good deal of wine, and wine makes most men ill-tempered rather than jovial; they came into the chambers with noise and pomp, and called coarsely to Beldia to aid them, and show them where the linen was kept, and the china and the hardware. She did not move.

'There is nothing hidden,' she replied calmly. 'You have eyes; use them.'

'You are bound to assist the law!' screamed the usher, thumping his hand down on an old brass-bound escritoire. 'Bring out all your keys, or I summon the carabineers to enforce my right.'

She rose, knowing that her father would not be

benefited by any brawl or disturbance, and fetched the keys and laid them down beside Gigi Fanno.

He took them up savagely, and tossed them to his colleague Dessi.

'Make her show you which is which,' he said to his coadjutor, 'or we shall never get through all this work by nightfall.'

'Come, my girl,' said Beppe Dessi insolently, 'get up and show us which is which of all these keys, and maybe, if you are pretty behaved, we will let you take out some finery and trinket of your own and hide it.'

But she did not stir. She might have been deaf and dumb for any reply which they could obtain from her. They tried the keys, one after another, for themselves, and set the doors and drawers of every bureau and chest and cupboard and closet in the rooms wide open.

Then began a havoc, such as to an orderly and careful housekeeper like herself would have been at any time torture, even without the shame which it now brought with it to her.

They ransacked the place, as soldiers do in a sacked city in search of plunder. They dragged everything out from its resting-place, and held everything up to the light, and chuckled and grumbled, and scoffed and swore; appraising all the objects at miserable prices, and setting the young clerk to catalogue them at their estimate. All the fair linen, made and marked by her mother's hands, with its odour of dried lavender and ground orris-root, was held up and pulled about by their dirty fingers. The old solid silver plate, with its date of

1620, was weighed and rubbed, and jeered at and thrown together in a drawer. The old pottery—some of Gubbio and Casteldurante—was grinned at, and pushed together on shelves, and written down as common earthenware. The flowered pot which Vestuccio had eyed on the dinner-table, enviously, months before, was first of all secured and shut up in a wardrobe. The iris-root and orange petals, laid up with the wearing apparel to keep out moths, were shaken out upon the floors, and every article made the object of coarse gibe and jest.

They dawdled their errand out over four long hours; and lighted candles, and poked them into dark corners and empty closets, to see that there was nothing hidden there. Then, leaving some places vacant and others over-filled, they locked up the latter and pocketed the keys, and sat all three at a table conning over the lists which they had made.

'Verify and sign them,' they said to Beldia.

She did not answer.

They went into the inner book-room, and bade her father rise and come and sign. He took no notice of them. Made furious by such disobedience, they ordered the boy Poldo to do so, and Poldo, shamefaced and frightened, yet very important, exchanging grins and winks with the young tribunal clerk, came up to the table and scrawled his name, in witness to the inventories and acts of seizure, as the law in its sapience required that someone present in the house should do.

All was disorder, nakedness, and discomfort: their tobacco was spilled upon the floor, their ink upon the table; the old familiar household things were locked away from their owners, two or three necessary objects were alone left out for daily use, and the empty cupboards—of which the doors stood open—looked like graves; they were indeed the graves of peace, of credit, of all simple peace, and of all honest joys.

She roused herself to make a cup of coffee for her father, and poured a little brandy in it, and took it to him with a roll. To please her he tried to take it, but his throat refused to swallow; the slow, salt tears of age were rolling down his cheeks; he was cold, and trembled with the nervous shiver of intense emotion long repressed.

Folko came and laid his head on his master's feet.

The candles which the men had lighted shed a faint flickering light over the room.

The boy Poldo, seeing that he was unwatched, slipped down the stairs and into the street, and narrated to his comrades a wonderful tale of how the officers of the tribunal had selected him as witness to their *verbale*—a tale told with many inventions to the glorification of himself.

'I can be a writer at the tribunal to-morrow, if I wish,' said Poldo, very vain-glorious and self-admiring, whilst he chucked a halfpenny in the air, to see whether he or his friends should stand a treat of vermuth at the drinking shop opposite with the green bough above its door.

At last she knew as much as her father knew himself of his losses, of his liabilities, of his utter and irretrievable ruin.

Although her own fears and the words of others had in so large a measure prepared her for the worst, yet the truth came to her with a terrible shock as of some disgrace wholly incredible and unsuspected. Although she had perceived that much was wrong and much was ominous, yet the profound faith which she had always had from infancy in his wisdom, and the habit ingrained in her of never permitting herself to judge or criticise him, had made her persuade herself that it could be only some mere passing embarrassment which had been brought about by her brother's extravagance. But now that she realized the full extent, the irreparable nature, of these calamities, she could no longer strive to think that her parent was blameless, or their situation easy to mend.

Their resources were stopped short, their revenue from their farm was cut off; the slight trade ever done in the book rooms had ceased entirely, for customers will not go where the demon of liquidation has shown its grim and grinning head; the cupboards and desks and bureaus were all locked up, and the keys borne away by the bailiff.

She saw quite well how he had been brought to his plight by carelessness, by over-confidence in himself and others, by that absence of mind which is so often the accompaniment of intellectual devotion to an ideal or an art, and by that habit of reserve which, whilst admirable in its origin, is so frequently fatal in its results, shutting out those whom it isolates from the counsel and from the guidance of others. An immense pity for him took the vacated place of her perished trust, and she was almost insensible of the material losses and injuries to herself brought on her by his weakness, so entirely was she absorbed in her unselfish sorrow for him and in compassion for his poignant self-reproach.

'Oh, the cruelty of Cirillo!' she thought: had only Cirillo been that which he should have been, all these calamities would never have befallen them. He would have had ways, and means, and knowledge, which to her, a woman, obedient and ignorant, it had been impossible to possess; or, possessing, it would have been impossible to use.

For the first time since Odisio's departure she rejoiced that he was gone: he could have done no good, and it would have wrung his soul to have witnessed what it would have been out of his power to alter. For the ruin of her father seemed to her complete beyond any possibility of help.

Nothing which she could do to save her father was of any avail. Without money, and much money, there was no means of obtaining release or delay. There was the feeling abroad that the sooner the sales took place the better would it be for the creditors; and when such an impression as this is created, it were easier to stop the incoming tides of the sea than the insistence of those who have the power to insist.

She had at intervals tender and grave letters from Odisio's old mother in Brescia; and she answered them with gratitude and humility, but she feared that her replies might seem constrained and reserved to their recipient; for she could not bring herself to tell of her father's afflictions, and the reticence involved weighed on her frank and candid spirit.

Yet how could she reveal these sordid and vulgar calamities? They seemed to taint her with their own coarseness; how could she say to Odisio's mother, 'We are in misery, and soon shall starve,' without seeming to beg from her, without seeming to be a mere common scheming supplicant, unworthy of her son's troth? No, never, never, she thought, would she hint a word of their necessities to this unknown woman in Lombardy; sooner would she die for want of bread. Moreover, Odisio had often said that his mother had nothing but the little annuity which he had purchased for her, and her small house beside the Broletto.

It would but add to the distress and anxiety caused her by his absence, were she to know that the maiden to whom he was betrothed was travailing under the coarse and foul cares of indigence and debt. 'We may never meet in life,' thought Beldia; 'but, at least, she shall always think of me as what he has portrayed.'

She suffered keenly from the absence and the silence of her betrothed; and the material troubles which beset her were almost, in a sense, of service to her by distracting her from the visions and apprehensions which were for ever in her mind with regard to his fate.

Creditors are only patient if patience seems to them to be in their own interests, and it was not their interest here. Behind the scenes, Querci, and the other lawyers who served Vestuccio, were daily pressing for immediate sale, and setting afloat the rumour that only those who acted quickly would get any share of the proceeds.

Italian law is sharp and sudden when it deals with debtors; for assassins and other criminals it will creep gently and considerately by devious ways which leave the offender many a loophole of escape, but the debtor is a more abhorred and intolerable culprit; he is dealt with in a summary fashion, and has no escape, unless, indeed, he be indebted on a fine large scale, and has ruined a million or so of people, when the law will extend to him the indulgence it shows to the murderer.

With a protested bill, judgment against the acceptor is immediate; in five days execution is put in, and in ten more the sale takes place, unless the full amount, with heavy costs, be paid.

Ser Checchi, as a tradesman, had, of course, always known the state of the law and the penalty attached to dishonoured paper; but he was absent of mind, sanguine and yet timid, and had been too much inclined to trust all things to chance.

The sentences and the seizures had followed one on another with lightning-like rapidity, and had found him wholly unprepared to meet them. On legal grounds there was no resistance possible; his signatures were there, and he acknowledged them: there was no plea of opposition which he could lay before a lawyer; there was nothing to be done but to submit to execution, or pay the amounts.

He could no more pay them than he could have paid the vast deficit in the National Treasury. An old comrade, the Notary Reggiani, shook his head and groaned when he saw the documents.

'I cannot take up your case, because there is no ground in it to go upon,' he said; 'you have not honoured your signature to these bills, and your mortgagees were allowed to foreclose. What is there to say? Your pursuants, indeed, may be brutal and cunning, but they are wholly within the law. The law will not accept as an excuse that your wits were wool-gathering over commentaries and early editions, and so did not remember or perceive your liabilities.'

Other than this no lawyer would say; and there was reluctance in all the legal offices to accept the affairs of a man who admitted that he had no capital left, and showed that, as they considered, he had no capacity either. All the young advocates, who had come to the library so often on literary errands, shook their heads, and shut their office doors.

As for Pampilio Querci, he had accepted the landlord Saetta's affairs, and acted as that worthy's representative. A fledgling lawyer, who intends to be a counsellor and a deputy in due time, is not to be rejected in his suit by a maiden, without making her suffer for such want of appreciation. Querci was hand-in-glove with Vestuccio, and gave him much adroit assistance and advice, both officially and *ex cathedrâ.*

Rising men have a bond of sympathy between them; they climb in turn upon each other's shoulders. Old men, who are disappearing and decaying are only in their sight as sapless and leafless trees, which cumber the ground, and are best cut down ere they fall of themselves.

Uselessly, and with touching dignity in his humiliating martyrdom, Ser Checchi went to office after office, and spoke to this man and the other, whom he had benefited with his learning and the loan of his books. One and all turned their backs on him—some with a show of courtesy and regret ; some not even caring to assume so much decency as that ; some bidding him bluntly not take up their time.

He knew what his beloved Dante had known, how bitter it is to climb the stairs of others, to beg in vain for redress and justice ; and, if he had not yet known how hard it is to eat the bread of others, he felt that it would not be long before he did so.

For actual want was close at his door.

Had they been willing to sell or pawn anything, they could not have done so without being treated as criminals ; they had lost all right over their own possessions. Every other day the bailiff looked in, and walked about, and lit his pipe, and patted this object, and peered at this article and that, by way of earning the liberal fees with which his procreator, the law, endowed him. He wanted to be bribed into staying away, but this Beldia did not know, and, had she known it, had no means wherewith to bribe him ; and he, in vengeance, annoyed her as much as his position permitted—spat on her clean floors, sat and smoked on the edge of her bed, cut coarse jokes at her distress, and went to sleep in her father's own chair. Human nature, when it is hungry for a bribe and gets it not, is as a froward suckling denied its nurse's breast.

The serenity and self-restraint which were her habit only made her suffer more ; if she could have screamed and raved and torn her hair, as the women of her quarter would have done in similar circumstances, she would have suffered far less than she suffered silently in beholding the coarse and dirty figure of old Dessi pattering amongst her lavender-scented linen, or standing against the light amongst the neglected herbs and flowers of her garden on the roof.

'A proud-stomached hussy!' said Dessi to himself. 'How dare anybody be proud,' he thought, 'when he had the keys of their chests in his own desk at home?'

The world was divided into two races, in his opinion. There were the people who seized goods, and there were the people whose goods were seized. All his homage was given to the former; the latter he regarded as the ferret regards the rabbit. The ferret lives by the rabbit, indeed, but its scorn for the rabbit is boundless.

'We are human, if we are ruined,' a poor woman, whose bed had been sold from under her, had said once to him and his colleagues; and Dessi had cocked up his snub nose in the air.

'Ay, ay, ye're human,' he had answered, 'as a skinned eel in the frying-pan is still an eel.'

And the hard-hearted joke had wounded the poor woman more than the cold brick-floor on which her ill-covered bones were forced to lie.

Beppe Dessi had it in his power, by his mere presence, his mere interference, his mere legalized espionage, to torture the spirit of Beldia, as St. Agnes was tortured by the eyes and hands of the gaoler who bared her virgin breasts for the steel of the shears. Everything about her seemed sullied and profaned. Nothing seemed her own any more. The privacy of life was ended; her home was as public as the street.

Her father scarcely seemed to notice what was done. He had sunk into an apathy from which he was only roused at rare intervals.

The scholar, with his mind far away amongst the beauties and mysteries of the past, and lost in the impersonal and delightful meditations with which an old chronicle or a new reading of an obscure text filled him, had heeded too little the things of daily life, been too thankful to escape from their sordid cares and wearing pressure, and had fallen an easy prey to the sophisms and temptations of a shrewd and soft-spoken man of business.

'Antella must go,' Ser Checchi had thought often, with a cruel pang; but he had never dreamed that, Antella wholly lost to him, he would remain still in the same sad plight, still abandoned face to face with debts incurred he could not have said how.

Ever since he had yielded to Vestuccio in accepting aid for the purchase of the rare Codex of Giogoli, he had pursued a downward path, and he had never known in plain figures what he was engaged to pay. A bill, in skilful hands, with its renewals, interest, compound interest, and all its attendant obligations, grows like the beanstalk of fable, and fastens its suckers as securely as the cuttlefish. Ser Checchi, besides great absence of mind, had a tender and proud heart; he had shrunk from telling his troubles to his daughter and his friends, and it had been insupportable to him to make his household feel pecuniary strain or suffer the harshness of personal want,

He would now have sold his library by private contract or by voluntary auction had his creditors allowed him to do so, but they would not consent. In vain he strove to persuade them and their attorneys that such a course, by enabling the books to be sold at their proper value, would bring in twice, thrice, probably ten or twenty times as much money as if they were sold by the order of the tribunal. He knew well how the latter sales were controlled by the official and habitual frequenters of them, so that the finest work of art or literature can be knocked down as so much mere canvas or paper.

Sold to amateurs and experts, his library, which was in many ways quaint and rare, would almost certainly have brought in much more than he owed. With the salt tears in his eyes, he besought his persecutors to agree together and let him do this; his heart would be wrung to part from his treasures, but, at least, when dispersed, they would thus find asylum on the shelves of those who could appreciate and care for them, whilst, if they went by auction by order of the sheriff's officer, they would in all likelihood be bought by weight, and in bundles to line butter-tubs or travellers' trunks.

Oftentimes at such law-enforced sales, in lonely villages or on secluded hillsides, he had seen ancient objects of rare workmanship, chairs, settles, chests, copper vessels, iron work, pottery, porcelain, knocked down at the sound of the horn for a few copper pieces or a single silver bit. Thus, in early days, he had himself bought several of his volumes at such sales; though he had always, in pity and in honour, sought out the poor owner thus sacrificed to the teeth and claws of the law, and paid to him secretly the balance of what he had considered the due value of such purchases. But the measure which Ser Checchi gave, no one gave to him.

His entreaties were of no avail; he had waited too long. He had, in the innocent egotism of the bibliophile, shrunk from the mere thought of such a voluntary sale when he had been still at liberty to make it. Now he was no longer free to do so. The Codice and all the other valuable works were seized promiscuously, amongst the worthless ones, by distraint. And his creditors were too jealous of one another to consent to what might have been of profit to them all. True, had Vestuccio advised such a conciliatory course, and one so advantageous to the debtor, they might have been persuaded to unite and permit it to be followed. But Vestuccio publicly said, with frank surprise, 'Nay, I am not in this matter; I have nothing to do with it, thank God I have not; my heart would be too tender to rob the poor old silly scholar of his all.' And privately to those persons, his instruments, to whom he had passed on Ser Checchi's signatures, he whispered: 'It would not be prudent to allow a voluntary sale; to do so, all the acts must be dropped, all the sentences annulled. Personally, I would do anything in my power to help the old gentleman, but I could not, in conscience and honour, counsel you to throw away all the advantage you have gained by the verdicts of the Pretura; his books alone might sell for much, or they might sell for nothing, whereas, if all the goods are sold as well, it is impossible that there should not be realized at least some fifty per cent. of what he owes. Besides, to agree to what he wishes, you must all be of accord, and when are a group of creditors ever all of accord? Were his affairs in my hands alone, I could have arranged, I could still arrange them; but where there are many opposing creditors, a charitable combination is impossible.'

'Impossible,' added Pampilio Querci.

How was it that there were so many creditors? Ser Checchi could not understand this; he had thought that he had dealt solely with Vestuccio, and although he had put his signature to drafts drawn up in other persons' names, he had been assured that these bills would lie safely and unseen in Vestuccio's desk, and had imagined in his innocence that the mortgage given by him on the land of Antella would cover all these loans. After all, the sums were very small, and had he earlier had the courage to sell his rarer folios and earlier editions to foreign buyers with some little sacrifice, they could have been met and covered. But it had been no part of Vestuccio's interests to allow his victim to clearly comprehend his own position, and he had let him float on in uncertainty and indecision until it had become too late to take any decided step to struggle out of the meshes into which he had sunk.

CHAPTER XV.

'WILL you come to supper, madamigella? It grows late,' cried the rough voice of Veronica from the inner chamber, where their frugal table was spread.

She was a good-hearted woman, but in her manner she permitted herself to be rougher, ruder, more boisterous of late; she did not see why she should not add violence to her nature, why she should trouble herself to speak softly, and stir noiselessly, to please folks who had the sheriff's officer coming to their doors every day.

'Madamigella has always wanted as much observance as if she were a queen. Eh! much she will get of it now,' said the serving-woman, with her arms akimbo, and a frown and a laugh together on her face, to her devoted listener, the boy Poldo. She was angered that the evening meal was thus delayed, and her own work thus prolonged.

'Nobody lets you be proud if you are poor,' added Veronica, with accurate knowledge of human nature.

'The signorina is not proud, not a bit proud,' said Poldo; 'but she has a way with her which makes you feel small, and when she looks at you she cows you, though she is kind.'

'Ay, ay, and won't they pay her off for all that now?' said Veronica, who was vexed and pained by the woes of her employers, yet found a certain relish in them. It fretted her to think that the whole quarter would see the hateful *Banda* swinging under the majolica angels and amorini; and yet it brought her importance and excitement to gossip about it all at the greengrocer's and the cheesemonger's, the butcher's and the tinman's, and to say with satisfaction : ' It does not matter to me—no, no—I have a fine nest-egg of my own in the savings bank, and I am torn in two with people who want me to go to them. I want nobody's bed or board; it would be well for them if they could say as much, poor souls! but the master was always up in the clouds, and never saw the dirt which lay in his path, or the stones that he stumbled over. Leave? oh yes, I shall leave, of course ; the saints befriend them when I am gone! They will want help sorely.'

Between her humiliation at such disasters befalling a family which she served, and her importance at being the bearer of such dreadful news to the gossips of Santo Spirito and San Jacopo, she did not know whether she was the more glad or the more grieved, at the events which had cast such a gloom over the peaceful life in the tower. The boy was wholly sorrowful. Nowhere would he find another mistress so thoughtful for his creature comforts as Madama Beldia.

It was dull work, indeed, copying and yawning amongst those musty old volumes, where never a laugh was heard or a joke was made. But then, in compensation, what abundance of good wheaten bread, of sound red wine, of fritters, of pickles, of macaroni, of polenta, and of summer and winter fruits! The Vestuccio children would henceforth devour those grapes and figs, those nuts and walnuts of Antella, which had been his summer and autumn joys; and he had heard the chandler say to the charcoal-seller : ' I shall give the tower folks no more of anything unless they pay ready-money; they have not a penny, they say, so down on the nail they shall pay before a grain of rice or a stick of paste goes out to them.'

And the heart of the lad had been heavy, as he had heard, because what he heard meant short commons and an empty stomach for himself. No one had ever understood, as Madama Beldia had done, that a growing boy's hunger is bottomless, and restless as the sounding sea. Poldo would willingly have struck down the chandler amongst his tubs of beans and seeds, his little round cheeses, his savoury brown sausages, his smoked tongues, and his flasks of olive oil. No credit to Madamigella Beldia, who had paid, every Saturday morning, her little weekly accounts at the shops as regularly and as surely as the strokes of the old Dutch house-clock tolled out the hours!

'It is a shame, a crying shame!' said Poldo, with red eyes and burning cheeks.

'It is the way of the world,' said Veronica. 'If you can drive a coach and six when you choose, everybody you meet on the road offers you a lift; everybody, from the Archbishop in his chariot to the dustman in his donkey-cart; but if you are a poor devil limping along the highway with a sore foot and a ragged jacket, why, then, nobody ever sees you on the path, neither his Grace nor the sweeper!'

'It is an infamous shame!' repeated the boy with fury.

Veronica was less touched to wrath: she saw matters as the small traders saw them.

'They will send nothing, nothing, unless you pay for it; there are no weekly credits now,' she said to Beldia, with the sort of triumph which a coarse nature always feels in hurting the dignity of a delicate temper.

Beldia shrank as from the touch of a hot iron, but she soon recovered her self-command.

'It is very natural that they should feel afraid to trust us,' she answered. 'I will give you the ready-money every morning.'

'For how long?' said Veronica. 'If you have got ready-money, madamigella, you had best hide it upon your person when Gigi and Beppe come round next. They poke into every hole and corner, nothing escapes them, and if they see any money they will take it.'

Beldia looked at her with the bewildered, harassed look of the tracked hare.

'They cannot deny us a little money for food,' she said stupidly. 'Even the galley-slaves are fed.'

'The galley-slaves? ay, ay!' said the woman roughly. 'But they have the wit to break the law and make the nation maintain them. Poor master has only made away with his own, you see; so he may go and starve, and it is nobody's business if he starve to death. If you have any money, hide it, or give it to me, and I will keep it about me.'

'I will hide nothing,' said Beldia firmly; but her eyes did not lose their strained and hunted expression. The woman's words had brought home to her with startling distinctness the fact that all her father possessed had been seized in the name of his creditors; and that nothing, not even the sheets they slept in, or the platter on which they cut their loaf, was their own any more.

'You have jewels and pretty things, madama,' said Veronica; 'they can't touch them, they are yours; you can pawn or sell them.'

Beldia was silent.

All her little personal treasures had gone, one by one, to satisfy the leechlike craving of her brother, and at the last the pearls had gone. She had nothing left, except her body-linen and her wearing apparel.

Everything in the tower was her father's, and thus, now, belonged to his creditors.

'If the master had had a grain of sense,' said Veronica, 'knowing the plight he was in, he would have made a deed of gift of it all to you, or a deed of sale to Messer Odisio; and Messer Odisio would have stayed at home, and wedded you, and all would have gone well.'

'My father would never do a dishonourable thing,' said Beldia quickly, with a sigh. 'That would have been dishonourable.'

'Ah!' said the serving-woman, with brusque contempt. 'Fine words fry no fish, and mend no holes. Is it honourable, think you, to write away his children's patrimony, and bring a maiden like you face to face with a vulgar shame and contumely like this, because he never had courage or strength to look his affairs in the face, and leave off buying mouldy parchments and mice-gnawed books? Honour—honour! 'tis a mighty big word; but it seems to me as how Ser Checchi, who is so rare and fond of it, has read its reading upside down!'

'Be silent!' said Beldia sternly. 'Cannot you respect my father's name? You have eaten his bread and known his goodness twenty years and more. Is it not infamy enough that his old age is betrayed and tormented by strangers, without the foulness of his servants' tongues daring to soil his stainless name?'

'What I say is true, signorina,' said Veronica doggedly, yet abashed.

'Yes, it is quite true,' said the voice of Ser Checchi behind them.

Veronica screamed, and let fall the knife and the carrot which her hands held.

'I thought you were out of the house, sir,' she stammered, confused and terrified.

'I am no eavesdropper,' said Checchi, with a

faint, sad smile. 'But you spoke so loudly, Veronica, that I heard you on the stairs. You are quite right; I have dishonoured myself and robbed my daughter. Believe me, you cannot censure me as doth my conscience by day and night.'

He spoke gently and humbly, with the meekness of a chidden child, yet with the dignity of a discrowned king.

Veronica stood and stared at him in irresolute amaze; then, with a gasp, she threw her rough apron over her head, turned her shoulder to the wall, and sobbed aloud.

'I was a beast to say it,' she muttered between her sobs. 'And I never meant it—I never thought it, dear master!'

'I have told you that you were right,' said Ser Checchi. 'Yet I cannot let such things be said in my house, so long as I have a house at all. There is your wage for a month. Let this be the last night that you sleep here.'

And he laid on the table beside her the amount of her wage; it was the last money that he possessed.

'No, no, master, no, no!' she cried, her voice choked by her sobs. 'I have an ill tongue, but I have not a base heart. I have eaten your bread in your prosperity; I will not leave you in your misery. I have laid by six hundred francs in your service; I will lend them to you, if you will take them. No, no, I will not go. Madamigella Beldia, speak for me! I will not go. I will not touch that money. He says that what I said was true. Then, why turn me from the door because I said it?'

Ser Checchi put the money into her unwilling hand.

'The truth is truth, by whomsoever spoken,' he

said briefly; 'but we love not those who chasten us. Go; and leave us to our fate. You are a strong woman and a capable servant; you will find service elsewhere. We can keep none to serve us now.'

And he put the weeping woman gently but firmly out from the chamber, and closed the door upon her. Then his firmness deserted him, and his age and his sorrows overcame him. He sank, broken and tremulous, upon the nearest seat.

'She was right,' he said hoarsely. 'I am dishonoured. My daughter—my dear daughter!—forgive me all I bring upon you!'

Beldia kissed his hands.

CHAPTER XVI.

LIFE in the tower of Taddeo had been hitherto always so peaceful, orderly, and regular, with an almost puritanic method in all its ways and habits, that the disorder of poverty, and the irregularity entailed by it, were the most cruel tortures and trials which could have befallen Beldia. Never in her life had she left a small or large payment over-due, a household bill neglected; their living had been simple, but generous and unstrained; she had never thought twice before giving an alms or offering a meal, and the utmost exactitude had been observed in the discharge of all obligations which came before her in the daily routine of her management.

The difficulties, the embarrassments, the small, mean, trivial troubles which go with need of money, now harassed and embarrassed her at every step. She felt lowered by them and defiled by them.

Every morning since she had been a child of fifteen she had set the house in order as soon as she had risen for the day; and, although her father had bade her avoid extravagance, she had always had plenty for the homely and comfortable needs of life, and had never been forced to deny herself the pleasure of getting a flask of superior wine for a guest, a dish of fruit for the table, or a bunch of market flowers for herself. To be obliged to pause before she bought a few eggs or a little rice, to have to divide a few copper pieces anxiously between bread for to-day and bread for to-morrow, was a trial so new, so unimagined, that she felt herself the prey of some oppressive nightmare; sunk by it to the level of the beggars at the street corners, the poor begars for whose improvidence her pity alone had prevented her disdain. All the heavy manual work also of the house fell upon herself alone. True, Veronica was not far off indeed, and was constantly offering her assistance, as did some of the neighbours out of curiosity rather than pity; but Beldia did not accept these offers, and all the household work fell on herself. She had to sweep, to dust, to make the beds, to cook, to fetch water, to do everything which there was to do, and which the strong woman servant and the boy had done before for her; and the hard manual labours were almost a relief to the torturing mental anxiety which was upon her night and day. They fatigued her physically so intensely that, when she lay down at night, some hours of heavy sleep came to her.

'Oh, my love, that ever you should, through me, be brought to such degradation!' said her father once, as he saw her pass with a pan of charcoal, a coarse apron wound about her skirt, and her hair covered with a linen kerchief.

She smiled faintly.

'It is no degradation, father. The women of old Greece thought it none. Did not Penelope spin, and Nausicaa wash clothes?'

'You are a brave child, and merit a better fate than I have given you,' he said in a broken voice.

But even in his grief for her he did not realize how difficult it was to even obtain that pan of charcoal, and the frugal food which she cooked upon it. No one would give her credit even for so much as these, and her little personal trinkets and trifles, such as even so serious a maiden as she cherished, had all gone one by one in other years under Cirillo's draining exigencies.

One day when she saw him look more careworn, ill, more heartbroken than ever, a sudden idea sprang up within her breast. She said nothing to her father, but wrapped a black shawl round her head and shoulders, and went out into the street. It was growing dark and Vestuccio's shop would be closed, she knew; she took her way to his private house. The lamps were lighted, and their reflections were trembling in the river, which was full from a storm in the previous night.

There are few things in nature and art more beautiful than is the Arno, lighted thus, when above head there is a starry and moon-illumined sky. Even in the distraction and distress of her mind, she could not help looking westward and eastward at the scene, so long familiar, yet ever so fresh in beauty, the darkness beneath the arches of the bridges and of the masses of building above them

THE PONTE VECCHIO.

contrasted with the luminance of the heavens and the waters. Deep shadow veiled all which was poor, or base, or trivial; nothing was seen but what was majestic, mysterious, and noble. On such a night had Buondelmonte left the chamber of his love; on such a night had Ginevra wakened from the tomb; on such a night had Luisa Strozzi ridden down on her palfrey to the masked supper at Casa Nasi. Beldia looked at the loveliness of the river, and the tears rose in her eyes and choked her throat in thinking of the happy, harmless years which she had passed beside these fair, familiar scenes.

She ceased to look, and hurried onward across the Ponte Vecchio between the closed shutters of the jewellers' and goldsmiths' little shops. The door stood open of the house in which Vestuccio occupied the first floor; a modest but commodious house in the Via dei Benci. She mounted the stairs with a sick heart and rapped. Within she could hear voices and laughter. A good-looking wench opened the door to her, and said, with evident falsehood, that her master was away. There was a scent of tobacco, of garlic, of wine, of fried fish ; and, being pressed hard, the servant girl admitted reluctantly that the master was at home, but had friends, and had bidden her deny him to all visitors. Then she showed Beldia into a close little room, with its window shut, and its petroleum lamp flaring, and left her and sought her employer to interrupt his revels. The voices on the other side of the wall ceased, and the laughter also ; and in a few moments Vestuccio appeared, a little red, as a man may be after a good supper, but smiling pleasantly and deprecating her apologies with a courteous gesture,

'Your servant, madamigella,' he said, lifting the smoking-cap which he wore. 'My wife is in the country with the little ones; God be with them, the darlings!—an old friend or two were supping with me to pass the time in their absence. Is your good father taken unwell that you come to me at this hour?'

Beldia threw off her black shawl and stood before him.

'Oh, for the pity of heaven do not play with me, Ser Aurelio!' she said passionately. 'You know of the great wretchedness in which my father is plunged. The truth was only made known to me the other day. They seized his books. He was obliged to tell me then what it meant, and all the woe which is upon him. You know how good he is, how simple, how guileless, and how, despite all his wisdom, he may easily be deceived and undone. I have come to you now because you are his chief creditor, it seems, and you have already taken Antella: can you not be content? Can you not spare him, give him time? He trusted you. He liked you. How could you betray his trust?'

Vestuccio listened in an attitude of respect and deference; but his eyes sparkled with anger, even whilst his countenance wore an expression of faint astonishment and of profound regret.

'Betray!' he repeated. 'Betray? I! Oh, signorina mia, could ever a word so base be said in seriousness to me? My honour is writ on granite, in sight of the whole town. I grieve for Ser Checchi's misfortunes; my heart bleeds for them; but I have been powerless to stop him on a road which never hath but one end.'

'To stop him!' echoed Beldia. 'You have driven

him onward in it! It is you who hold all his paper.'

Her soul had acquired nothing of the cunning, and cuteness, and finesse which are so needful in the commerce of the world. She felt that the man before her was the origin of all their woe, and she stripped his mask off and let him see that she knew him as he was.

It is a discovery which is never pardoned.

'I thought you were so attached to my father!' she cried in an ingenuous reproach which she repented of, as soon as she had yielded to it. Vestuccio joined his hands together impressively and looked up to the ceiling with pious invocation of the Most High who reads all hearts.

'I am truly devoted to your most saintly and noble father, signorina,' he said devoutly. 'But, when one's interests are in question, what would you expect? One must sacrifice one's own brother to one's self!'

'I quite understand that *you* would do so!' said Beldia curtly and coldly, as she made a movement towards the door.

'Everyone would do so, signorina,' said Vestuccio, unabashed. 'Do not believe them if any say the contrary.'

For to Vestuccio it seemed so natural, so holy, so beautiful a thing to allow interest to rule existence, that he did not see that there was anything but what was most creditable in the avowal that it did so. To reproach an Italian with his love of his own interests is to speak to him in an unintelligible language. 'Who should love me if not myself?' he will say, with perfect good faith. 'We are entirely sure of no one except of ourselves; therefore, in the name of all justice and prudence, let us first of all consider that best of all friends, our own advantage and advancement.'

Love thyself first: afterwards, a long way afterwards, love thy neighbour, if thou canst do so without hurt. So ran the law to him.

'You are a hypocrite and a rogue then!' said Beldia with scorn and passion. 'If you be only a self-seeking usurer, why do you pretend to care for others?'

Vestuccio preserved his deferential attitude; he spread out his hands in a gesture of deprecation; his eyes alone, which looked downward, glittered with the anger which was in his soul.

'You mistake, madamigella,' he said humbly. 'You wholly mistake. I have no power to arrest the course which the law takes. It is your venerable father, who has never comprehended that business is business, and that the closest friendship must give way to self-defence and to self-interest. I have done for him what I would not have done for my own father. I have given time and care, and thought and money, and if he had listened to me, things would not be now with him as they are. What would you? He has indulged the elegant taste and costly whims of a scholar, whilst he was only a poor bookseller on the brink of bankruptcy. How could the end be other than it is? He has spent his days and nights in the useless illusory pursuit of a learning which is not worth the farthing match that a child sells in the streets. In other times there were monasteries open for such vain dreamers as he. No one knows nowadays what to do with them; they are out of date, and the world walks over them while they remain distraught at their studies. It is many years now, Madama Beldia, since your father began to sign his name to bills and acts, without weighing well enough to what he put it. One thing or another has always dragged him down. There were his son's follies in one way, and his own in another; and he never could see an old book or manuscript but what his it must be; and he never noticed that it was all going out and nothing coming in, and he always liked to give you ready money to keep the house going, and he never could bring himself to grudge a bit or sup to anyone, or deny anybody the pick of his own brains, and it has come to this at last—such things always do; and if the crash have been staved off so long, why, it is solely due to the efforts of your poor servant Vestuccio, whom you rashly and unkindly are inclined to blame.'

He spoke so frankly, so clearly, and so openly, that any stranger hearing him would have been ready to swear to his truth and integrity. Almost they made Beldia herself waver in her belief against him.

Every word he said so exactly portrayed her father's faults and foibles that it wrung her heart to hear him; she stood close to him motionless, gazing at him as if her eyes would fain plunge into his inmost soul.

He moved uneasily under that intense and prolonged gaze, and on the pretext that the lamp was flaring, he turned down the flame so that the room grew dusky.

Beldia drew a deep breath, as she replied to him:

'You speak plausibly, you speak with apparent candour; I cannot deny that my father's errors are such as you have said. But you have taken a cruel advantage of them. You have turned to your own profit his trustfulness and absence of guile. You have filled your strong box with his signatures, and when the time was ripe to most profit by them you have pulled the cord and let the axe fall. You cannot deny it. You cannot deny it; all these men who bring these claims and charges and protested paper are your creatures.'

She paused, and looked to see him abashed, unmasked, ashamed. The innocent always expect to behold the guilty overwhelmed by the mere charge of guilt. She was wise, and clear of reason in many ways, but she knew not the heart of a rogue. She drew her pure, straight weapon of truth, and thought to see him shrink before it as Mephistopheles before the cross. But Mephistopheles, in the person of Vestuccio, was not so simple. He smiled within himself to see the maiden so frankly and so foolishly laying bare her soul to him, and showing him how much, and yet how little, she knew, how dangerous and yet how impotent she was.

'Never show your cards, madamigella!' he murmured, and then, with a pained expression, added in a colder tone: 'Your language is strange and full of offence to me. But I can understand that you are agitated, and so are unjust and confused. These troubles have fallen on you without warning. Often and often would I have warned you myself, but your father would never allow me to do so, and he was master of his own secrets. Believe me, madamigella, believe me, by the souls of my children, whom you know that I love so well, if Ser Checchi has been thus far saved from utter ruin, it is due to me and to the influence which my townsfolk are so good as to let me exercise in the counsels I give to them. I am a hard-working man, who has risen from the lowest state, by energy and frugality, and the city knows it and honours me.'

Vestuccio's face beamed, his figure dilated; he had in his own eyes the nimbus about his head of successful and prosperous virtue. He was never so happy or so eloquent as when he lauded himself.

Beldia's gaze was riveted upon him, trying to read his hidden mind, and failing, because the candour and integrity of her own nature had no gauge by which to measure the duplicity and hypocrisy of his.

'If this be true,' she said simply, 'if you have had neither hand nor head in this cabal against my father, save him. He has always trusted you. You have always advised him. His ruin must be due to you, directly or indirectly, since you were so often his adviser. Save him.'

'And how, madonna mia?' cried Vestuccio, acting innocent ignorance and bewildered surprise.

'Get him time; get him loans; speak to those who seize his goods, who hold his signatures, if it be not you indeed who hold them. You are a man of business; you must know a thousand ways in business, by which men on the brink of ruin can be saved from the lowest depth of all. Save him, save him, as I saved Gemma when the fungus of death was growing in her throat.'

She spoke with intense and fervid feeling, whilst her voice thrilled with the intensity of her dread and of her hope.

Vestuccio looked downward on the floor. For one brief second his heart was touched; he loved his child, and he remembered how this woman, who pleaded with him now, had remained in the contagion of the horrible disease, when Gemma's own mother had fled shrieking away from what was deemed a dying bed.

He remembered, and he knew that he could save her father without the outlay of a farthing, merely by renunciation of gain, merely by lifting up his hand to the pack which he had let loose, and bidding them take their fangs off their quarry and wait.

For one moment he wavered, remembering and regretting. The next moment nature, habit, the instinct of avarice, the passion of acquisitiveness, the cruel, insatiable hunger of the usurer, which is like the appetite of the horse-leech, were all stronger than the alien and evanescent impulse of mercy.

He looked away from Beldia, and answered: 'You are labouring under some sad illusion, madamigella. I could not stay judgment against your father for a day. I have no power, no means. I am grieved, grieved to the heart, but I can do nothing. The law of debt must take its course.'

He had spent eight years in careful preparation for the catastrophe which had now fallen on Beldia and her father. Little by little he had built up the scaffolding, step by step he had drawn near the edifice; he could not lay down unlit the slow match with which he had made ready to set it ablaze for the warming of his own hands and heart.

He loved his child, but he loved money, intrigues, and acquisition more. In the actual moment of her danger he would have renounced anything to save her; but years had gone by since then, and his gratitude had cooled.

After all it was Providence which had saved her; so he thought to himself, and hardened his heart. It was not only gain which he would lose if he yielded, but self-respect. He would for ever despise himself, and be despised by those who acted with him, if he now held back and spared the dwellers in the tower. It is not by mercy and long-suffering, by kindness or grateful memories, that the fortunes of industrious people like himself are made. A short memory for benefits and a long memory for figures are the two essentials to monetary success.

He looked upon the floor, his pleasant smile stereotyped upon his mouth.

'You have taken a wholly wrong view of the matter, *signorina mia gentilissima*,' he added respectfully. 'I might take exception at your expressions, but I pass them by; you are agitated and unhappy, and know not what you say. I am powerless in this matter, which you seem erroneously to think that I control. It is not I who move the law, it is the men of law. I have no power to stop them in what they deem their duty. As I understand it, all which Ser Checchi suffers from are the legal and logical consequences of his own acts. If he had not signed these papers, these bills, these drafts; if he had not purchased costly works, and mortgaged all he possessed to pay for them, no one would molest him now. People complain of the law, but wrongly; the civil law never touches those who have not first violated some moral law written in their conscience, but broken in their acts.'

He paused to see the effect of his words; he was pleased with the last phrase; it filled him with the calm complacency of a man who has been always careful to be himself on the right side of the law, ever to be creditor, and never to be debtor.

Beldia shuddered as she heard. From violence may come mercy, from fury may be born pity; but never, never, never, she knew, could any good or gentle thing arise from the accursed smoothness of a self-admiring hypocrisy, from the cruelty of a damnable avarice.

'Answer me one thing only, in one word,' she said, looking always at him with her straight, clear gaze, which he had now braced himself to meet. 'Is it not you who have seized Antella?'

'Madamigella,' said Vestuccio, with dignity and rebuke, 'I had lent out my own honest gains upon that land. I had lost upon it; I had waited long, very long; if at the last I have entered into my own, I have done no more than that. Nay, so true a friend am I to your father, that to-morrow, if he pay me my capital and interest and costs, I will give the land back to him, as though there had been never any question of it between us. Can I say more? Who else would say as much? I have six children who look to me for bread. I cannot make gifts to right and left, as childless men may do.'

She looked at him in silence, reading his soul in all its meanness and baseness, and trickery and cruelty.

'My heart is but too tender,' he continued, warming to his own self-praise, as he ever did. 'It is a heart of gold. I maintain my old parents in every comfort, I have made the fortunes of my family; I rejoice to give; I am full of benevolence as the fresh melon of its juice; but there are limits— there are duties—one may be indulgent, but one must not be a dupe. Who will pay me for all the time which I have thrown away in your honoured father's affairs? No one, not a farthing; I am sacrificed in every way. Others have the law on him, not I. The land? What is the land? All clay and rock, yielding nothing, and taxed at fifty per cent. It is a dead loss to me to be forced to take it instead of my good, sound, national notes. If all business were done as I have done this thing, lenders would be beggars. Had I only had the money which I lent Ser Checchi, I could have turned and turned it over and over a score of times, and made hundreds, thousands, tens of thousands out of it. To help him, to succour him, I have robbed myself and my children, and the child unborn that my wife goes with now. And what do you give me in return? Abuse, suspicion, shameful and unjust reproach.'

His eyes filled, his hands spread themselves outward in the gesture of one wrongly accused, who repudiates a dishonouring charge; he stood erect and self-satisfied, a very model of calumniated, and upright, and self-respecting manhood.

He waited for her to reply, but she said nothing; her gaze was still fixed upon him. She was thinking bitterly how long a viper may dwell in the ivy by your gates, and you have no chance to see him shed his skin.

Vestuccio, being only thus answered by a silence which reproached and condemned him more overwhelmingly than any words could have done, replaced his smoking-cap on his head, set his eyeglass in his eye, and banished the kindliness and sadness from his face.

'Pardon me,' he said curtly; 'I can waste no

more time. My friends in the next room are waiting for me. Offer my respects to your honoured father; it is useless to remind him that, had he attended to the disinterested counsels of a practical man, he would not now be in the strait he is.'

Then he opened the door sharply.

'Lucinda, my girl,' he said to the servant maid, 'light the Signorina Beldia down the stairs.'

CHAPTER XVII.

BELDIA went home through the lamplit and moonlit streets, sick at heart with that weary sense of the futility of truth, of the nullity of justice, of the incapacity for right to struggle against wrong, which is the most enervating and torturing of sorrows. She knew, as plainly as though it were written on the walls, that all hope was over for her father and herself.

She realized with a horrible shock that their position was neither higher nor better than that of the many debtors whose names were printed up at the doors of the Pretura, to be talked of all over the city. To her nature, so delicate, so proud, and so reserved, the discovery was a torture none the less acute because she endeavoured to bear it bravely. She knew that Vestuccio had adroitly schemed for and compassed her father's destruction, but she had no proofs that he had done so; no one would have heeded her protestations, and the law was on the side of the evil-doer. To the tribunals, as to the crowd, Vestuccio was but a prudent and provident man asking only for his own; and her father was the imprudent and improvident one, who is always a criminal in the sight of others, because he can no longer benefit or purchase his contemporaries. To the lender of money all were ready to doff their caps and bend their backs; the borrower of money was only a poor, played-out, uninteresting, useless creature in their sight. The world always respects power, and never asks the means and methods by which it has been gained.

In the streets and squares and shops and offices of the city, Vestuccio was a power: he had many men in his grip, and fortune in his future. Ser Checchi could not be of any further use or profit to anyone; naturally the town took the former to its bosom, and left the latter alone, like the dead ass by the wayside.

When she went up the stairs of her home, the door of the back-room was open, her father stood in the doorway, a brass lamp in his hand, waiting for her.

'You have been to ask grace of Vestuccio?' he said sternly.

Beldia did not reply; to prevaricate or deny never occurred to her.

'You did wrong,' said Ser Checchi. 'Long centuries ago, in yonder street, a woman asked the escaped lion to spare her babe; and the desert animal heard her prayer. But had she spoken to the usurer she would have spoken in vain. I did not think you would have so abased me.'

'It was not abasement,' she said, wounded by the word. 'I did but tell him the truth: that he had abused your trust, that he had taken Antella unjustly by abrupt foreclosing, that he was behind all these other men who now attack you. I did but ask him time and patience, and such influence as it would cost him nothing to use. That was all.'

Ser Checchi smiled faintly.

'Poor innocent! Could you provoke him more? He will only go in the morning to the attorneys, and bid them hurry on their acts.'

'Why? Why should he hate you so? You have done him no evil.'

'I trusted him and he betrayed me. Who wrongs never pardons.'

CHAPTER XVIII.

EVERY half-year Beldia had, of late years, gone herself to pay the rent on the twentieth day of August, and on the twentieth day of February, as the Florentine law mercilessly exacts; and now, when these cruel documents came to their door, in these scorching days of the late summer, she thought with relief that the money for the coming half-year was safe in the hands of the old Canon of the Duomo, Don Gervasio, with whom it had always been her habit to lodge it well in advance of the date at which it would be needed. This year her father had given it to her earlier than usual, foreseeing the troubles which were to come upon him, and desiring that this matter at least should be at rest. It was almost the last money which remained to him out of that small capital which he had inherited from his progenitors.

'You gave the rent money to Don Gervasio?' he asked her anxiously one day.

'Oh yes,' she answered; 'shall I get it from him, and pay Saetta beforehand?'

'It would be well,' said Ser Checchi. 'Better early than late.'

So she went that self-same day and got the small sum from the old Canon, who kept it, with his funds for charitable purposes, in an iron box with a silver figure of an Apostle on its lid, and a secret to its lock.

The Canon was banker to all the poorer neighbours, and, when he kept the children's pence, produced them multiplied, and told their young owners that, if let alone, the *soldi* grew, just as endive did, or cresses.

When he gave her roll of notes to Beldia now out of his iron box, he looked anxiously in her face.

'If I could be of any use, you would tell me, my daughter?' he asked wistfully. 'I have heard with pain of your father's troubles. I owe him many years of good neighbourliness and peaceful communion of the intellect. I would do anything in my power to lighten his burdens. You know that?'

'I know it well, most reverend,' said Beldia, with a deep sigh. 'But my father is very proud in some ways, although so humble in others. He would not take a loan.'

'And it would be wrong in me to question you as to that which he chooses to keep secret,' said the Canon. 'Nor would I do so. But when the men of law are knocking loudly at your gates, and you have not wherewithal to pay them and send them thence, there is no secret any more, alas! The very lads in the street know your sorrow.'

Beldia bent her head in ashamed assent; her pale cheeks burned with crimson colour.

'I know not how this misery has come upon me,' she said sadly. 'My father was ever most punctual, most exact, most honourable.'

'He has fallen amongst thieves,' said Don Gervasio, 'and he has been too long mute under his wounds. But I cannot pardon him for his oblivion of his daughter's interests,' he added, a shade of severity and censure passing over his benignant features. 'Books are very dear to me myself, and good books and great books are the benison of the world; but not even to the wisdom of all the ages should your peace and prosperity and his own fair name have been sacrificed.'

'It does not matter for me,' said Beldia quickly. 'What matters is, that the books will be lost, and his good name, as your reverence says, lost with them.'

Then she turned away to hide the agitation which she could ill control, and slipped the bank-notes within the bosom of her gown, and left the good priest to go down into the street and homeward. But on the threshold the Canon stopped her.

'Wait one moment. You go to pay the rent?'

'Yes, you know that I do,' said Beldia wonderingly, a vague fear fluttering at her heart.

'But I have heard,' murmured the Canon, 'that Maso Saetta means—wishes—intends to—to—to send you a notice to quit.'

Beldia uttered a sharp cry.

'He cannot!' she cried aloud.

'Oh, pardon me, my child, he can.'

'He cannot!' she repeated wildly. 'He cannot, father! He cannot!'

'My poor girl, consider. You hold the tenements by no contract, no term of years; you have always held it loosely, as your forefathers did, with nothing written, paying from half-year to half-year. True, "*l'uso fa légge*," saith the proverb. But usage is against you here. Believe me, Saetta can turn you out in November, if he chooses to give you dismissal now; and—and I have heard it said in the town that he will do so. I grieve to pain you more, my dear daughter; but I would not have you go on a fool's errand to this graceless and unkind old man.'

'But he would never be so cruel as to take the very moment of our misfortune to make us homeless?'

'My dear maiden, adversity tests our friends; but few bear the test; and Saetta was never a friend of yours or anyone's. He is a greedy, hard, and ignorant person, who will only conclude from your father's present position that he is not a desirable tenant any more.'

'A tenant!'

She repeated the word stupidly. It seemed to her to have no fitness in connection with themselves; the tower was theirs; they had lived in it, loved it, cherished it, laboured for it; it had had the mornings and the evenings of their days; it had harboured their joys and sorrows; it had seen their births and their deaths; it had heard the cry of the new-born child; it had seen the dead whom they loved borne across its threshold; it had heard the words of their prayers, the laughter of their lips, the sobs of their lamentations, the gladness of their delight, the deep-drawn breaths of their slumbers: they belonged to it, and it was theirs by the tender tie of a thousand days, by the sacred bond of a thousand nights.

It was theirs—theirs—theirs—by every bond which binds the heart of man to the roof which shelters him and to the walls which guard his sleep.

She was at home there, as were the swallows under its eaves, and the owls in its loopholes and gargoyles. To dwell elsewhere than in the tower seemed incomprehensible to her; her father and grandfather had been born there before her, and her great-grandfather had watched the entry of Bonaparte's battalions from its grated casements.

She also had been born there, and cradled and reared there; and although she had always known, indeed, that the tower was not actually part of her father's possessions, but belonged to Tomaso Saetta, yet so used was she to her old home, and so long, she knew, had it been occupied by her family, that she felt rooted in the place like any tree in its native soil. She would have as soon expected to see the angels from its niches take wing across the Arno, as have thought it possible that she could live elsewhere. Whenever she dreamed of her future with Odisio, it was always framed in this antique setting which she loved so well; whenever she thought of children who might be born to her, it was always of them as they would flit to and fro down these dusky stairs, which had felt her own feet so long, and as they would stand beside her at sunrise and at sunset amongst the flowers on this roof, whence she had so often watched the stars.

The Saetta family had become the proprietors of it, indeed, because the necessities of the old patrician race to which it belonged had thrown it on the market at a low price, and even that low price had been too high for Ser Checchi to be able to purchase it, dearly as he would have loved to have done so. But although Saetta had become the legal owner of it, both she and her father had always felt that it did far more truly and entirely belong to themselves by all the ties which long affection and occupation can create between the dwelling and the dweller in it. They had taken Saetta every six months five hundred francs, for the half-year's rent paid in advance, and had received his receipt in return; but there his interest in it began and ended as far as they were concerned. He let its ground-floor to the charcoal-seller and the chandler, and the mezzanino to the cobbler and the tailor and the cabinet-maker, and the rest to Ser Checchi, and never spent a penny on its repair, or attended to any fissure in its masonry or rot in its timber. The tower took care of itself, and having been built by the great master, Gaddi, could do very well and very long without any other care ; and its wonderful majolica decorations of Messer Luca's bore wind and rain, sun and heat, and even that insidious enemy, frost, without any apparent dulling of their brilliant colours, or any blunting of their fine outlines.

Once a year Ser Checchi, from love of these angels and loves and shields and wreaths, paid a mason to climb and brush the dust and dirt off these lovely ornaments; but Maso Saetta would never have wasted a franc in doing anything of the sort. His old father had bought the tower because it had come in his way to buy it very cheaply, but he himself despised it, thought it only fit for bats and rats, and much preferred a square little house with green shutters, a slate roof, and walls a few inches thick, which he had built for his use outside the San Gallo gate, and which stuck up its pert and paltry vulgarity amidst ruined vineyards and desolated gardens.

CHAPTER XIX.

She went down into the hot and shadeless ways of the city with a sense of confusion and stupor upon her, as if someone had struck her on the head. She did not go to the landlord, but wended her way straight homeward, intending to take counsel with her father. But even as she mounted the stairs and opened the door of the book-room, she met, face to face, the usher of the tribunal, who grinned as he passed her, and pointed his thumb over his shoulder at Ser Checchi, who stood holding a printed document in his hand, and stared down on its lines as though they were written in some characters unknown to him.

'Not this! not this! not to us,' he said stupidly.

'May I see it?' she asked timidly, frightened by his distraught look; he let the paper pass from his hand to her.

She understood it at a glance. It was the *disdetta* with which the Canon had warned her that they were menaced, a notice to quit the tower within two months and twelve days' time. At the expiration of that term, unless the premises were vacated and surrendered to the owner, the law would turn the occupier, and all his goods and chattels, into the street by force, if they did not go willingly.

Beldia read it twice and thrice, unable to believe her own sight. She had often seen such documents brought to her poorer neighbours, carrying consternation and destitution in their train, for two months is but a brief space in which to pack up your tents and go to unknown ground.

'But we owe him nothing?' she said, meaning their landlord.

Ser Checchi shook his head.

'Nothing. You remember you took the last rent, last February, to him yourself. I suppose he is afraid for the one now coming due.'

'But when he has always been paid, can he send us away?'

'Oh yes! we have no contract with him. Our people have lived here two hundred years and more, but that does not count. He bought the tower; he can do as he likes with his own.'

He spoke wearily, drearily, stunned by this new calamity, feeling too helpless under it to rebel or protest. He was tired of his troubles; he was an old man, and they were too many for his strength.

He took the paper again into his hands and turned it to and fro stupidly, as though he were an illiterate man who could not read.

'I did not think that Maso would have done it to me, to me,' he said feebly and wonderingly.

He and Maso Saetta, the owner of the tower, had been play-fellows and school-fellows in their youth, and cronies in their older years, often talking of their early days over a cup of coffee or a glass of lemonade.

'Oh, it is impossible, impossible!' said Beldia, her face scared and white. 'Go away?—you and I —oh, it is impossible! Go away! Leave the tower? Oh, no—no—no! anything but that, anything but that! He has always been paid; the law cannot let him do such a monstrous thing. The tower is ours, ours, ours!'

For the first time she had lost her reasonableness, her patience, her intelligence. She was stung to the heart. She was beside herself with pain. The tower had been her home from birth. It had had all her life, all her care, all her love. She could not realize that a little old man, who had no love for it and no place in it, could have superior title over it to hers, and power to drive her and her father from the hallowed shelter of its roof.

Her father folded up the document, and placed it with the other law-papers in a drawer.

'He can do as he likes with his own,' he said in the same low, broken, tired voice. 'All these acts have frightened him. Proprietors love not debtors under their roof-tree.'

'But we owe him nothing!'

'That makes no difference. He is afraid that we shall. When a hound is lamed and falls, the rest of the pack turn on him and rend him. It is the law of life.'

'And you will do nothing?'

'There is nothing to do.'

He knew that there was nothing to do; against a *disdetta*, signified by the tribunal in the landlord's name, no man can appeal. It is a decree immutable and unalterable; if the tenant has not vacated the house on the date appointed, the law casts him and all he possesses into the street. He cannot complain; he was duly cited and warned.

She felt as though the world itself was slipping from beneath her feet, and the solid earth giving way and vanishing into space.

'But I have the money to pay him,' said Beldia piteously. 'Surely, surely he would not turn us out if he saw the money?'

Ser Checchi lifted his dulled, sad eyes and sighed.

'The sight of money sometimes works miracles,' he said hesitatingly. He had seen it act like an incantation on his countrymen, making the savage meek, the timid bold, the unkind full of loving-kindness; he had seen truth forsworn, peace signed away for ever, certainty thrown aside for possibility, and solid value bartered for shining dross, at the mere magical sight of money in the palm.

'But no, no,' he added imperatively; 'since he has done us this outrage, let it so remain. Seek no redress. He does but exercise his legal right. I would not humble myself or you to plead for any respite.'

'But there may be some error? He may think we cannot pay. What can he want more than to have his money's worth? Oh, let me see him, father, let me see him!' she cried, with unwonted passion, losing her power of self-control and self-effacement. 'If we are here we will be happy even with bare walls. Things will mend. Trade will return. We spend so little that we shall be able to live. But it must be *here*, oh, it must be here! If I go hence, I shall leave my heart in the very stones!'

She trembled violently, her pale face was violently flushed; being a true woman as she was, the calamity which struck at her associations and affections affected her far more intensely than the privations and miseries which touched her material welfare. To die of hunger in her old beloved home seemed to be a sweeter and fairer fate than to dwell in riches and abundance elsewhere.

Her father looked at her for a moment, and then averted his eyes, unable to endure the sight of her anguish.

'Do what you will,' he said to her; 'I, who have brought you to this pass, have lost all title to dictate to you. You may easily be wiser than I. More unwise you cannot be.'

CHAPTER XX.

On that vague permission she acted. She took the money for the rent from the old priest, to whom she had confided it, and went to the dwelling of Maso Saetta.

He was an old man, who lived on his own small means, frugally, had never married, and led the monotonous, trivial, tedious life led by so many of his country people, toddling between his chamber and his coffee-house, amusing his forenoon at his barber's, and in the evenings going to one of the cheap theatres or the puppet show, or sitting on the bench by Goldoni's statue to see the fine folks drive down the Lung Arno.

She had always seen Maso Saetta as easily as she saw the communal clock, whenever she wanted to do so. But now again, and again, and again, he eluded her; was neither at his own house or at his usual haunts, and seemed to have altogether altered the routine of his days. She began to divine that he avoided her on purpose, and redoubled her efforts, going again and again in the same day to the street where he dwelt. Time was passing, months are but as an instant when they are bringing what we dread upon their wings; and a ghastly, choking terror seized her, when she thought that, if she could not turn or soften him, the tower would soon be no more theirs. She awoke from a short and troubled sleep every morning with this dread suffocating her; her once peaceful nights were broken, her once happy waking was over; when she heard the bells chiming in the clear dusk of the dawn, she no more rose gladly because another day had begun. She rose in apprehension, and with oppression, dreading what the coming hours should bring.

Her father never asked her if she had seen Maso. He knew well that she had not, or she would have told him.

'Aren't you thinking of getting a new roof to cover you?' said Dessi, the bailiff, officiously to her. 'Time flies, and you won't be wise if you provoke *the sfratta*.'

The *sfratta* is the corollary and colophon, as it were, of the *disdetta*, the last act of all which tells the refractory tenant that the carabineers are coming to drive him out into the street, and pitch his goods out after him.

Beldia did not answer; she ignored Dessi as utterly as it was possible to do. 'The proud-stomached wench!' he thought angrily. 'How dare she hold her head in the air like that, when I have locked up her very jam-pots and bed-linen, and have even got her saucepans and fish-kettle in my keeping?'

'Out you'll go, mind that,' he said spitefully one day. 'You won't turn Maso more than you'll melt the bronze boar. Not a bit of it. Don't you hope to do it. Vestuccio has got hold of Maso.'

Beldia sighed heavily, but she had self-command enough to ask him nothing. She knew that it was most probable that what he said was true; the influence of Vestuccio spread far and wide.

She only doubled and trebled her efforts to see the landlord; the time it took up to do so she could ill spare, for all the household work was now hers to do, and such food as she could obtain she had to prepare; and she strove to make it as tempting and delicate as she could to attract her father's failing appetite. At length, all other means proving useless, she resolved to wait at the barber's shop, where, from the time that he had reached puberty, Saetta had never neglected to go as the city clocks tolled noon; and there at last, although his hour was changed to escape her, she saw him come, looking furtively from side to side as he hurried across the threshold.

She hurried after him, and caught the lappets of his long coat.

'Ser Maso, Ser Maso, hear me; for pity's sake stop and hear me!'

He looked down on her in terror; he was a little, red-faced, plump, merry-looking man; but he lost his colour and frowned as he said nervously, trying to pluck his coat from her grasp:

'I cannot listen—I cannot indeed. You must go to the lawyers if you want anything. Everything is in the lawyers' hands. Let me go. Pray let me go.'

'But I have brought the money for the half-year to come,' said Beldia, taking the bank-notes from the bosom of her gown. 'You cannot send us away if we are ready and willing to pay. Our people have been there two hundred years, and you are my father's friend; perhaps you feared we could not pay, and so you did this cruel thing; but here is the money for the half-year to come.'

The eyes of Maso Saetta twinkled, winked, and leered as they saw the crisp bank-notes so near his grasp; he longed to snatch them, he ogled them as any satyr a nymph; he made a little clawing, grasping, unconscious movement of his hands, which is a frequent gesture with Italians when they behold money. But he turned his head away resolutely, and shut his eyes tightly to shut out the temptation.

'It is not that,' he said quickly. 'Oh, not at all, not at all! It is quite another matter. I want the tower empty; I have other uses for it. I have other tenants. Very likely I may sell it. Very likely the municipality will pull it down——'

'Pull it down?'

'Eh!' said the owner, with a deprecating outward curl of his lips. 'It is very old; it is dirty and grim and ugly; it takes up room, and they want everything smart and wide, and clear and whitewashed. All the water-side of the Borgo San Jacopo is marked for demolition, and if they pull down the tower I shall have large compensation, and the della Robbia will sell alone for a vast deal.'

'Pull down the tower!'

She echoed the words faintly, leaning against the doorpost of the barber's shop to keep herself from falling.

'*E antico!*' repeated Maso Saetta, with that boundless scorn which the Italian can put into those two words.

'It is old!' he repeated, chuckling in cynical derision of its age, and then, seeing her pained, scared face, her appealing eyes, the bank-notes in her hand, he grew angry at the unreason and untimeliness of this absurd appeal to him, which tempted him and worried him, and made him feel ashamed of using his own unquestionable rights.

'My good maiden,' he said breathlessly, thrusting his face close to hers, and waving his shaking fingers in the air, 'this is unreasonable, this is unkind, this is preposterous! You should have more consideration. When a man employs a lawyer, he does so because he wishes to be put to no trouble in the matter himself. I respect your father, and I pity him, and no one can understand how he has lost his wits, and come to such a pass as he has. But one must think of one's own interests before all. You cannot expect me to forget my own interests. I have acted on good advice, and I shall not draw back from what I have done. You should not try to unnerve me in this manner. It is unkind. Besides, how could you and your father keep up a place like that, when your books are all sold, and your trade at an end? Be reasonable, my dear. Be reasonable. It is not honest what you want to do: to live on at my expense and cheat the piper of his pay. Oh-h-h! Do not set your back up like that. When folks cannot pay they must go softly and meekly; they walk on broken bottles. Yes, yes; I see the money; but I suppose it belongs to the creditors. If Gigi Fanno saw it, he would take it and lock it up. I shall not say anything about it, but you had best hide it in your gown. Yes, yes; I know all you want to say. I have been a friend of Ser Checchi's; I never said I have not, but friendship is one thing, and interest is another. One must consider one's own interest before all. I want the tower emptied; I want the tower vacant. You have had your notice to quit. It is quite regular, quite legal. What have you to complain of? Am I, or am I not, the owner of the place? Ay, you cannot dispute that. Then go back to your father, and tell him so, and tell him that, when one employs a lawyer, one does not expect to be worried out of one's life by women. No—no—no! I have said it and I stick to it. You have the notice to quit. Out you go! out you go! Of course a week more or less we will not make a fuss about, for old acquaintance' sake. But out you go. I have other views for the tower. And you, hearken to a word of sense—go you and take a couple of little rooms. It is as much as you can afford, and maybe you won't be long able to pay for even those; and, I am told, everything except your beds is seized. The idea—the idea of poor folks without a table or chair wanting to go staying on at the tower! Two hundred years? I know you say so. Yes, I believe it is so. But your people were only tenants all that while. My father —rest his soul!—bought it forty years ago, and the deed of sale was registered, and may be seen by whoever will. I am the master—I am the master! and out you go. No—no; no—no! It is of no use to torment me; you ought to have more feeling, you ought to have more consideration. You will cause me an apoplexy; I must go home unshaven, and take a purging dose. You should not excite one so. I feel a booming in my ears. If I perish of a stroke, you will have killed me.'

And he began to cry, for he was exceeding frightened.

'It is a shame, signorina, to torment a poor, good, kind man thus,' said the barber, who had been listening all the while, a brass pot of hot water swinging in his hand. 'It is a shame to importune him so, and it may cause him a stroke, as he says. Like enough, alack! Ser Maso has a heart of gold, and it irks him to deny the smallest thing to man or child. Come into my inner room, sir,' he added, 'and lie down on my sofa a bit, and let me make you a cooling draught. If you walk home in the agitation you are in now, you may very well not reach your house in safety.'

'You are right,' said Maso Saetta, with a kind of pride in being so near his end, mingled with a great commiseration for himself. 'My feelings are always too much for me, and to be obliged to seem unkind to an old friend is very painful. But when one has had good advice, and has set the law in motion, no reasonable being would be turned aside from his own interests.'

Here his tottering steps bore him across the threshold of the inner room of the barber, and the door of it was closed on him, and Beldia was left alone in the shop with some curious passers-by, and some round-eyed street urchins crowding round the door to see what was the matter.

'What can that maiden be thinking of? She and her old fool of a father must be mad,' said the barber in the inner chamber, as he mixed a lemon-juice and citrate of magnesia; 'they have nothing in the world; they are cleaned out like disembowelled rabbits, and they expect to stay on in such a fine place as Taddeo's tower. They are a disgrace to the town. You do well, sir, to get rid of them. The man has always been a poor, dreamy, feckless creature, looking for noon at twilight and thinking twelve is thirteen; and as for the signorina,

Madonna Beldia as they call her, why, there is naught to say against her virtue, but she is a wench who thinks herself a queen, and nobody good enough to speak to; my woman once takes her a piece of harmless gossip, as women will, and she reads her a sermon on back-biting and bearing false witness! She is like a starched coif, and I for one shall not be sorry to see her roughly handled and the starch creased. Drink this, dear and good sir, and lie quiet a little; she cannot come in hither.'

'She is a good young woman enough, but head-strong,' said Maso Saetta faintly. 'She does not realize her own situation. If Gigi Fanno knew she had that money in her breast, I misdoubt the law would not let her finger it. Debtors cannot secrete large sums.'

'Nay, it is a fraud,' said the barber. 'How is your head now, sir? If you would like a leech or two I could run over to the apothecary's opposite.'

'No, no, the ill is passing. Are you sure she cannot come in here?'

'Sure and certain, sir. The bolt is shot.'

'It would be only right that the creditors should know she has that money. Really and truly it is theirs.'

'It is theirs, sir, yes. If I said a word to Gigi? I shave him twice a week.'

'It might be well; the law must never be defrauded. Yes; I think it would be well.'

'Then I will say the word, sir, before the day is over,' said the barber with virtuous unction, and that mysterious pleasure in doing harm to people with whom he had no concern, which is frequent in human nature.

CHAPTER XXI.

SER CHECCHI had courage and integrity in his blood, and at first, for the sake of his daughter and of his own good name, he struggled against his adversity. But he could not bring himself to stoop very low, or to beg very humbly; words of supplication choked him. Though a man of great intellectual humility, he had been always proud and sensitive, having accorded many favours but asked none; so that he petitioned ill, and did not understand the trick of greasing the palms of those middlemen who are always supreme in such circumstances; moreover, the covert influence of Querci and of Vestuccio was always opposed to him, closing any doors he strove to open, and hastening on what he tried to retard, so that he could do little, very little; and the time grew close at hand for the actual sales to take place. The neighbours had a sore sense of deception, when they still involuntarily felt unwilling respect for that slight, bent, feeble figure, with its soft gray hair touching the shoulders, and the luminous large eyes looking so far beyond them and theirs, as Ser Checchi went on his weary way through the streets to beg mercy and delay from his torturers.

The very reverence which he had inspired among those who saw him in his daily walks in the city went against him now, for to the vulgar it is always irritating to have been subdued into feeling respect where there is no money to warrant their feeling it, or to reward them for having done so.

'What an artful old hypocrite to look so venerable,

and buy choice copies as if he were some rich scholar, whilst all the while he was head over ears in debt!' said the tradesfolk of the neighbourhood; and this, or something like this, was the general sentiment amongst the small number of persons who were interested in observing the decline and fall of his fortunes.

Once in her despair, feeling that no personal reluctance or pride should prevent her essaying any means which could possibly alleviate her father's distress, Beldia went to the offices of Pampilio Querci, situated in the Canto dei Nelli. His name was attached to the suit of more than one creditor, and she knew that, although not officially, he was virtually the adviser of Vestuccio. The attorney, a little, dapper, spruce, pert figure, bald at twenty-six years old, and pallid as a candle, received her with elaborate and frigid politeness, sitting behind a writing-table strewn with legal papers, and the manuscripts of the archæological articles which he was preparing for a learned Roman review.

He listened to her politely, but evidently wearied as by a twice-told tale. He was grieved, he was inconsolable, he was in despair, but he could not defer execution: he was but the instrument of his clients; was Dessi insolent and overbearing?—he was pained to hear it, but he could do nothing; custodians were independent citizens, under no one's orders; they had heavy responsibilities, they could scarcely be blamed if they were anxious to protect themselves; in the event—an absurd hypothesis, she would excuse him for even putting it forward—in the utterly impossible event of anything seized in the name of the law being made away with by the debtor, or anyone belonging to him, Giuseppe Dessi was responsible for its disappearance.

He might, therefore, be excused, if he were over-solicitous and somewhat impertinent; nevertheless, if she thought she had any real ground of complaint, she might address a petition against him to the most worshipful the Pretore of the tribunal of the section; he could not guarantee that such an application would meet with success, but it might do so, if respectfully and humbly worded.

All this he said in long, involved, pompous and deliberate phrases, balancing a paper-knife on his forefinger, and looking at her impertinently through his eyeglasses, as he leaned back in his office chair.

He had been as amorously moved towards her at one time as a cold-blooded and cautious little egotist can ever be so moved to anyone; and it consoled his wounded vanity and his balked passion to see this serene and stately maiden a supplicant before him, and to be able in turn to reject her suit.

Had she not deserved every humiliation and tribulation which could befall her? What vengeance of 'the handless and footless goddess' could be too great upon a woman so blind and so ingrate.

'It is well that my fancy was restrained from fulfilment,' he reflected. 'She grows plain, quite plain, and she looks old.'

He did not say in so many words, 'If you had listened to my suit, all these miseries would have been spared to you;' but his attitude, his smile, his bland reproof, his frigid condolence, all said it for him in unmistakable meaning.

She might have possessed him, and his dapper person, and his checked suit, and his bran-new house amidst the tramway lines and the jute factories, and she had preferred a wandering Lombard scholar, with loose chestnut curls and an old velvet jacket, and no house at all anywhere, except in outlines upon his drawing-board.

Beldia was mute under the malignant ingenuity which made her parent's misfortunes seem traceable to her. It was possible enough, she knew, that had she accepted the young advocate's suit, the affairs of Ser Checchi would never have drifted to so desperate a ruin.

'If it be your vengeance, it is a poor, and paltry, and cruel one,' she said at length. 'My father had no part or act in my rejection of your hand. He showed you hospitality, kindness, liberality; and in return you steal his thoughts, and hawk them to the public press, and hound on his enemies against him. It is you who have counselled Maso Saetta to drive us from the tower.'

'That is wholly untrue, signorina; you are cruelly unjust. As a man I feel, and feel poignantly; but of my feelings you were pleased once to make no account; as a lawyer I am a mere machine, I can listen to no entreaties, I can neither pause nor waver in my course. My duty, my sole duty, is towards my clients, and, whatever it may cost me, I must do their bidding, and follow what I conceive to be their interests.'

'You need not have accepted their affairs,' said Beldia, weary of the long, pompous, and empty periods. 'You owe my father much, signore: you have learned much from him, and your learning has brought you other wages than those of that pure intellectual delight which it has always been sufficient for him to feel.'

She glanced as she spoke at the manuscript ready for press, and at the printer's proof which lay beneath his hand upon the table, between the summons-papers. Over Querci's pallid face there passed a quiver of embarrassment. Though his hand had written, and his name had signed, these scholarly articles, he knew well enough that it was of her father's scholarship, and her father's suggestions and discoveries, that those papers were full; though from their initial letter to their colophon no allusion was made, no reference was hinted, as to the man who had in reality inspired them.

'I have sat at the feet of Ser Checchi in certain studies with pleasure and profit,' he said, with some faint confusion disturbing for a moment the starch of his stiff and self-satisfied manners. 'I would never deny it for a moment. But it is not my fault if he has been so engrossed in those studies that practical matters have been lost sight of by him. I cannot afford to imitate his error, precious although such learned pursuits and investigations are to me. If he has not had at his side a practical adviser, who would have saved him from the consequences of such absence of mind, it is not my fault either. If you had chosen, I would have united my interests to his. But you preferred that it should be otherwise. It is the greatest pain to me that I have been compelled by my professional obligations to assume an attitude offensive, and apparently hostile, to you. But I am, of a truth, no more responsible for it than is this paper-cutter for the opinions of the volume upon which it is employed.

Had they not come to me, these adversaries of yours, they would have gone to some other solicitor, who would probably have shown less delicacy and patience in a painful duty than I have done.'

Then she turned away from him as she had done from Vestuccio, and went out of the office. Querci rose and hastened after her to open the outer door.

'Signorina,' he murmured, when I can befriend you conscientiously, believe me that I shall ever rejoice to do so. I am not Signore Saetta's keeper, nor Ser Checchi's, nor was I ever, allow me to remind you, attorney for the latter. Messer Tomaso has, on the contrary, always honoured me with his confidence. I owe a duty to my clients which I must fulfil, and he is one of them. But if you can obtain from him, or from them all, or from any one of them, an order to suspend proceedings, I shall be relieved and glad.'

He extended his hand as he spoke; she did not take it.

She had seen his clients again and again before this day, and one and all they had replied to her that they could move in no way, that the advocate Querci held their affairs in his hands, and that they dared not meddle with him. Her life swung like a pendulum between the thresholds of creditors' houses and lawyers' studies; she was worn out by the ceaseless and useless swing to and fro betwixt these men, who sent her backwards and forwards from one to another as the players at pallone sent their ball.

Querci closed the door upon her, and returned to his desk.

'Plain—yes, she grows plain,' he thought once

more with unction. 'And she must be four-and-twenty years old by now. When the old man is dead, she will have to go out to domestic service in some capacity; she has nothing, and her Lombard will be wise enough to keep the ocean between them. To think that I ever wished to marry her! and that I might have been taken at my word!'

Then he lit a cigarette, and felt that fortune had protected him, and dreamed of himself as he would be in future years—town councillor, provincial councillor, deputy, secretary of finance, commander of civil orders, even—who could say not?—even cousin of the King, by virtue of the Annunciation Insignia. Why not? A Sicilian notary is so now.

The bean-stalk climbing of a Messer Crispi makes ambitions ferment, like new wine, in the brains and bosoms of all youthful lawyers.

Then he roused himself from his dreams, took up his pen, and resumed his essay, looking every three minutes at the memoranda which he had taken down a year or two before from the teachings of Ser Checchi, concerning the African origin of the Sardinian race, and the epoch of the Etruscan invasion of Latium.

Half an hour after there was a tap at his door, and a man entered.

'Good-day, Messer Vico,' said Querci, with cheerful politeness, slipping his manuscript into his blotting-paper. 'I am at your service; what is it?'

Ludovico del Beni, a tall, bony, brown man, with a weak mouth and kindly eyes, wiped his forehead, spat on the floor, twirled his hat in his fingers, and then said sheepishly:

'Please, sir advocate, I do not like this business.'
Querci looked at him sharply.
'Why not?' he inquired.

Ludovico del Beni, called Vico by all who knew him, who kept a small shop of mattings, and cordage, and brushwork, stood first on one foot and then on the other, and spat again on the floor with great ceremony and solemnity.

'Well, sir,' he said, with a pause, 'he is an old man, and a gentle one; and my mind misgives me that he has not got long to live, and it seems to me that I'm neither here nor there in this business, and I'd like to be out of it; and why don't Ser Aurelio do his own jobs, and put his name to them? And the young woman, she came to me last evening, and she is very pretty spoken, and she is fond of the old man, and so I wanted to say, sir—can't they be given time, and let off a bit? It is not a business as I like; no, I never was a hard man, and I don't care to look like one; and I said to the young woman, if the sales could be stopped, and if the matter could be arranged in any other way——'

'It cannot,' said Querci, with a sharp click of his teeth, like the shutting of a steel trap. 'Confine yourself to your own affairs, my friend; they are like enough to cause you trouble.'

The tradesman looked at him nervously, and, with a meek and deferential pleading in his voice, said timidly:

'The prosecution is in my name, is it not?'

'Of course. It is you who hold the bill.'

'To please Ser Aurelio. I have never had a penny of the money.'

'That is not the present question. You are the

actual and apparent holder of the bill. You obtain judgment and levy execution. A sale follows, as night follows day.'

'But I do not like to look like a knave.'

'A knave!'

Querci was shocked; nothing alarms men of his kind so much as plain language.

'There is no question of knavery,' he said coldly. 'If there be any knavery at all, it is on the part of the debtor, who made himself responsible for sums which he knew he could not meet. I would advise you not to talk in this way; you yourself have paper out which is not worth very much. It may prove necessary to see how much, if your compassion for the old man in the tower runs away with your common-sense.'

The tradesman trembled as he heard, and took out his large cotton handkerchief, and wiped the perspiration from his forehead.

'But, sir,' he said piteously, 'we ought all to be merciful, and not judge our neighbours; and it is quite true what she says, that Ser Checchi has always been a most quiet, harmless, honest citizen, and if his craze for books ran away with him, and he had a bad son to drain him dry, why, so may anybody; and my own lads cause me trouble enough, and I have a fellow-feeling.'

'Your reflections come late in the day, my friend,' said Querci with cutting contempt. 'The notice of sale will be out on Friday.'

'In my name?'

'In your name, and in the names of others. It is impossible, you see, for Ser Aurelio to wait any longer. There is too much danger in delay. Other creditors may arise, and the chance of enforcing full payment will be lost. Besides, the orders are given.'

The man stood silent, regretful, and disturbed.

'But I have nothing to do with it,' he said timidly. 'I am put forward as if I had, but you know well, sir advocate, none better, that I have no more to do with it than the babe unborn.'

Querci frowned ; the imbecility and obstinacy of the man incensed his higher intelligence.

'Why talk this nonsense at the eleventh hour?' he said with severity. 'If you speak in such a way to anyone besides myself, you will have unpleasant communications from Vestuccio yourself. Remember all that you owe to his forbearance and to his good nature.'

The unhappy tradesman drooped his head and shifted nervously from one foot to another, and seemed to shrink into himself as a young shy dog will do when he sees a whip.

'Very well, sir,' he said humbly. 'If it must be, it must be. But I am sorry for that maiden and the old man !'

He was one of the many humble tradesfolk who were of so much use to Vestuccio in his financial transactions, people necessitous and easily moulded, who, having been assisted by him in the beginning of his intimacy with them, became in due course his creatures, his instruments, his marionettes, moved by him either through their terror or their cupidity. He would not for worlds have figured in law courts himself as a persecuting and usurious creditor, but it was in no way against his reputation to pass on the bills which he received to his puppets, and guide unseen their manœuvres in the tribunals, and secretly impose on them an inexorable severity, whilst openly and publicly he lamented their rigour.

When a bill has passed out of your hands, what can you do about it? Nothing, clearly, were you king or emperor. Whoever holds it is the headsman who strikes when he chooses. You may express your grief that it has gone out of your hands; but, once put in circulation, you can no more stop it than you can stop the rolling and exploding of a cask of petroleum, if you have set it alight and started it down a slope.

No one ever saw the match in Vestuccio's hand; people only saw him running with a bag of sand to put out the flaring barrel, and always arriving too late, and expressing his regrets with touching pathos for the carelessness with which others left inflammable oils within reach of ignited fuses.

True, there were a few who were not dupes of his comedy; there were even many who knew the whole truth, but such persons respected him the more for his dexterity and duplicity. The public is not angry with a good citizen who purrs pretty phrases in its ear, whilst he leads it by the nose wherever he pleases.

'If he had trusted all his affairs to me,' he said often at this juncture, with tears in his eyes, 'Ser Checchi would not now be in the position he is. I was grieved to foreclose on Antella, it cut me to the heart to do anything harsh; but when there are also many creditors, one dares not lag behind, one's duty to one's family is paramount.'

This was the kind of speech which enchanted and enslaved his fellow-townsmen. Disguise is usually popular. It expresses deference for your neighbour's opinion. If you did not care for his opinion, you would not dissemble to propitiate him. Human nature forgives anything except bluntness. Bluntness offends; it is the brother of truth. Vestuccio was never blunt, and he was always popular.

Ser Checchi ceased to struggle, desisted from all effort. He accepted his fate, and bent his head to the storm meekly, ashamed, bitterly ashamed, of the folly which had drawn it on his head.

He ate scarcely anything, slept but rarely and fitfully, and his hands had a continual tremor in them; he wrote illegibly, and grasped his pen with difficulty.

'Why was not my hand paralyzed ere I put my signature to any bill?' he said bitterly to his daughter. 'Everything comes too late, even infirmity!'

When she heard him say this, she burst into a passion of weeping.

'It is not paralysis, father,' she cried piteously; 'no, no—no, no.'

'It will be,' said Ser Checchi quietly.

He did not deceive himself; he knew that his strength was failing, his health giving way.

'Only let my body die before my brain!' he said in his heart, in the scholar's terror of aphasia.

One day a registered letter was brought to Beldia; her heart leaped up in sudden hope, thinking that it bore news of her betrothed; but before her eager hands could take the packet her face fell—she recognised the handwriting of Cirillo.

She opened the letter with fear; nothing but trouble had ever come to them from him.

Out of the envelope dropped a bank-note. There were a few hurriedly written lines with it:

'I won fifty thousand francs last night. I send you twenty of them. Your pearls enabled me to play. I am well, and hope that what I send may get my father out of trouble. You see the devil is not as black as your maiden fancy paints him. Acknowledge this, Poste Restante, Monaco.'

The letter was dated from Monte Carlo, and the French bank-note was for twenty thousand francs.

Beldia sat still with them both on the table before her, the sunshine falling on the paper-money. Here was deliverance; here was relief; here was succour.

The motes of the sunbeams swam and circled before her sight; there was a dull noise in her ears; she was strangely moved to relief, and yet to terror.

A gambler's money!—would her father take it?

She did not hear his voice calling to her until he had called thrice. She rose and went to him, the letter and money crumpled in her hand.

Ser Checchi stood at the head of the stair.

'You have had a letter; is it from Odisio?' he cried to her; for the Lombard, with his pure scholarship and his loyal manhood, was dear to him.

Beldia stood before him with a strange sense of guiltiness upon her; as if she had come out of some shameful place; and yet of gladness too, seeing the means by which all their mourning might be changed to rejoicing, and their woes undone.

Without daring to say one word in either joy or fear, she held out the letter to him. He glanced sharply at the money in her hand, a flush of hope and warmth passing over his wasted features.

Then he read Cirillo's writing once, twice, thrice, very slowly, as if he could not fathom its meaning, or believe his own senses. He stretched out his hand and took the bank-note from her and folded it up with the letter; his face had grown cold and stern, as though it were cut in stone. Looking on him, she had no need to ask him if he accepted the gift.

'Give me an envelope and sealing-wax,' he said harshly.

She went to her chamber and brought both. He put the letter and the money together in the envelope, and sealed it with his big seal, and addressed it to his son's name at the post-office of Monaco.

'Send it to be registered,' he said sternly. 'If there be not a franc in the house to pay the postage, pawn my shirt.'

Beldia grew very pale.

'Father, he means well,' she said timidly. 'He has never seen as we see. He will only lose it at play if it go back to him; and—it would save all, it would save the books!'

The sunken blue eyes of Ser Checchi flashed their lightnings of terrible wrath upon her. For one moment she thought that he would strike her.

'Take the alms of my son! The spawn of a gambling hell! Dare you tempt me?—you? Let the books go; let the last stick and thread and crust which belonged to me go, but do not play the devil's part for him, and try to buy my soul with a gambler's gold!'

She dared not argue more; and the letter went back to Cirillo by that evening's post, sealed with the big onyx seal of his father, with which he had played when he was a little curly-haired child, and stood at Ser Checchi's knee on Sunday afternoons at Antella.

Beldia knew that her father was right, that he was only true to himself in this act of inexorable honour. Yet, woman-like, she mourned for Cirillo, in whose hard heart she knew that there must have been a soft place, when he had penned that letter and parted with that large sum; she knew that there must have been in him some awakening to conscience, some regret for his faults and follies, some yearning for his kindred and his birthplace.

She wished that it had been returned to him less harshly. She wrote herself, and strove to soften the rejection of his aid, but to her letter she received no answer, neither then nor at any other time.

She never doubted that her father had done rightly, or that his choice was the only one possible to a man reared in the strong and pure ethics of the great writers whom he loved. But that rescue had been so near, succour so close, seemed to make their fate more cruel. It would have been a delight so exquisite, a pleasure so honest and so just, to have barred the door against the invasion of the law and had their home once more intact and inviolate. To put down this sweetness untasted, to thrust away this healing draught untouched, made their torture only harder to endure.

CHAPTER XXII.

The days wore on, each one sadder, harder than the previous day; the men of the tribunal came, fussing and fuming, peeping into and roaming in and out of every room, and Beppe Dessi swelled with more insolence and more importance as the period of probation allowed by the law drew nearer and nearer to its end.

The bare walls with a few of the necessaries of daily life were soon to be all which would be left to them, and soon even those walls were to shelter them no more; they would be driven out to a new home.

Unknown to them, Don Gervasio had taken a few humble chambers near his own dwelling, so that they should not find themselves utterly houseless; but he dared not speak of this even to Beldia; the thought that she could live elsewhere than in the tower seemed to paralyze all her energies and stupefy her intelligence.

'Oh, never elsewhere!—never elsewhere!' she said piteously to the old priest. 'We have done no harm that we should be forced away like slaves to be sold in a market, and the money for the rent is there.'

But the money for the rent was not there; since Gigi Fanno, warned by Saetta's barber, had obtained an order from the tribunal for Don Gervasio to deliver it up in the name of the creditors which the priest had been forced to obey. But he had not the courage to tell her this; he knew that she would learn it soon enough; he knew that, were it still in his possession, it would be powerless to move their landlord to mercy; he knew that Maso Saetta would send them out by main force if they did not go voluntarily; and, therefore, unknown to her, he hired the little chambers looking on a shady monastery garden near Porta Romana, so that when the inevitable eviction should take place, there should be some shelter ready for her and for her father.

As though the terrible force of the temptation which had assailed him when he had refused his son's gift had broken down his moral and physical strength, Ser Checchi from that hour grew feebler and sicklier, and less able to meet the woes which pressed on him. As though the contrast of what was with what might have been, had he stooped to retain his son's gift, made the bitterness of his lot too much even for his fortitude, he passed whole days shut up in his bed-chamber, lost in apathetic meditation, and at times his eyes would fill with sudden tears, which he did not strive to conceal; something of the pathetic weakness of an innocent animal, harassed and tortured without resistance, had come into him. It seemed as if his last forces had spent themselves in the rejection of Cirillo's gold.

Once she heard him mutter to himself:

'Even her pearls—even her mother's pearls—gone in a foreign hell!'

He did not view his son's action as she saw it; it only seemed to him an insult, an outrage, a degradation the more.

On one of these weary, empty, yet laborious, days in early autumn, when the city is at its dreariest, and dustiest, and dullest, Beldia, looking from a back casement which opened from the kitchen on the river, saw a boat come up and station itself under the tower wall, whilst the men who were in it fastened a rope's end to one of the iron stanchions in the basement. She watched them unconsciously

for a little time; her mind was dulled as by an opiate by the continued succession of sorrows, anxieties, humiliations, and miseries; as far as her thoughts were awake at all, they were dwelling in fancy on the vintage fields of Antella, with the white and dun oxen pacing through them, and the yellow dragon's mouth, and the lilac colchicum growing in the grassy furrows. It was the first autumn in all her life that she had not been amidst those fields when grapes were ripening in late summer suns. But, lost as she was in pain and in remembrance, the movements of these men below ended by arresting her attention; they had a pot of white paint on the bench of their little shallow boat, and with a big brush they were making a broad white line along the brown stones of the tower at as great a height as they could reach. The terror which was now always with her as to the loss of her old home, made her watch with puzzled fear this singular marking of the ancient place.

'Good people, what are you doing there?' she asked them, leaning as far out of the window as she could.

They looked up, and the one who held the brush, standing at rest a moment, answered her civilly:

'We are marking the river-wall: where this line runs everything is to be pulled down. We have been below already, as you may see, signorina, if you look over yonder.'

'Pulled down!' she echoed the words stupidly.

'Ay, ay,' said the man. ''Tis a pity, I do think myself; there is a lot of life in these old stones still; but, you see, at Palazzo Vecchio they want to have everything spick-and-span new; they want to make a quay here, they say, with electric light, and a tramway, and new houses, all whitewashed, just like the quay on the other side, where the old Zeccha, and the trees, and the Alberti chapel used to be. And like enough, when all's been cleared, they'll choke it up with factories and gas works, just as the shore is choked up down yonder. But there! 'tis no business of mine, and the gentlemen want to turn some money—what else do they get themselves made town - councillors for? Why, madamigella, how queer you look! Have you not heard of it before?'

And the good man, confused and troubled at the effect of his news, splashed his big brush into the iron pot again, and went on drawing his broad white line along the stones welded together so firmly by the artisans of Taddeo Gaddi.

Beldia sank down on the window-seat of the kitchen, and hid her face in her hands, as one who hears a death-warrant.

She did not doubt the workman's story. She remembered what Maso Saetta had said, and she knew the frightful apathy of the city before its own undoing, wrought for the greed and gratification of its Jacks in office.

Destroyed! the tower destroyed! The blood surged in her ears and the tearless sobs strangled her breath like knotted cords.

CHAPTER XXIII.

MEANTIME of Odisio Fontana there had entirely ceased to come any tidings whatever, since the day that the ship in which he had sailed had touched at the island of Madeira. Gathering courage from her desperate dread, Beldia had written to his old master in Milan, and he to her had replied, formally, as to a stranger, that he also knew and had heard nothing, and shared her fears as to the fate of the vessel, of which no tidings had been rumoured by the underwriters. He told her that the poor mother of Odisio had been spared the sorrow, for she had died, suddenly and painlessly, in her sleep, in the summer heats, and her small income had died with her. The Milan architect added that he had taken charge of the few things which she had left, and had placed them in safety to await communication of the wishes of her son.

Although Beldia had never had directly any word from her, she had heard so much from Odisio of his mother that she felt a personal pain and loss, when she learned that she would never see in life this gentle and learned northern woman, who had chosen to give her son rather the riches of the mind than the goods of the world, the freedom of the spirit rather than the servitude of wealth.

It was a minor sorrow, lost in the deeper grief of her father's woes, and her own ignorance whether the man she loved were living or dead; but it was the one drop which filled her cup to overflowing.

She had not known how much solace and support she had unconsciously derived from the thought of Odisio's mother, until now that she learned of her death.

Nor either of Cirillo did she know aught. From the night when he had vanished down the dusky street with her pearls upon him, he had given no sign of life. She supposed that he had got safely out of the country, since, had he been arrested, it would have been publicly known. But his fate was hidden in obscurity. Her father never named him. From time to time he roused himself from his depression and apathy to question her of her betrothed; but of his son he said never a word.

'Your mistress's Lombard is lost at sea, they tell me, good Nica,' said Beppe Dessi to Veronica one afternoon, when, as his wont was, he swaggered through the rooms, prying here and there, locking and unlocking, peering and fingering, jabbering and grinning. In that curious way in which bad news travels swiftly and cruelly, it had become known in the quarter that the Genoese vessel was reported missing.

'Were he dead on land, we would not ask you to pay for his burying,' said Veronica, who had come in, as she often did, to linger about her old kitchen, and try and coax her late mistress into eating some tit-bit which she brought with her; she had a coarse and shrewish tongue, but her heart was neither hard nor unfaithful.

'Ships be often silent for many a month, and come safe into port after all,' she added; 'anyhow, 'tis better to drown at sea than live to get fat on other folks' pain, and gnaw other folks' loaves, as you do, Beppino.'

Old Dessi chuckled, shaking his broad stomach.

'You have a vixen's tongue, but a witless one, my dear,' he replied. 'Few men are as merciful as I. Haven't I left your good people the use of their rooms and their things, when I might have locked them all up, and left nothing out but a mattress and a pipkin, and a knife and fork, as the law doth prescribe?'

He was seated as he spoke in Ser Checchi's own chair; he had his pipe in his mouth; with his fat, dirty fingers he was turning over a fair copy of the 'Bellezze di Firenze.' Not that he knew one book from another, or could tell a copper-plate engraving from a lithograph; but he liked to look important, and he could see the librarian in the inner chamber wince and move nervously, whenever a fine volume was roughly and rudely handled thus.

He had no personal ill-will to Ser Checchi, with whom he had never had any interviews until the executions levied on the books; but the low mind hates the higher spirit by instinct, and with ferocity, and gloats over its torment, as the grinning yokel loves to see the stately and gracious stag pulled down by hounds in a muddy lane.

Veronica, who was no respecter of persons, and whose temper was quickly roused, snatched the volume of Cinelli from him with no gentle hand, and banged it upon his shoulders.

'You porpoise!' she screamed, 'would you ape a scholar? Look at the black marks your paw has left on the margins! Custodian you may be, and a fine farce it is, if you be so; but you have no right to damage the goods you have charge of with that soot you have got on your fist from the grasp of your godfather the devil.'

Beppi Dessi laughed, because he always laughed at everything; but he was angry too; had Veronica not been a big, buxom, brown widow, much to his liking, he would have made her feel his anger as a representative of the sanctity of the law.

'Jest away, sauce-box,' he said jocosely, chucking her under the chin. 'You won't laugh when you see the books go to sale on the carts on Friday, and all the pots and pans you used to see here swinging and jingling atop of them.'

Veronica turned gray under the healthy brown and red of her complexion.

'Friday? 'Tis not as near as that; the saints help us!'

'Ay, that it is!' said Dessi, smacking his lips as over some savoury morsel. 'To-morrow I shall put up *bande*, and, you know, five days after, out everything goes, if the King's liege himself was the debtor.'

'The *bande!*' echoed Veronica, as in old days in that old tower women might have said with bloodless lips 'The plague!' or 'The headsman!'

When the *bande*—the declarations of the date of sale—are pasted on the walls and hung up by a string to the door of the doomed dwelling, nothing can arrest the sale of the debtor's possessions. It is the funeral knell over the burial of credit and of honour.

Bribes, prayers, tempted cupidity, hope of other modes of payment, may retard the bringing of the *bande*, but once brought, nothing except payment can avert the sale which they announce.

'Not the *bande!*' shrieked Veronica. 'Not yet, not yet! Oh, Beppino—dear, good, kind Beppino—you will put off the day, you will persuade the people, you will not bring these horrible, thrice accursed *bande* here?'

Dessi's fat sides shook with contented facetiousness.

'Ay, ay, ay! It is "dear Beppino"—"good, kind Beppino" now, is it? Is the devil my godfather now?'

'The devil is your godfather, and your father too, if you bring those vile things here. You know well enough when those papers are out there is nothing to be done—no hope, no help, no anything. Look ye, Beppe, you never dare——'

'Dare!' said the great man, swelling bigger and bigger with his own importance. 'Dare! That is a fine word to use to me! If you don't take care to keep a civiller tongue behind your teeth I will clap you in prison for the maltreatment of a peaceable citizen in the orderly pursuit of the duties which the law entails on him. My shoulders ache now with your bang of that big book; and were you not a passable, good-looking wench for your years——'

'What are my looks, bad or good, to you? I am not come to such a pass that I need take a gouty old bailiff for my lover!' screamed Veronica, hissing in her rage like the hot water in her own boiling coppers. 'You are a monster, Beppe!—a beast, a pig, a raging tiger! What! bring the salesmen here to my honoured master, to my dear and saint-like mistress! You never can, you never shall. I will tear the coat off your back, and your hair off your head in the street with my hands and my teeth——'

'These folks are not your master or your mistress any more, so you need not fuss about them; and it is not I who force the sales; it is the creditors,' said Beppe Dessi sullenly, for his dignity was hurt by her invectives. 'And neither Gigi nor I have aught to do with hurrying on or holding off the sales, as you would know without being told, if you weren't an ignorant vixen; and I know not what good could be got out of waiting any longer, if we could wait, for these people have not a farthing left, and every day the costs run on, and so every day which is wasted is a theft to the creditors, and to me myself, as one may say. For, as it is, there will be precious little to divide between us when all this lumber of musty books is sold.'

Veronica's nerves gave way; she fetched him a sounding box on the ear, then threw her apron over her head, as her habit was under emotion, and sobbed aloud.

The *bande!*—how often in that poor quarter of the town were these words heard like a tocsin tolling in ruin and death!

The sound of the blow and the cries roused Ser Checchi where he was seated in the little dining-room, whither he had gone to avoid seeing the profanation and pollution of his volumes by the hands of the bailiff.

He rose and approached them.

'Woman, what do you here? You are no more in any service of mine,' he said to her. 'Yes, I know you mean well; but you have no place here now, and I cannot have this brawling in my chamber.'

'Ser Checchi! Ser Checchi!' sobbed Veronica, 'the old beast swears that he will put up the papers to sell on Friday. Who ever heard the like? The papers once up, what can you do? There will be only five days to find help, and you will not find it; everything will go, from your books which have ruined you, to the stewpans and pipkins that I used fifteen long years in this house come Barnabas' Day!'

Ser Checchi wavered slightly, like a man who has been struck a heavy blow. But he steadied himself, feeling the eyes of Beppe Dessi staring with curiosity and triumph upon him.

'Is it true?' he asked the man briefly.

'Ay, ay, sir; it is true,' said Dessi, for once serious, and forced into respect, he knew not why.

'And—you sell—everything?'

'Everything, sir,' replied the bailiff; and he added with his audacious fat chuckle: 'I suppose you think much of them, but they'll make a mighty poor show in the auction-room.'

Ser Checchi made one passionate movement, as though he would have struck the blasphemer to the ground; then, with a violent effort controlling his impulse, he left the room in silence. He felt as one who hears his children insulted, his friends dishonoured in his presence, and is powerless to avenge them.

All those dear companions of his studies! All those precious assistants of his labours! All those valued ministers to his meditations! The Seneca, the Pindar, the Cicero, the St. Augustine, the Tertullian, the Villani, the Vitruvius, the Aldine Horace, the Etienne Plato, the Giuntini Avicenna, the Labacco, the Cicoonara, the Pistolesi, the scores and scores of familiar and beloved brethren of his heart and mind, which were now for ever to pass from their honoured rest within his walls, and be flung into unworthy hands, perchance be torn and tossed piecemeal to some shameful fate! And it was his own fault, his own clumsy, stupid, foolish fault, his own ignorance, carelessness and witlessness, which had brought him to this pass, and made him powerless to protect himself or them!

CHAPTER XXIV.

DON GERVASIO did his best to help his old friend, but he was a poor priest with no money but that which he held in trust for others; and though he stooped to use expostulation and supplication in Ser Checchi's cause, which he would never have used in his own, he could effect little, except to obtain some slight delay in the execution of the sentences. Ser Checchi deserved no enemies, but he had few friends: men who are at once shy and proud do not easily make friends, and his absorption in his intellectual and interior life had seemed like arrogance and stiffness to the other tradesmen of the neighbourhood. The few who valued and cared for him—like the old churchmen and professors who frequented his rooms, and were of like tastes with himself—were poor indeed in worldly goods, and, even were they willing to aid him, were without any means to do so. The simplicity and solitude of his life had been such as to isolate him from all practical men of affairs, except indeed from Vestuccio. But Vestuccio, though his name did not figure on these fatal documents, was the instigator and director of all their misfortunes. That Beldia felt; even her father confessed it; the appropriation of Antella proved it.

'If Aurelio Vestuccio had kept faith with me, no

ill would have ensued,' said her father; and she forbore to press him for details; she had not lived amongst tradesfolk all her life without knowing the misery and ruin which come of protested bills, of overdrawn accounts, of unpaid interest, of worthless paper. Their lives had indeed been detached almost completely from that of their neighbours; yet still she had always been acquainted with these things which she witnessed daily, weighing on the mind, and eating away the savings of the small people of her quarter. She was conversant enough with the aspects of commercial failure to understand that her father had no chance of rising above his bankruptcy.

He had no credit.

He was an honest man; indeed, he had never had wit enough to be otherwise, said the wags of the neighbourhood; but he had no commercial credit; everyone knew him to be a dreamer and a scholar, to whom nobody in their senses would have dared to lend a five-franc piece. At least, not now that the deeds of sale had been hung above his door.

If it be a golden rule to kick a man when he is down, it is none the less so never to lend a penny to anyone who wants it.

Had the lands of Antella been in the case, things would have gone differently; both bankers and lawyers love a property which is immovable. But Antella, from its topmost branch to its lowest ditch, from the tiles on its roof to the cress in its runlets of water, was wholly and absolutely given over to Vestuccio. His claims were paramount; he was its mortgagee; his name appeared on the deeds of mortgage openly, and on the surface of things he seemed to have conducted himself with as much forbearance and benevolence as were possible to a cautious man of business, who was bound to consider prudence and self-interest. Everyone who spoke of this matter on piazza, and in studio and office, said with one voice, that Messer Aurelio had behaved excellently well, and if he had at the last entered into his own, it was only just that he should do so; and everyone applauded his past moderation.

If many in the town knew or guessed that the other lenders were but his allies and instruments, if it were generally understood that his masterhand loosened or tightened the meshes of the web in which the weakness of Ser Checchi had been drawn, no one failed to respect him the more for that. It is thus that fortunes are made in these days, when everyone is content to measure the golden fruits, and no one asks or cares what filthy rags or foul excrements may have manured the roots of the tree which bore them. Besides, no one cared about Ser Checchi at all, except a few bookworms, archæologists, and antiquarians like himself, who were as poor as they were learned. Everyone cared about Aurelio Vestuccio—a rising man, a promising citizen—in whose success many other interests were involved, from those of the bankers and private gentlemen who found it lucrative to be behind him in his larger mortgages and loans, to the little tradesfolk who saw in his success the triumph of their own class, and never found him reluctant to lend them a hundred francs in their hard moments.

The actual day of sale soon arrived, as Beppe Dessi had declared that it would do, seeming so sudden in its crash of doom, although such cruel torment had preceded and foreshadowed it.

All the neighbourhood was aware of the date, for the printed announcements swinging under the doorway shield, and at the public tribunal, had made it public, and all the men and women in the street got up between times to lose no portion of the tragedy, which was a comedy to them.

As soon almost as the sun arose, the men of law gathered at the great door of the tower, and leaving carts and hand-barrows waiting for their loads on the stones below, climbed the stairs in company with their hired men, stalwart, rough, brawny porters with hairy arms and sun-brown skins and coarse voices, who pushed, noisy and hot and turbulent, up the dusky staircase. The people who lived within sight of the tower were all out of their own dwellings, and gathered in the street agog and gaping, the baker's wife foremost among them; and in the house itself, the charcoal-seller, the chandler, the cobbler, the tailor, and the cabinet-maker craned their necks to watch, and doffed their caps to the minions of the law, with nervous smiles and eager salutations, ' Good-day, good gentlemen ! We hope we see you well !'

The lookers-on crowded below amongst the sacks and cheese and charcoal, the lad Poldo amongst them; there was a great uproar of voices and a great pushing and struggling to see what would first be brought down the stairs; in the streets the mules harnessed to the carts were stamping, and shaking their bells ; the usual street cries were unheard, for the vendors had come in with the crowd, the fair morning sunshine poured its light on the loves and garlands and shields of Messer Luca; the men tramped on up the stairs, under the noble Latin inscription of the library door.

Beldia, shut in her own chamber, kneeling at prayer, heard the noise and confusion, and rose to her feet and listened breathlessly.

Even up to this very latest moment she had always thought that some miracle would happen, that the books would in some way be saved.

She hurried to her father's room. He was up and clothed; indeed he had not lain down all the night.

'Oh, father,' she murmured with dry white lips. 'Oh, father! they are come!'

'I hear them, my love,' he answered gently. He was quite still, save only for the nervous trembling and twitching of his hands.

She put her arms about his throat, and pressed her head against his breast.

He stroked her hair tenderly.

'Good child, good child,' he said in a low and dreamy voice. 'You have never rebuked me.'

Then he put her with gentleness away from him and went out across the passage and into the bookroom, and sat down in his great leathern chair.

'You cannot bear to see them taken away, father,' murmured Beldia. 'Come elsewhere, come into my room, they will not dare disturb you there.'

He waved her aside.

'They shall find me in my place,' he answered. 'I am a feeble and foolish spendthrift, but I am not a coward.'

And he waited, seated in his big, black, leather chair, where so often he had sat to follow and enjoy the abstruse learning of his cherished studies, and trace the handwriting of penmen dead seven centuries and more.

'Keep your chamber, my dear,' he said to her. 'I would not have their cruel eyes fall on you in your sorrow.'

'But let me stay with you, father. Pray let me stay! I will be calm and silent; I can control what I feel. You may trust me.'

'I never distrust you. But I will not have you seen by those coarse men. Shut yourself in your chamber; let me not be disobeyed by *you*.'

The neighbours meanwhile were all staring out of their doors, eager to see with their cruel relish for the misfortunes of others, which is not confined to the courtly world which Rochefoucauld knew. Only the cobbler, he who had used to take care of the plants and the pigeons, had tears in his eyes, and cried aloud, 'Alack the day! who would ever have believed to see the like of this after all these years of honoured solvency!'

Whereupon Beppe Dessi cuffed him on the ear, half in joke, half in anger.

'You fool!' said the bailiff, 'anybody with the eye of a fish might have seen what was coming ten years ago. A tradesman cannot buy books like a Pope and all his Cardinals without going bankrupt.'

'Alack, alack, so good a soul to come to such a pass!' cried the cobbler, the big tears coursing down his nose.

'What good doth goodness?' said Beppe Dessi. ''Tis but a poor soft thing which gets hunted like a hare.'

And they went on up the stairs with Gigi Fanno and the porters, and the young clerk with the pen behind his ear, and all their followers, trooping noisily, chattering and holloaing in their wake; but they stopped on the threshold of the door, surprised and taken aback to see the old librarian in his accustomed place.

'The impudent old idiot!' muttered Beppe Dessi, and his coadjutor, blustering, yet in his secret soul afraid, advanced to the table at which Ser Checchi sat, and producing the acts and authorities of sale, recited the usual formulas in a pompous, unintelligible gabble, concluding with the usual interrogation:

'You are unprepared to pay these just demands—capital, interest, and costs?'

'I cannot pay,' replied Ser Checchi coldly. There was a coarse laugh, led by Dessi and echoed by the other men, which Gigi Fanno silenced with a gesture.

'You had best then not molest or hinder the proceedings of the law,' he said pompously. 'We have come to remove the goods which are forfeited by sentence and order of the civil and correctional tribunal of this city.'

'Obey your orders,' replied Ser Checchi. His hands had ceased to tremble: they were clasped before him upon his desk. His face was colourless but calm. Something in his tone awed and hushed the boisterous and offensive humour of the men. Beppe Dessi alone, chuckling and thrusting out his paunch, said, with a tap of his pipe-bowl on the cover of a quarto Tertullian, 'They've cost you dear, your ugly old books, but they'll only sell for waste paper, I warrant me. If I'd wished to ruin myself, I'd have done it better than that—good wines now, or good dishes, or plump women——'

'Enough chatter, Beppe,' said his colleague, putting up his papers in his pocket. 'Get to work. The rooms must be cleared by eight. The sale is at ten o'clock. Quick!'

He made a sign of impatience to his followers, and the men threw themselves on the first bundles of volumes which were near them. Already corded together, pell-mell, with no reference to their dates, or values, or titles, the books, which had taken fifty years of assiduous toil and patient devotion to collect, were rapidly divided, seized, hoisted on the rough men's shoulders, and carried down the stairs, to be thrown into the carts waiting for them as though they were bales of straw or sacks of beans. Warming to their work of devastation, as soldiers to the sacking of a town, they cleared away parcel after parcel with an alacrity wholly contrary to their usual lazy, dawdling, sleepy ways, and the folios and manuscripts, which had been as neighbours and brethren on the same shelves so long, were torn from one another, and borne out of that tranquil atmosphere of learning and of peace down into the brawling and dirt of the narrow pavement below, and flung, even as the Pisan captives, bound hand and foot, had once been carried through these very streets, on the planks and straw of the barrows and waggons.

The shelves had long been empty. Now the floors were cleared. Ser Checchi sat motionless at the table: not a word or a gesture escaped him.

The vulgar souls of the men were frightened by that calm and dignified attitude; the carters instinctively moved a little more quietly, carried their burdens away a little more carefully. Only Beppe

Dessi going to and fro shouting his orders, swearing his oaths, grinning, laughing, calling out now a blasphemy, and now a joke, came up to him and struck him familiarly on the shoulder: 'Hi! old book-worm, get up! Your chair goes too, you know. We've left you a stool in the kitchen. Get up, I say!'

Ser Checchi rose slowly, and turned, and faced him. The tough hide of the bailiff winced under his regard. The porters made a muttering sound of rebuke and protest. Gigi Fanno whispered in his colleague's ear: 'Softly, softly! the chair can wait for to-morrow's sale!'

But the old man laid his hands upon it, as if in blessing; it was an old friend, and had been in his house two centuries and more; then he pushed it towards them in silence, and went to the embrasure of the kneeling window and seated himself on its stone step.

''Tis a shame, a crying shame to take even his chair from under him!' muttered one of the porters; but Beppe Dessi struck the grumbler a sharp blow with his stick.

'You are a beast of burden, not a counsellor, Tonino,' he said to the man; 'when we ask your opinion you can give it; speak again, and you shall go before the Questura for contumacy. Take out the old fool's chair.'

The poor fellow, grumbling inaudibly, hoisted, with effort, the large leathern seat upon his shoulders, and staggering under its weight carried it through the doorway and set it down with a crash upon the stone landing at the head of the stairs.

Then they bore away the table, with its desk, the

volumes which had been upon it, the large old brass inkstand and the bronze cup for sand, and the other chairs which stood about the chamber, and the cypress wood shelves and fittings of the book-cases.

Ser Checchi looked on in silence; seated on the embrasure of the high-barred window, the light of earliest morning shining on his brow and eyes.

'The old man is stronger than I thought,' muttered Gigi Fanno to Dessi. They were chagrined; they had hoped for some scene of resistance and violence, or at least for one of tears and of supplication.

This calm and dignified silence baffled their malignity and gave their coarse natures no pleasure.

The tramping tread of the carters up and down the stairs, the loud angry voices in dispute, the dust which rose in gray clouds, the noise, and haste, and clumsy bustle continued for a time, then ceased; to be succeeded by the grinding of the wheels on the stones below, and the oaths of the men to their mules and their stable boys. Then all was still beneath; the little curious, indolent crowd of spectators had moved away after the carts and barrows. Ser Checchi was left alone in the empty rooms, filled with the choking smell of dust, and sweat, and unwashed human flesh.

He tried to rise, but his limbs failed him; he could not get up from the stone seat; he ceased to try to move, and waited, knowing that his daughter would soon come to him.

'May I come in, master?' asked the harsh voice of the woman servant Veronica, as her broad, brightly-coloured figure stood in the doorway. Her voice was gentle now, and broken with sobbing, her face was swollen with tears.

'Forgive me, master! Oh, forgive me!' she said with a loud cry, as she fell on her knees. 'Never did I think to see a martyrdom like this. I will serve you day and night on no wage, if you will let me. I have never had a moment's peace since I left you and the damagella.'

He seemed not to hear, or not to understand: his mind was not with her: it was with his lost books.

'Get me my hat and stick,' he said hoarsely. 'Quick; go, get them, I say.'

'What would you do, master?' she asked, terrified at something in his look and voice.

'What is that to you? Go, get my hat and stick, I say.'

Trembling, Veronica went and got them, and brought them to him.

'Help me up,' he said irritably with the first irritation he had shown. She put her strong arms under his, and raised him up. He stood a moment, but his limbs failed him; he knew they would answer to his will no longer.

'Call my daughter,' he said, again sinking heavily on to the stone seat. 'Say nothing to her of me; mind you, nothing; only tell her that the men are gone, that she may come to me. Do what I tell you, and do no more.'

Frightened, the woman hastened from the room.

In another moment Beldia came, followed by Folko, growling as he lingered over and smelt the traces of the many steps.

Her father motioned her back as she would have

come to him. 'Go to the salesroom in the piazza of San Firenze,' he said imperatively. 'Cover yourself so that none recognise you, and stay there until my Dante Codex be bid for, then return and tell me to whom it is allotted.'

'But you are ill, father! Do not send me from you for pity's sake!'

'I am not ill. Go, as I bid you, and stay the whole day if needful, until you learn that which I tell you.'

Beldia obeyed without more protest.

'Keep Folko in,' she said to Veronica; 'and if you have indeed any love for us, stay with my father till I return.'

'That will I; never fear,' replied Veronica. The woman was sobbing noisily, with a loud but sincere sorrow; she could not understand their tearless eyes, their calm, low voices, their self-control under their torture.

The morning wore away; Veronica prepared some food for the dog and gave it to him, made some coffee for her late master which he did not touch, brought a pillow to place behind his shoulders, and put to the wooden shutter to keep out the sun.

Then there was nothing more for her to do; she took out her straw plaiting and sat down at the head of the stairs, whence she could see Ser Checchi without annoying him by her presence. The hours wore away, she counted them by the tolling of Santo Spirito; the old Dutch clock in its tall lacquered case, which had sounded the hours for so many years in those rooms, had been taken away to the auction-rooms.

'To be sold for a song, I dare say,' she thought; she knew well how sales are controlled and conducted; that long ere the auctioneer's signal has sounded, the cabal of professional buyers have agreed amongst themselves what to run up and what to run down, and how to play into each other's hands, so that, go the sale how it may, they alone will be gainers by it.

The day wore away and seemed as though it would never end. Ser Checchi did not move, his head leaned against the pillow which she had placed for him, and its linen was not whiter than his features; she took him a little red wine, he put his lips to it, but could not drink. Every moment was torture to him, every moment something which had been his was passing away into the hands of strangers, never to return.

When Beldia's step was heard on the stairs his pale cheeks flushed, the nervous trembling in his hand returned; his eyes had a pitiful longing in them.

'The Dante?' he muttered faintly, as she entered the room. She was clothed in black, and had a black shawl drawn over her head like a hood. Great slow tears were now rolling down her cheeks.

'The Dante?' he said, more loudly, as he raised himself on his elbows and gazed at her.

She answered him, unwillingly; but in obedience and truth.

'It went with other old books in a lot for forty francs; there was no competition; Vestuccio's clerk bought it.'

'As I thought!' he murmured. 'As I thought.'

Beldia fell at his feet.

'Oh, my father, my dear father!—what a wretch I am to tell it you, but you would have it so!—alas, alas! of what use is one's love for you, if it cannot save you from these miseries!'

'This wretchedness is none of your fault,' he answered feebly, while his hand touched her hair. 'And it is always well to be loved and obeyed.'

Half an hour passed by in silence; and they watched there, afraid to move, afraid to disturb him; the sun fell through a chink across his eyes, and he looked up at it vaguely with failing sight.

Then he was silent: his head bent, his eyes closed.

The two women watched him in awe and fear, the white dog crept up to his feet.

Veronica thought he was cold; and opened the shutter to let in the flood of early evening light.

'The sun can give me no warmth,' he said faintly. 'The cold is coming upward—soon it will reach my heart, so far it is well; I shall not leave the tower! But you—you—all alone—ah, Beldia!'

It was the last word he ever spoke. By the fall of night he was dead.

CHAPTER XXV.

THEY buried him at Trespignano, the graveyard of the poor; and at the same hour as that of his burial, Aurelio Vestuccio, seated at his desk in his little office, wrote out a receipt for two thousand pounds of English money; the price paid for the Codice of the 'Divina Commedia' by an English bibliophile, who was more learned in black-letter than in commerce, and who was ignorant that the volume had been bought at a public sale only a few days earlier for as many pence.

The bibliophile was sworn to secrecy in the matter of this purchase on account of the law which forbids the sale of antique and precious things to foreigners. In the city of Dante no one ever knew or heard what had become of the folio.

Once the smith of Giogoli, asking troublesome questions of him in the Piazza della Signoria, Ser Aurelio said to him, shaking his head: 'Ah! my good friend, I shall never see back those five hundred francs which I gave you for that rusty volume which our poor old blind bookseller so stupidly thought such a treasure. I bought it in at his sale as you know; but I had to give it away for ten francs. I was poor old Ser Checchi's dupe always! Well, well! we will say no harm of the dead.'

CHAPTER XXVI.

A YEAR and six months passed away; the winds of spring once more were on the air, the showers of spring once more were on the soil, and everywhere, in the duskiest shadows of the house walls and palace parapets, the flowers of spring were lying in dewy sheaves and moss-lined baskets all over the city.

It was a brilliant forenoon in the month of March, the river, brimming and green, rolled rapidly beneath its bridges to its fall over the weir; the sky was of purest azure, flecked with little, light, snowy clouds; the bronze Bacchus of San Jacopo had blossoming boughs of pear and peach leaning up against his stone water-trough, and bunches of Narcissus poeticus were heaped in rush-skips underneath the stern walls of the old Manelli tower. Baskets full of early primroses were carried down the narrow ways, and the field daffodils blazed in their deeper gold, tied up by their own blade-like leaves, and brought to die of drought and dust, far from their pleasant nests at the foot of olive-tree or maples in the grassy paths of the hillside farms. The bells above-head were chiming in melodious riot, and the sparkling sunshine shone through the open portals of churches, and on the gray wings of pigeons of the house-roofs, on the silver dishes and jewelled trinkets of the goldsmiths' stalls, and on the yellow head and white shirt of a little chorister walking and ringing his bell before the Host.

A man went quickly past the jewellers' and goldsmiths' shops upon the bridge built by Taddeo Gaddi, and the flower and fruit stalls under the Bacchus.

He moved with a light step, as of one who was happy and eager; his face was sunburnt, and his clothes were worn; his bright clear eyes glanced from the old walls to the blue sky, from the primrose and daffodil baskets to the iron stanchions and the stone machicolations, seeing in one and all dear and familiar friends. He went on his way rapidly, until a few paces farther onward the shadow of the Tower of Taddeo fell across the narrow causeway which it dominated. Whilst he was still some yards away from its lofty walls, he stared at them, doubting his own sight; all its ornament, its shields, its garlands, its amorini, and its angels, in their canopied niches, all were gone; its balconies and its gratings were gone also; its windows were blank and dark, like eyes which are wide open but sightless, and in the arch where its Madonna had sat throned, there was a mere vacant, gaping aperture.

He stood upon the opposite side of the way, and gazed at its desecrated walls in stupefaction; a woman, in a baker's shop which fronted it, came out and looked at him, and said to herself, with her hands resting on her hips:

'Holy Jesus save us! If it be not the Lombard come back, who they said was drowned!'

He at whom she stared had already crossed the street and was knocking violently with the heavy bronze knocker on the great oaken nail-studded door, which used to stand open all the day long, with the mastiff, Lillo, as the guardian at its threshold. The loud knocking resounded through the street, echoed by the high walls around. But there was no response to it other than its own echo. The tower was as mute as a grave.

Amazed and terrified, he turned to the baker's wife, who stood in her doorway, and recognised her.

'What has happened? Where are they? What has been done here? Why is it silent and ruined thus?'

The woman, nothing loath to be a bearer of ill-tidings, crossed the road and stood beside him.

'Why, man, you look as white as a ghost under your brown skin! I thought you were a ghost. They said you were lost at sea in some outlandish parts. Eh! it's no use your staring at the tower; there is no one in it; Ser Checchi is dead, and the place is empty.

The municipality have bought it, and are going to pull it down. They pull down everything they can, you know; the old stones are gilt gingerbread to them.'

'Dead! dead! Ser Checchi?'

He echoed the words in horror, and staggered and leaned against the doorway, with a sick sense of faintness upon him.

'Beldia?' he said hoarsely.

'She is alive; she lives hard by,' answered the baker's wife. 'She has not a bronze halfpenny, and she works for her bread. Lord! how odd you look! Did you never hear that the old tower was sold up before he died? Ay, he lost everything; and they do say that what killed him was the sale of his old musty books. Anyhow, he died on the very day of the sale: he had been ailing some time. Some say Vestuccio, the dealer, was at the bottom of all. 'Tis he bought those garlands and loves of Luca's off the wall yonder, and chipped them out of their niches, and took them away. He has sold them to some foreign museum. There was talk of the authorities stopping him, but he squared them, and made a fine picking. He bought the old iron, too. Holy Mary! how ill and scared you look! Come across to my shop and take a drink of wine. It will put heart into you.'

He thanked her, but refused her by a gesture; his features were contracted and his chest heaved with tearless sobs.

'Ser Checchi! my dear, innocent, generous Ser Checchi!' he murmured, 'shall I never see his face, hear his voice? Oh, my God! what he must have suffered before he died! And she!'

'You think of her still, then? Where have you been all this while? Some said you were drowned. Most thought you only kept away to get rid of her, and keep out of her father's troubles.'

'The ship went down in mid-ocean,' he answered briefly. 'I saved myself by swimming. I have been on a desert island, and was only rescued a few weeks ago by a barque which was bound for Valparaiso. I did not write, because I have travelled as fast as any post could come. All that matters nothing now. Tell me of her; where can I find her?'

'In the Canto dei Santi over yonder. Number eighty, fourth floor. But she looks old and ill. She is not worth a thought from a comely gallant like you. Why should you go after her? Come in and have a drink of something, and tell me all about your wreck and the strange things on land and water which you have seen.'

For this Calypso, with her buxom shape, her bold amorous eyes, and her curling red-brown locks, thought that she could easily console this stranded Odysseus.

But he put her roughly away, as she laid her hand upon his arm, and with a backward look of longing at the old tower in its mutilated strength, he went on to find the place which she had named: a narrow passage-way connecting two side streets behind the dome of the Carmine, shaded by the adjacent trees of a palace garden, and frequented by the pigeons circling around the cupola of Massaeio's church.

'Ser Checchi dead!' he murmured to himself as he went. 'Ser Checchi dead! and the books dispersed!—oh, vile beast that I was to leave them alone in their helplessness and their sorrow for sake of gain! Well have I merited to return poorer even than when I sailed!'

With a beating heart, torn between joy and grief, between hope and fear, he climbed the steep and uncleanly stair, foul with noxious odours and slippery from the continual tread of many feet.

He struck on the panel of the low wooden door which was shown to him as hers; the barking within of a dog, in which he recognised the voice of Folko, answered him.

'Who is there?' asked Beldia, as she withdrew the bolt of the door.

Then he feared to be too sudden for her, and to startle her too perilously as one risen from the grave; he hung back a moment, thinking how he could best prepare her for their meeting; but in that instant of time the white dog, thrusting his nose through the open chink of the door, pushed it further open and sprang on him in instantaneous joy of recognition; then Beldia saw him also.

She would have fallen on the stones insensible, had he not caught her and raised her to his heart.

She was in truth so changed that he would scarce have known her. She had lost her bloom, her youth, the gloss on her fair hair, the light in her serene eyes; she had grown old before her time from sorrow and from solitude. Through winter and summer, autumn and spring, she had dwelt here alone with the dog; visited only by Don Gervasio and by Veronica, copying papers and sewing linen to buy her daily pittance of food; hearing all through these latter days, as they echoed to her ear over the roofs, the blows of the pickaxes and hammers which were routing out and beating down, under a cloud of dust, the beauty and the strength of that beloved old home which was passing from its place in the city as her father had passed from his place amongst living men.

It had been a life of extreme misery, of incessant toil, of endless anxiety; oftentimes she had gone without bread herself that she might give some to the dog, and she had no supper but a glass of water; and the sole thought which had sustained the breath of life in her was her belief that her lost betrothed would still return to her.

'You never doubted me?' asked Odisio, an hour later.

She answered:

'Nay, love—had I doubted you, I should not have found strength to live till now.'

Colophon.

On the site of the Tower of Taddeo there is now standing the chimney of a factory, belching forth its stinking vapours to the sullied waters and the outraged heavens.

The change is called Progress.

THE END.

21 BEDFORD STREET, W.C.

Telegraphic Address,
Sunlocks, London

A List of
Mr. William Heinemann's Publications and Announcements

May 1890.

The Books mentioned in this List can be obtained to order by any Bookseller if not in stock, or will be sent by the Publisher on receipt of the published price and postage.

Index of Authors.

	PAGE		PAGE		PAGE		PAGE
Alexander	30	Ely	17	Knight	18	Renan	11, 17
Allen	27	Evans	11	Kraszewski	29	Ricci	10
Anstey	18			Kroeker	20	Richter	17
Arbuthnot	21	Farrar	17	Landor	15	Riddell	31
Aston	6	Ferruggia	29	Lawson	10	Rives	31
Atherton	31	Fitch	22	Le Caron	13	Roberts (A. von)	29
Baddeley	13, 20	Fitzmaurice-Kelly	6	Lee (Vernon)	26	Roberts (C. G. D.)	16
Balestier	24, 26, 32	Forbes	16	Leland	14	Robinson	24
Barrett	25, 31	Fothergill	31	Le Querdec	9		
Battershall	25	Franzos	29	Leroy-Beaulieu	17	Saintsbury	15
Behrs	13	Frederic	17, 24, 30	Lie	29	Salaman (J. S.)	17
Bendall	20	Furtwängler	10	Linton	24	Salaman (M. C.)	18
Benedetti	11	Garmo	22	Locke	25, 27	Sarcey	13
Benham	23	Garner	21	Lowe	13, 16	Scidmore	16
Benson	15	Garnett	6	Lowry	32	Scudamore	16
Beringer	27	Gaulot	12	Lynch	30	Serao	29
Björnson	28, 29	Gontcharoff	29	Maartens	31	Sergeant	23, 24, 30
Bowen	22	Gore	21	McFall	15	Somerset	15
Boyesen	17	Gounod	11	Macnab	25	Southey	5
Brandes	6, 7	Gosse	6, 8, 12,	Maeterlinck	19	Steel	25
			15, 19, 20, 26	Malot	30	Stevenson	19, 23, 25
Briscoe	32	Grand	23, 25	Marey	21	Sutcliffe	24
Brooke	24	Gray (Maxwell)	25	Marsh	27		
Brown	16	Gras	23	Masson	12	Tadema	27
Brown & Griffiths	21	Griffiths	21	Maude	16	Tallentyre	18
Buchanan	16, 19,	Guyau	9	Maupassant	29	Tasma	30
	31, 32			Maurice	16	Thompson	16
Burgess	14	Hall	20	Merriman	18	Thomson	15
Butler	22	Hamilton	24, 27	Michel	10	Thomson (Basil)	23
Byron	3	Hanus	22	Mitford	31	Thurston	21
Caine (Hall)	15, 23, 25,	Harland	32	Monk	27	Tirebuck	24
	30	Harris	25	Moore	25	Tolstoy	17, 19, 29
Caine (R.)	20	Hauptmann	19	Murray (D. C.)	16	Tree	19
Cambridge	30	Heine	13, 14	Murray (G. G. A.)	6	Turgenev	28
Challice	8	Henderson	32				
Chester	18	Henley	19	Nordau	14, 23, 24	Upward	27
Clarke	26	Hertwig	21	Norris	23, 26		
Coleridge	14, 15	Heussey	13	Nugent	7	Valera	29
Colmore	31	Hichens	24, 27			Vandam	8, 13
Colomb	16	Hirsch	9	Ogilvie	19	Vazoff	29
Compayré	22	Holdsworth	24, 27	Oliphant	18	Vincent	15
Compton	27	Howard	26	Osbourne	25		
Coppée	32	Hughes	22	Ouida	26	Wagner	17
Couperus	29	Hungerford	26, 30			Waliszewski	12
Crackanthorpe	25, 32	Hyne	26	Paget	4	Walker	14
Crackanthorpe				Palacio-Valdés	29	Ward	31
(Mrs.)	27	Ibsen	19	Patmore	20	Warden	32
Crane	9, 23, 27	Ingersoll	16	Pearce	30	Waugh	12
		Irving	19	Pendered	24	Weitemeyer	15
Davidson	22			Pennell	17	Wells	24, 26
Dawson	20	Jacobsen	29	Phelps	31	West	22
De Broglie	11	Jæger	13	Philips	32	Whibley	7
De Goncourt	13	James	23, 24	Pinero	20	Whistler	18
De Joinville	12	Johnstone	5	Pritchard	23	White	24
De Quincey	14			Pugh	23, 27	Whitman	16
Dixon	25	Keary (E. M.)	10			Williams	10
Dowden	6	Keary (C. F.)	24	Raimond	23, 27	Wood	26
Dowson	25	Keeling	25	Rawnsley	15		
		Kennedy	31	Raynor	18	Zangwill	13, 26
Eeden	18	Kimball	21	Rees	23	Zola	24, 26, 32
Ellwanger	18	Kipling	26	Rembrandt	10	Z. Z.	23, 24

THE WORKS OF LORD BYRON.

EDITED BY WILLIAM ERNEST HENLEY.

IN TEN VOLUMES.

VOLUME I. LETTERS, 1804-1813.

To be followed by

VOLUMES II.-IV. LETTERS AND SPEECHES.

VOLUME V. HOURS OF IDLENESS, ENGLISH BARDS AND SCOTCH REVIEWERS.

VOLUME VI. CHILDE HAROLD.

Small cr. 8vo, price 5s. each.

Also an Edition limited to 150 sets for sale in Great Britain, printed on Van Gelder's handmade paper, price Five Guineas the set net.

It is agreed that Byron's Letters, public and private, with their abounding ease and spirit and charm, are among the best in English. It is thought that Byron's poetry has been long, and long enough, neglected, so that we are on the eve of, if not face to face with, a steady reaction in its favour: that, in fact, the true public has had enough of fluent minor lyrists and hide-bound (if superior) sonnetteers, and is disposed, in the natural course of things, to renew its contact with a great English poet, who was also a principal element in the æsthetic evolution of that Modern Europe which we know.

Hence this new Byron, which will present—for the first time since the Seventeen Volumes Edition (1833), long since out of print—a master-writer and a master-influence in decent and persuasive terms.

It is barely necessary to dwell on Mr. Henley's special qualifications for the task of editing and annotating the works of our poet.

THE PAGET PAPERS.

DIPLOMATIC AND OTHER CORRESPONDENCE

OF

The Right Hon. SIR ARTHUR PAGET, G.C.B.

1794–1807.

[WITH TWO APPENDICES, 1808 AND 1828–1829].

ARRANGED AND EDITED BY HIS SON

The Right Hon. SIR AUGUSTUS B. PAGET, G.C.B.,

Late Her Majesty's Ambassador in Vienna.

With Notes by Mrs. J. R. Green.

In Two Volumes, Demy 8vo, with Portraits, 32*s.* net.

These volumes deal with the earlier Napoleonic Wars, and throw a new light on almost every phase of that most vital period of European history. They are the Dispatches of one of His Britannic Majesty's Envoy-Plenipotentiaries at different European Courts during that period, and are unique probably as the account of an hostile eye-witness of the Campaign, which has so persistently been described from the side of the victorious intruder. "The Paget Papers" explain much that has been unexplained so far of the complicated policy of that time of shifting alliances, and especially the attitude of the lesser Courts. The policy of Prussia between Holland and Poland, the attitude of Bavaria, the temper of the Neapolitan Kingdom, were all brought under Sir Arthur Paget's notice in his successive embassies from 1794 to 1800. After the Peace of Amiens he watched from the Court of Vienna the building up of the Third Coalition, and was with the Emperor during the Campaign of Austerlitz; while his final mission carried him to the Dardanelles, where, curiously enough, the same political play was then being gone through as has been witnessed there quite recently. The volumes will be edited by Sir Arthur Paget's son, the Rt. Hon. Sir Augustus Paget, G.C.B., late Her Majesty's Ambassador at Vienna, and illustrated with numerous Portraits of the chief contemporary figures of the time.

LIFE OF NELSON.

By ROBERT SOUTHEY.

A NEW EDITION

Edited by DAVID HANNAY.

Crown 8vo, Gilt, with Portrait.

SOUTHEY'S LIFE OF NELSON is an acknowledged masterpiece of literature. It can never cease to have value, even if it is at any future time surpassed in its own qualities. Up to the present it has never been equalled. While we are waiting for the appearance of a better Southey, the old may well be published with a much-needed *apparatus criticus*. The object of the new edition is to put forth the text, supported by notes, which will make good the few oversights committed by Southey, the passages in Nelson's life of which he had not heard, or which he, influenced by highly honourable scruples, did not think fit to speak of so soon after the hero's death, and while some of the persons concerned were still living. A brief account will also be given of the naval officers, and less famous soldiers or civilians mentioned, though it will not be thought needful to tell the reader the already well-known facts concerning Pitt, Sir John Moore, or Paoli. Emma Hamilton, of whom Southey said only the little which was necessary to preserve his book from downright falsity, will have her history told at what is now adequate length. The much debated story of Nelson's actions at Naples will be told from a point of view other than Southey's. It is not proposed to write a new life of Nelson, but only to set forth the best of existing biographies with necessary additions and corrections, as well as with some comment on his qualities as a commander in naval warfare.

THE LIFE OF THE LATE SIR JOSEPH BARNBY.

W. H. SONLEY JOHNSTONE.

In One Volume, with Portraits, 8vo.

SIR JOSEPH BARNBY was a personality and an influence; music was only a part of him. He was an arduous worker, a brilliant talker, a *raconteur* of merit, a good speaker, and a popular favourite in society. The period through which he lived was one of the most important and fruitful in the annals of English music, and Mr. Johnstone will receive the assistance of composers and others in making this work as comprehensive as possible.

The main divisions will be: Music in England Half-a-Century Ago—Early Life of Barnby—His Eton Career—His Albert Hall Career—As Composer and Conductor—His Social and General Life—The Academy and Guildhall.

Literatures of the World.
EDITED BY
EDMUND GOSSE.

MR. HEINEMANN begs to announce a Series of Short Histories of Ancient and Modern Literatures of the World, Edited by EDMUND GOSSE.

The following volumes are projected, and it is probable that they will be the first to appear:—

FRENCH LITERATURE.
By EDWARD DOWDEN, D.C.L., LL.D., Professor of English Literature at the University of Dublin.

ANCIENT GREEK LITERATURE.
By GILBERT G. A. MURRAY, M.A., Professor of Greek in the University of Glasgow.

ENGLISH LITERATURE.
By THE EDITOR.

ITALIAN LITERATURE.
By RICHARD GARNETT, C.B., LL.D., Keeper of Printed Books in the British Museum.

MODERN SCANDINAVIAN LITERATURE
By DR. GEORG BRANDES, of Copenhagen.

JAPANESE LITERATURE.
By WILLIAM GEORGE ASTON, M.A., C.M.G., late Acting Secretary at the British Legation at Tokio.

SPANISH LITERATURE.
By J. FITZMAURICE-KELLY, Member of the Spanish Academy.

WILLIAM SHAKESPEARE.
A CRITICAL STUDY.

By GEORG BRANDES.

Translated from the Danish by WILLIAM ARCHER.

In Two Volumes, demy 8vo.

Dr. Georg Brandes's "William Shakespeare" may best be called, perhaps, an exhaustive critical biography. Keeping fully abreast of the latest English and German researches and criticism, Dr. Brandes preserves that breadth and sanity of view which is apt to be sacrificed by the mere Shakespearologist. He places the poet in his political and literary environment, and studies each play not as an isolated phenomenon, but as the record of a stage in Shakespeare's spiritual history. Dr. Brandes has achieved German thoroughness without German heaviness, and has produced what must be regarded as a standard work.

ROBERT, EARL NUGENT:
A MEMOIR.

By CLAUD NUGENT.

In One Volume, demy 8vo, with a number of Portraits and other Illustrations.

A BOOK OF SCOUNDRELS.

By CHARLES WHIBLEY.

In One Volume, crown 8vo, with a Frontispiece.

In "A Book of Scoundrels" are described the careers and achievements of certain notorious malefactors who have been chosen for their presentment on account of their style and picturesqueness. They are of all ages and several countries, and that variety may not be lacking, Cartouche and Peace, Moll Cutpurse and the Abbé Bruneau, come within the same covers. Where it has seemed convenient, the method of Plutarch is followed, and the style and method of two similar scoundrels are contrasted in a "parallel." Jack Shepherd in the stone-room of Newgate, reproduced from an old print, serves as a frontispiece.

IN CAP AND GOWN.
THREE CENTURIES OF CAMBRIDGE WIT.

EDITED BY CHARLES WHIBLEY.

Third Edition, with a New Introduction, crown 8vo.

SEVENTEENTH-CENTURY STUDIES.
A CONTRIBUTION TO THE HISTORY OF ENGLISH POETRY.

By EDMUND GOSSE,

Clark Lecturer on English Literature at the University of Cambridge.

A New Edition. Crown 8vo.

PROTESTANTS IN SPAIN
IN THE SIXTEENTH CENTURY

By RACHEL E. CHALLICE.

WITH AN INTRODUCTION BY

HIS GRACE THE ARCHBISHOP OF DUBLIN,

And a Preface by CANON FLEMING.

In One Volume.

UNDERCURRENTS OF THE SECOND EMPIRE.

By ALBERT D. VANDAM,

Author of "An Englishman in Paris" and "My Paris Note-book."

Demy 8vo, 10s. 6d.

MADE IN GERMANY.

REPRINTED WITH ADDITIONS FROM *THE NEW REVIEW*.

In One Volume.

The Industrial Supremacy of Great Britain has been long an axiomatic commonplace; it is fast turning into a myth.

These papers are not prompted by the Bimetallic League, nor by devotion to fair trade, nor by any of the economic schemes and doctrines which reformers are propounding for the cure of our commercial dry-rot. It is the Author's object to proceed on scientific lines, to collect and arrange the facts so that they may clearly show forth the causes, and point with inevitableness to the remedies, if and where there be any.

THE BLACK RIDERS

VERSES.

By STEPHEN CRANE,

Author of "The Red Badge of Courage."

LETTERS OF A COUNTRY VICAR.

Translated from the French of YVES LE QUERDEC.

By M. GORDON-HOLMES.

In One Volume, crown 8vo.

This translation of a work which, in the original, has evoked a quite exceptional measure of attention, will be welcomed for its vivid pictures of country life in France, and of the relations subsisting between Church and laity.

THE AGNOSTICISM OF THE FUTURE.

FROM THE FRENCH OF

M. GUYAU.

In One Volume, 8vo.

GENIUS AND DEGENERATION:

A PSYCHOLOGICAL STUDY.

By DR. WILLIAM HIRSCH.

With an Introduction by Professor E. MENDEL.

Translated from the Second German Edition.

In One Volume, demy 8vo, 10s. net.

MR. HEINEMANN'S LIST.

ANTONIO ALLEGRI DA CORREGIO: His Life, his Friends, and his Time. By CORRADO RICCI, Director of the Royal Gallery, Parma. Translated by FLORENCE SIMMONDS. With 16 Photogravure Plates, 21 full-page Plates in Tint, and 190 Illustrations in the Text. In One Volume, imperial 8vo, £2 2s. net.

*** *Also a special edition printed on Japanese vellum, limited to 100 copies, with duplicate plates on India paper. Price £12 12s. net.*

REMBRANDT: His Life, his Work, and his Time. By EMILE MICHEL, Member of the Institute of France. Translated by FLORENCE SIMMONDS. Edited and Prefaced by FREDERICK WEDMORE. Second Edition, Enlarged, with 76 full-page Plates, and 250 Illustrations in the Text. In One Volume, Gilt top, or in Two Volumes, imperial 8vo, £2 2s. net.

*** *A few copies of the* EDITION DE LUXE *of the First Edition, printed on Japanese vellum with India proof duplicates of the photogravures, are still on sale, price £12 12s. net.*

REMBRANDT. Seventeen of his Masterpieces from the collection of his Pictures in the Cassel Gallery. Reproduced in Photogravure by the Berlin Photographic Company. With an Essay by FREDERICK WEDMORE. In large portfolio 27½ inches × 20 inches.

The first twenty-five impressions of each plate are numbered and signed, and of these only fourteen are for sale in England at the net price of Twenty Guineas *the set. The price of the impressions after the first twenty-five is* Twelve Guineas *net, per set.*

MASTERPIECES OF GREEK SCULPTURE. A Series of Essays on the History of Art. By ADOLF FURTWANGLER. Authorised Translation. Edited by EUGENIE SELLERS. With 19 full page and 200 text Illustrations. In One Volume, imperial 8vo, £3 3s. net.

*** *Also an* EDITION DE LUXE *on Japanese vellum, limited to 50 numbered copies in Two Volumes, price £10 10s. net.*

THE HOURS OF RAPHAEL, IN OUTLINE. Together with the Ceiling of the Hall where they were originally painted. By MARY E. WILLIAMS. Folio, cloth. £2 2s. net.

A CATALOGUE OF THE ACCADEMIA DELLE BELLE ARTI AT VENICE. With Biographical Notices of the Painters and Reproductions of some of their Works. Edited by E. M. KEARY. Crown 8vo, cloth, 2s. 6d. net; paper, 2s. net.

A CATALOGUE OF THE MUSEO DEL PRADO AT MADRID. Compiled by E. LAWSON. In One Volume, crown 8vo:
[*In preparation.*

MR. HEINEMANN'S LIST.

BROTHER AND SISTER. A Memoir and the Letters of ERNEST and HENRIETTE RENAN. Translated by Lady MARY LOYD. Demy 8vo, with Two Portraits in Photogravure, and Four Illustrations, 14s.

Mr. GLADSTONE has written to the publisher as follows : " I have read the whole of the Renan Memoirs, and have found them to be of peculiar and profound interest."

The Illustrated London News.—" One of the most exquisite memorials in all literature."

The Daily Telegraph.—" A faithful record of a perfect friendship."

CHARLES GOUNOD. Autobiographical Reminiscences with Family Letters and Notes on Music. Translated by the Hon. W. HELY HUTCHINSON. Demy 8vo, with Portrait, 10s. 6d.

The Daily News.—" Interwoven with many touching domestic details, it furnishes a continuous history of the dawn and development of his genius down to the period when his name had become familiar in all men's mouths."

The Globe.—" Will, of course, have many interested readers, and will find its way into the libraries of all musical enthusiasts."

STUDIES IN DIPLOMACY. By Count BENEDETTI, French Ambassador at the Court of Berlin. Demy 8vo, with a Portrait, 10s. 6d.

The Times.—" An important and authentic contribution to the history of a great crisis in the affairs of Europe."

AN AMBASSADOR OF THE VANQUISHED. Viscount Elie De Gontaut-Biron's Mission to Berlin, 1871-1877. From his Diaries and Memoranda. By the DUKE DE BROGLIE. Translated with Notes by ALBERT D. VANDAM, Author of "An Englishman in Paris." In One Volume, 8vo, 10s. 6d.

The Times.—" The real interest of the book consists in the new contributions which it makes to our knowledge of the dangerous crisis of 1875."

The Daily Telegraph.—" A book at once teeming with accurate information, and free from emotional indiscretion ; marked by coolness of tone and impartiality of judgment."

ANIMAL SYMBOLISM IN ECCLESIASTICAL ARCHITECTURE. By E. P. EVANS. With a Bibliography and Seventy-eight Illustrations, crown 8vo, 9s.

The Manchester Courier.—" A work of considerable learning. We have not often read a book that contains more quaint and unusual information, or is more closely packed with matter. It is very pleasant reading and may be commended to all who are interested in the by-paths of literature and art."

Great Lives and Events.

Uniformly bound in cloth, 6s. each volume.

A FRIEND OF THE QUEEN. Marie Antoinette and Count Fersen. From the French of PAUL GAULOT. Two Portraits.

The Times.—"M. Gaulot's work tells, with new and authentic details, the romantic story of Count Fersen's devotion to Marie Antoinette, of his share in the celebrated Flight to Varennes and in many other well-known episodes of the unhappy Queen's life."

THE ROMANCE OF AN EMPRESS. Catherine II. of Russia. From the French of K. WALISZEWSKI. With a Portrait.

The Times.—"This book is based on the confessions of the Empress herself; it gives striking pictures of the condition of the contemporary Russia which she did so much to mould as well as to expand. . . . Few stories in history are more romantic than that of Catherine II. of Russia, with its mysterious incidents and thrilling episodes; few characters present more curious problems."

THE STORY OF A THRONE. Catherine II. of Russia. From the French of K. WALISZEWSKI. With a Portrait.

The World.—"No novel that ever was written could compete with this historical monograph in absorbing interest."

NAPOLEON AND THE FAIR SEX. From the French of FRÉDÉRIC MASSON. With a Portrait.

The Daily Chronicle.—"The author shows that this side of Napoleon's life must be understood by those who would realize the manner of man he was."

ALFRED, LORD TENNYSON. A Study of His Life and Work. By ARTHUR WAUGH, B.A. Oxon. With Twenty Illustrations from Photographs specially taken for this Work. Five Portraits, and Facsimile of Tennyson's MS.

MEMOIRS OF THE PRINCE DE JOINVILLE. Translated from the French by Lady MARY LOYD. With 78 Illustrations from drawings by the Author.

THE NATURALIST OF THE SEA-SHORE. The Life of Philip Henry Gosse. By his son, EDMUND GOSSE, Hon. M.A., Trinity College, Cambridge. With a Portrait.

MR. HEINEMANN'S LIST.

MY PARIS NOTE-BOOK. By ALBERT D. VANDAM, Author of "An Englishman in Paris." In One Volume, demy 8vo, price 6s.

EDMUND AND JULES DE GONCOURT. Letters and Leaves from their Journals. Selected. In Two Volumes, 8vo, with Eight Portraits, 32s.

ALEXANDER III. OF RUSSIA. By CHARLES LOWE, M.A., Author of "Prince Bismarck: an Historical Biography." Crown 8vo, with Portrait in Photogravure, 6s.

The Athenæum.—"A most interesting and valuable volume."
The Academy.—"Written with great care and strict impartiality."

PRINCE BISMARCK. An Historical Biography. By CHARLES LOWE, M.A. With Portraits. Crown 8vo, 6s.

VILLIERS DE L'ISLE ADAM: His Life and Works. From the French of VICOMTE ROBERT DU PONTAVICE DE HEUSSEY. By Lady MARY LOYD. With Portrait and Facsimile. Crown 8vo, cloth, 10s. 6d.

THE LIFE OF HENRIK IBSEN. By HENRIK JÆGER. Translated by CLARA BELL. With the Verse done into English from the Norwegian Original by EDMUND GOSSE. Crown 8vo, cloth, 6s.

RECOLLECTIONS OF MIDDLE LIFE. By FRANCISQUE SARCEY. Translated by E. L. CAREY. In One Volume, 8vo, with Portrait, 10s. 6d.

TWENTY-FIVE YEARS IN THE SECRET SERVICE. The Recollections of a Spy. By Major HENRI LE CARON. With New Preface. 8vo, boards, price 2s. 6d., or cloth, 3s. 6d.

*** *The Library Edition, with Portraits and Facsimiles, 8vo, 14s., is still on sale.*

THE FAMILY LIFE OF HEINRICH HEINE. Illustrated by one hundred and twenty-two hitherto unpublished letters addressed by him to different members of his family. Edited by his nephew, Baron LUDWIG VON EMBDEN, and translated by CHARLES GODFREY LELAND. In One Volume, 8vo, with 4 Portraits, 12s. 6d.

RECOLLECTIONS OF COUNT LEO TOLSTOY. Together with a Letter to the Women of France on the "Kreutzer Sonata." By C. A. BEHRS. Translated from the Russian by C. E. TURNER, English Lecturer in the University of St. Petersburg. In One Volume, 8vo, with Portrait, 10s. 6d.

QUEEN JOANNA I. OF NAPLES, SICILY, AND JERUSALEM; Countess of Provence, Forcalquier, and Piedmont. An Essay on her Times. By ST. CLAIR BADDELEY. Imperial 8vo, with numerous Illustrations, 16s.

CHARLES III. OF NAPLES AND URBAN VI.; also CECCO D'ASCOLI, Poet, Astrologer, Physician. Two Historical Essays. By ST. CLAIR BADDELEY. With Illustrations, 8vo, cloth, 10s. 6d.

LETTERS OF SAMUEL TAYLOR COLERIDGE.
Edited by ERNEST HARTLEY COLERIDGE. With 16 Portraits and Illustrations. In Two Volumes, demy 8vo, £1 12s.

DE QUINCEY MEMORIALS. Being Letters and other Records here first Published, with Communications from COLERIDGE, the WORDSWORTHS, HANNAH MORE, PROFESSOR WILSON, and others. Edited with Introduction, Notes, and Narrative, by ALEXANDER H. JAPP, LL.D., F.R.S.E. In Two Volumes, demy 8vo, cloth, with Portraits, 30s. net.

MEMOIRS. By CHARLES GODFREY LELAND (HANS BREITMANN). Second Edition. In One Volume, 8vo, with Portrait, price 7s. 6d.

LETTERS OF A BARITONE. By FRANCIS WALKER. Square crown 8vo, 5s.

THE LOVE LETTERS OF MR. H. AND MISS R. 1775-1779. Edited by GILBERT BURGESS. Square crown 8vo, 5s.

PARADOXES. By MAX NORDAU, Author of "Degeneration," "Conventional Lies of our Civilisation," &c. Translated by J. R. McILRAITH. Demy 8vo, 17s. net. With an Introduction by the Author written for this Edition.

CONVENTIONAL LIES OF OUR CIVILIZATION. By MAX NORDAU, author of "Degeneration." Second English Edition. Demy 8vo, 17s. net.

DEGENERATION. By MAX NORDAU. Ninth English Edition. Demy 8vo, 17s. net.

THE PROSE WORKS OF HEINRICH HEINE. Translated by CHARLES GODFREY LELAND, M.A., F.R.L.S. (HANS BREITMANN). In Eight Volumes.

The Library Edition, in crown 8vo, cloth, at 5s. per Volume. Each Volume of this edition is sold separately. The Cabinet Edition, in special binding, boxed, price £2 10s. the set. The Large Paper Edition, limited to 50 Numbered Copies, price 15s. per Volume net, will only be supplied to subscribers for the Complete Work.

  I. FLORENTINE NIGHTS, SCHNABELEWOPSKI, THE RABBI OF BACHARACH, and SHAKESPEARE'S MAIDENS AND WOMEN.
  II., III. PICTURES OF TRAVEL. 1823-1828.
  IV. THE SALON. Letters on Art, Music, Popular Life, and Politics.
  V., VI. GERMANY.
  VII., VIII. FRENCH AFFAIRS. Letters from Paris 1832, and Lutetia.

THE POSTHUMOUS WORKS OF THOMAS DE QUINCEY. Edited, with Introduction and Notes from the Author's Original MSS., by ALEXANDER H. JAPP, LL.D., F.R.S.E., &c. Crown 8vo, cloth, 6s. each.

  I. SUSPIRIA DE PROFUNDIS. With other Essays.
  II. CONVERSATION AND COLERIDGE. With other Essays.

CRITICAL KIT-KATS. By EDMUND GOSSE, Hon. M.A. of Trinity College, Cambridge. Crown 8vo, buckram, gilt top, 7s. 6d.

QUESTIONS AT ISSUE. Essays. By EDMUND GOSSE. Crown 8vo, buckram, gilt top, 7s. 6d.
*** *A Limited Edition on Large Paper, 25s. net.*

GOSSIP IN A LIBRARY. By EDMUND GOSSE, Author of "Northern Studies," &c. Third Edition. Crown 8vo, buckram, gilt top, 7s. 6d.
*** *A Limited Edition on Large Paper, 25s. net.*

CORRECTED IMPRESSIONS. Essays on Victorian Writers. By GEORGE SAINTSBURY. Crown 8vo, gilt top, 7s. 6d.

ANIMA POETÆ. From the unpublished note-books of SAMUEL TAYLOR COLERIDGE. Edited by ERNEST HARTLEY COLERIDGE. In One Volume, crown 8vo, 7s. 6d.

ESSAYS. By ARTHUR CHRISTOPHER BENSON, of Eton College. In One Volume, crown 8vo, buckram, 7s. 6d.

THE CHITRAL CAMPAIGN. A Narrative of Events in Chitral, Swat, and Bajour. By H. C. THOMSON. With over 50 Illustrations reproduced from Photographs, and important Diagrams and Map. Second Edition in One Volume, demy 8vo, 14s. net.

WITH THE ZHOB FIELD FORCE, 1890. By Captain CRAWFORD MCFALL, K.O.Y.L.I. In One Volume, demy 8vo, with Illustrations, 18s.

THE LAND OF THE MUSKEG. By H. SOMERS SOMERSET. Second Edition. In One Volume, demy 8vo, with Maps and over 100 Illustrations, 280 pp., 14s. net.

ACTUAL AFRICA; or, The Coming Continent. A Tour of Exploration. By FRANK VINCENT, Author of "The Land of the White Elephant." With Map and over 100 Illustrations, demy 8vo, cloth, price 24s.

COREA, OR CHO-SEN, THE LAND OF THE MORNING CALM. By A. HENRY SAVAGE-LANDOR. With 38 Illustrations from Drawings by the Author, and a Portrait, demy 8vo, 18s.

THE LITTLE MANX NATION. (Lectures delivered at the Royal Institution, 1891.) By HALL CAINE, Author of "The Bondman," "The Scapegoat," &c. Crown 8vo, cloth, 3s. 6d.; paper, 2s. 6d.

NOTES FOR THE NILE. Together with a Metrical Rendering of the Hymns of Ancient Egypt and of the Precepts of Ptahhotep (the oldest book in the world). By HARDWICKE D. RAWNSLEY, M.A. Imperial 16mo, cloth, 5s.

DENMARK: its History, Topography, Language, Literature Fine Arts, Social Life, and Finance. Edited by H. WEITEMEYER. Demy 8vo, cloth, with Map, 12s. 6d.
*** *Dedicated, by permission, to H.R.H. the Princess of Wales.*

THE REALM OF THE HABSBURGS. By SIDNEY WHITMAN, Author of "Imperial Germany." In One Volume, crown 8vo, 7s. 6d.

IMPERIAL GERMANY. A Critical Study of Fact and Character. By SIDNEY WHITMAN. New Edition, Revised and Enlarged. Crown 8vo, cloth, 2s. 6d.; paper, 2s.

THE CANADIAN GUIDE-BOOK. Part I. The Tourist's and Sportsman's Guide to Eastern Canada and Newfoundland, including full descriptions of Routes, Cities, Points of Interest, Summer Resorts, Fishing Places, &c., in Eastern Ontario, The Muskoka District, The St. Lawrence Region, The Lake St. John Country, The Maritime Provinces, Prince Edward Island, and Newfoundland. With an Appendix giving Fish and Game Laws, and Official Lists of Trout and Salmon Rivers and their Lessees. By CHARLES G. D. ROBERTS, Professor of English Literature in King's College, Windsor, N.S. With Maps and many Illustrations. Crown 8vo, limp cloth, 6s.

THE CANADIAN GUIDE-BOOK. Part II. WESTERN CANADA. Including the Peninsula and Northern Regions of Ontario, the Canadian Shores of the Great Lakes, the Lake of the Woods Region, Manitoba and "The Great North-West," The Canadian Rocky Mountains and National Park, British Columbia, and Vancouver Island. By ERNEST INGERSOLL. With Maps and many Illustrations. Crown 8vo, limp cloth, 6s.

THE GUIDE-BOOK TO ALASKA AND THE NORTH-WEST COAST, including the Shores of Washington, British Columbia, South-Eastern Alaska, the Aleutian and the Seal Islands, the Behring and the Arctic Coasts. By E. R. SCIDMORE. With Maps and many Illustrations. Crown 8vo, limp cloth, 6s.

THE GENESIS OF THE UNITED STATES. A Narrative of the Movement in England, 1605-1616, which resulted in the Plantation of North America by Englishmen, disclosing the Contest between England and Spain for the Possession of the Soil now occupied by the United States of America; set forth through a series of Historical Manuscripts now first printed, together with a Re-issue of Rare Contemporaneous Tracts, accompanied by Bibliographical Memoranda, Notes, and Brief Biographies. Collected, Arranged, and Edited by ALEXANDER BROWN, F.R.H.S. With 100 Portraits, Maps, and Plans. In Two Volumes, royal 8vo, buckram, £3 13s. 6d. net.

IN THE TRACK OF THE SUN. Readings from the Diary of a Globe-Trotter. By FREDERICK DIODATI THOMPSON. With many Illustrations by Mr. HARRY FENN and from Photographs. In One Volume, 4to, 25s.

THE GREAT WAR OF 189—. A Forecast. By Rear-Admiral COLOMB, Col. MAURICE, R.A., Captain MAUDE, ARCHIBALD FORBES, CHARLES LOWE, D. CHRISTIE MURRAY, and F. SCUDAMORE. Second Edition. In One Volume, large 8vo, with numerous Illustrations, 6s.

THE COMING TERROR. And other Essays and Letters. By ROBERT BUCHANAN. Second Edition. Demy 8vo, cloth, 12s. 6d.

AS OTHERS SAW HIM. A Retrospect, A.D. 54. In One Volume. Crown 8vo, gilt top, 6s.

ISRAEL AMONG THE NATIONS. Translated from the French of ANATOLE LEROY-BEAULIEU, Member of the Institute of France. In One Volume, crown 8vo, 7s. 6d.

THE JEW AT HOME. Impressions of a Summer and Autumn Spent with Him in Austria and Russia. By JOSEPH PENNELL. With Illustrations by the Author. 4to, cloth, 5s.

THE NEW EXODUS. A Study of Israel in Russia. By HAROLD FREDERIC. Demy 8vo, Illustrated, 16s.

STUDIES OF RELIGIOUS HISTORY. By ERNEST RENAN, late of the French Academy. In One Volume, 8vo, 7s. 6d.

THE ARBITRATOR'S MANUAL. Under the London Chamber of Arbitration. Being a Practical Treatise on the Power and Duties of an Arbitrator, with the Rules and Procedure of the Court of Arbitration, and the Forms. By JOSEPH SEYMOUR SALAMAN, Author of "Trade Marks," &c. Fcap. 8vo, 3s. 6d.

MANNERS, CUSTOMS, AND OBSERVANCES: Their Origin and Signification. By LEOPOLD WAGNER. Crown 8vo, 6s.

A COMMENTARY ON THE WORKS OF HENRIK IBSEN. By HJALMAR HJORTH BOYESEN, Author of "Goethe and Schiller," "Essays on German Literature," &c. Crown 8vo, cloth, 7s. 6d. net.

THE LABOUR MOVEMENT IN AMERICA. By RICHARD T. ELY, Ph.D., Associate in Political Economy, John Hopkins University. Crown 8vo, cloth, 5s.

THE PASSION PLAY AT OBERAMMERGAU, 1890. By F. W. FARRAR, D.D., F.R.S., Dean of Canterbury, &c. &c. 4to, cloth, 2s. 6d.

THE WORD OF THE LORD UPON THE WATERS. Sermons read by His Imperial Majesty the Emperor of Germany, while at Sea on his Voyages to the Land of the Midnight Sun. Composed by Dr. RICHTER, Army Chaplain, and Translated from the German by JOHN R. MCILRAITH. 4to, cloth, 2s. 6d.

THE KINGDOM OF GOD IS WITHIN YOU. Christianity not as a Mystic Religion but as a New Theory of Life. By Count LEO TOLSTOY. Translated from the Russian by CONSTANCE GARNETT. Popular Edition in One Volume, cloth, 2s. 6d.

THE SPINSTER'S SCRIP. As Compiled by CECIL RAYNOR. Narrow crown 8vo, limp cloth, 2s. 6d.

THE POCKET IBSEN. A Collection of some of the Master's best known Dramas, condensed, revised, and slightly rearranged for the benefit of the Earnest Student. By F. ANSTEY, Author of "Vice Versa," "Voces Populi," &c. With Illustrations, reproduced by permission, from *Punch*, and a new Frontispiece, by BERNARD PARTRIDGE. New Edition. 16mo, cloth, 3s. 6d.; or paper, 2s. 6d.

FROM WISDOM COURT. By HENRY SETON MERRIMAN and STEPHEN GRAHAM TALLENTYRE. With 30 Illustrations by E. COURBOIN. Crown 8vo, cloth, 3s. 6d.

THE OLD MAIDS' CLUB. By I. ZANGWILL, Author of "Children of the Ghetto," &c. Illustrated by F. H. TOWNSEND. Crown 8vo, cloth, 3s. 6d.

WOMAN—THROUGH A MAN'S EYEGLASS. By MALCOLM C. SALAMAN. With Illustrations by DUDLEY HARDY. Crown 8vo, cloth, 3s. 6d.

STORIES OF GOLF. Collected by WILLIAM KNIGHT and T. T. OLIPHANT. With Rhymes on Golf by various hands; also Shakespeare on Golf, &c. *Enlarged Edition.* Fcap. 8vo, cloth, 2s. 6d.

THE ROSE: A Treatise on the Cultivation, History, Family Characteristics, &c., of the various Groups of Roses. With Accurate Description of the Varieties now Generally Grown. By H. B. ELLWANGER. With an Introduction by GEORGE H. ELLWANGER. 12mo, cloth, 5s.

THE GARDEN'S STORY; or, Pleasures and Trials of an Amateur Gardener. By G. H. ELLWANGER. With an Introduction by the Rev. C. WOLLEY DOD. 12mo, cloth, with Illustrations, 5s.

THE GENTLE ART OF MAKING ENEMIES. As pleasingly exemplified in many instances, wherein the serious ones of this earth, carefully exasperated, have been prettily spurred on to indiscretions and unseemliness, while overcome by an undue sense of right. By J. M'NEILL WHISTLER. *A New Edition.* Post 4to, half cloth, 10s. 6d.

*** A few copies of the large paper issue of the first edition remain, price £1 11s. 6d. net.

LITTLE JOHANNES. By F. VAN EEDEN. Translated from the Dutch by CLARA BELL. With an Introduction by ANDREW LANG. In One Volume, 16mo, cloth, silver top, 3s. net.

GIRLS AND WOMEN. By E. CHESTER. Post 8vo, cloth, 2s. 6d., or gilt extra, 3s. 6d.

Dramatic Literature.

THE PLAYS OF W. E. HENLEY AND R. L. STEVENSON: — DEACON BRODIE; BEAU AUSTIN; ADMIRAL GUINEA; MACAIRE. Crown 8vo, cloth. An Edition of 250 copies only, 10s. 6d. net.

LITTLE EYOLF. A Play in Three Acts. By HENRIK IBSEN. Translated from the Norwegian by WILLIAM ARCHER. Small 4to, cloth, with Portrait, 5s.

THE MASTER BUILDER. A Play in Three Acts. By HENRIK IBSEN. Translated from the Norwegian by EDMUND GOSSE and WILLIAM ARCHER. Small 4to, with Portrait, 5s. Popular Edition, paper, 1s. Also a Limited Large Paper Edition, 21s. net.

HEDDA GABLER: A Drama in Four Acts. By HENRIK IBSEN. Translated from the Norwegian by EDMUND GOSSE. Small 4to, cloth, with Portrait, 5s. Vaudeville Edition, paper, 1s. Also a Limited Large Paper Edition, 21s. net.

BRAND: A Dramatic Poem in Five Acts. By HENRIK IBSEN. Translated in the original metres, with an Introduction and Notes, by C. H. HERFORD. Small 4to, cloth, 7s. 6d.

HANNELE: A DREAM-POEM. By GERHART HAUPTMANN. Translated by WILLIAM ARCHER. Small 4to, with Portrait, 5s.

THE PRINCESSE MALEINE: A Drama in Five Acts (Translated by GERARD HARRY), and THE INTRUDER: A Drama in One Act. By MAURICE MAETERLINCK. With an Introduction by HALL CAINE, and a Portrait of the Author. Small 4to, cloth, 5s.

THE FRUITS OF ENLIGHTENMENT: A Comedy in Four Acts. By Count LYOF TOLSTOY. Translated from the Russian by E. J. DILLON. With Introduction by A. W. PINERO. Small 4to, with Portrait, 5s.

KING ERIK. A Tragedy. By EDMUND GOSSE. A Re-issue, with a Critical Introduction by Mr. THEODORE WATTS. Fcap. 8vo, boards, 5s. net.

THE PIPER OF HAMELIN. A Fantastic Opera in Two Acts. By ROBERT BUCHANAN. With Illustrations by HUGH THOMSON. 4to, cloth, 2s. 6d. net.

THE SIN OF ST. HULDA. A Play. By J. STUART OGILVIE. Fcap. 8vo, paper, 1s.

HYPATIA. A Play in Four Acts. Founded on CHARLES KINGSLEY'S Novel. By G. STUART OGILVIE. With Frontispiece by J. D. BATTEN. Crown 8vo, cloth, printed in Red and Black, 2s. 6d. net.

THE DRAMA: ADDRESSES. By HENRY IRVING. With Portrait by J. McN. WHISTLER. Second Edition. Fcap. 8vo, 3s. 6d.

SOME INTERESTING FALLACIES OF THE Modern Stage. An Address delivered to the Playgoers' Club at St. James's Hall, on Sunday, 6th December, 1891. By HERBERT BEERBOHM TREE. Crown 8vo, sewed, 6d. net.

THE PLAYS OF ARTHUR W. PINERO. With Introductory Notes by MALCOLM C. SALAMAN. 16mo, paper covers, 1s. 6d.; or cloth, 2s. 6d. each.

I. THE TIMES.
II. THE PROFLIGATE.
III. THE CABINET MINISTER.
IV. THE HOBBY HORSE.
V. LADY BOUNTIFUL.
VI. THE MAGISTRATE.
VII. DANDY DICK.
VIII. SWEET LAVENDER.
IX. THE SCHOOLMISTRESS.
X. THE WEAKER SEX.
XI. THE AMAZONS.

THE NOTORIOUS MRS. EBBSMITH. A Drama in Four Acts. By ARTHUR W. PINERO. Small 4to, cloth, 2s. 6d.; paper, 1s. 6d.

THE SECOND MRS. TANQUERAY. A Play in Four Acts. By ARTHUR W. PINERO. Small 4to, cloth, with a new Portrait of the Author, 5s. Also Cheap Edition, uniform with "The Notorious Mrs. Ebbsmith." Cloth, 2s. 6d.: paper, 1s. 6d.

THE BENEFIT OF THE DOUBT. By ARTHUR W. PINERO. Small 4to, cloth, 2s. 6d.: paper, 1s. 6d.

Poetry.

ON VIOL AND FLUTE. By EDMUND GOSSE. Fcap. 8vo, with Frontispiece and Tailpiece, price 3s. 6d. net.

FIRDAUSI IN EXILE, and other Poems. By EDMUND GOSSE. Fcap. 8vo, with Frontispiece, price 3s. 6d. net.

IN RUSSET AND SILVER. POEMS. By EDMUND GOSSE. Author of "Gossip in a Library," &c. Crown 8vo, buckram, gilt top, 6s.

THE POETRY OF PATHOS AND DELIGHT. From the Works of COVENTRY PATMORE. Passages selected by ALICE MEYNELL. With a Photogravure Portrait from an Oil Painting by JOHN SARGENT, A.R.A. Fcap. 8vo, 5s.

A CENTURY OF GERMAN LYRICS. Translated from the German by KATE FREILIGRATH KROEKER. Fcap. 8vo, rough edges, 3s. 6d.

LOVE SONGS OF ENGLISH POETS, 1500-1800. With Notes by RALPH H. CAINE. Fcap. 8vo, rough edges, 3s. 6d.
*** *Large Paper Edition, limited to 100 Copies,* 10s. 6d. net.

IVY AND PASSION FLOWER: Poems. By GERARD BENDALL, Author of "Estelle," &c. &c. 12mo, cloth, 3s. 6d.
Scotsman.—"Will be read with pleasure."
Musical World.—"The poems are delicate specimens of art, graceful and polished."

VERSES. By GERTRUDE HALL. 12mo, cloth, 3s. 6d.
Manchester Guardian.—"Will be welcome to every lover of poetry who takes it up."

IDYLLS OF WOMANHOOD. By C. AMY DAWSON. Fcap. 8vo, gilt top, 5s.

TENNYSON'S GRAVE. By ST. CLAIR BADDELEY. 8vo, paper, 1s.

Science and Education.

THE BIOLOGICAL PROBLEM OF TO-DAY: Preformation or Epigenesis? Authorised Translation from the German of Prof. Dr. OSCAR HERTWIG, of the University of Berlin. By P. CHALMERS MITCHELL, M.A., Oxon. With a Preface by the Translator. Crown 8vo. 3s. 6d.

MOVEMENT. Translated from the French of E. MAREY. By ERIC PRITCHARD, M.A., M.B., Oxon. In One Volume, crown 8vo, with 170 Illustrations, 7s. 6d.

A popular and scientific treatise on movement, dealing chiefly with the locomotion of men, animals, birds, fish, and insects. A large number of the Illustrations are from instantaneous photographs.

ARABIC AUTHORS: A Manual of Arabian History and Literature. By F. F. ARBUTHNOT, M.R.A.S., Author of "Early Ideas," "Persian Portraits," &c. 8vo, cloth, 5s.

THE SPEECH OF MONKEYS. By Professor R. L. GARNER. Crown 8vo, 7s. 6d.

Heinemann's Scientific Handbooks.

MANUAL OF BACTERIOLOGY. By A. B. GRIFFITHS, Ph.D., F.R.S. (Edin.), F.C.S. Crown 8vo, cloth, Illustrated. 7s. 6d.

Pharmaceutical Journal.—"The subject is treated more thoroughly and completely than in any similar work published in this country."

MANUAL OF ASSAYING GOLD, SILVER, COPPER, and Lead Ores. By WALTER LEE BROWN, B.Sc. Revised, Corrected, and considerably Enlarged, with a chapter on the Assaying of Fuel, &c. By A. B. GRIFFITHS, Ph.D., F.R.S. (Edin.), F.C.S. Crown 8vo, cloth, Illustrated, 7s. 6d.

Colliery Guardian.—"A delightful and fascinating book."

Financial World.—"The most complete and practical manual on everything which concerns assaying of all which have come before us."

GEODESY. By J. HOWARD GORE. Crown 8vo, cloth, Illustrated, 5s.

St. James's Gazette.—"The book may be safely recommended to those who desire to acquire an accurate knowledge of Geodesy."

Science Gossip.—"It is the best we could recommend to all geodetic students. It is full and clear, thoroughly accurate, and up to date in all matters of earth-measurements."

THE PHYSICAL PROPERTIES OF GASES. By ARTHUR L. KIMBALL, of the John Hopkins University. Crown 8vo, cloth, Illustrated, 5s.

Chemical News.—"The man of culture who wishes for a general and accurate acquaintance with the physical properties of gases, will find in Mr. Kimball's work just what he requires."

HEAT AS A FORM OF ENERGY. By Professor R. H. THURSTON, of Cornell University. Crown 8vo, cloth, Illustrated, 5s.

Manchester Examiner.—"Bears out the character of its predecessors for careful and correct statement and deduction under the light of the most recent discoveries."

The Great Educators

A Series of Volumes by Eminent Writers, presenting in their entirety "A Biographical History of Education."

The Times.—"A Series of Monographs on 'The Great Educators' should prove of service to all who concern themselves with the history, theory, and practice of education."

The Speaker.—"There is a promising sound about the title of Mr. Heinemann's new series, 'The Great Educators.' It should help to allay the hunger and thirst for knowledge and culture of the vast multitude of young men and maidens which our educational system turns out yearly, provided at least with an appetite for instruction."

Each subject will form a complete volume, crown 8vo, 5*s*.

Now ready.

ARISTOTLE, and the Ancient Educational Ideals. By THOMAS DAVIDSON, M.A., LL.D.

The Times.—"A very readable sketch of a very interesting subject."

LOYOLA, and the Educational System of the Jesuits. By Rev. THOMAS HUGHES, S.J.

ALCUIN, and the Rise of the Christian Schools. By Professor ANDREW F. WEST, Ph.D.

FROEBEL, and Education by Self-Activity. By H. COURTHOPE BOWEN, M.A.

ABELARD, and the Origin and Early History of Universities. By JULES GABRIEL COMPAYRÉ, Professor in the Faculty of Toulouse.

HERBART AND THE HERBARTIANS. By Prof. DE GARMO.

In preparation.

ROUSSEAU; and, Education according to Nature. By PAUL H. HANUS.

HORACE MANN, and Public Education in the United States. By NICHOLAS MURRAY BUTLER, Ph.D.

THOMAS and MATTHEW ARNOLD, and their Influence on Education. By J. G. FITCH, LL.D., Her Majesty's Inspector of Schools.

PESTALOZZI; or, the Friend and Student of Children.

Forthcoming Fiction.

MAGGIE. By STEPHEN CRANE. In One Volume.

A COURT INTRIGUE. By BASIL THOMSON. In One Volume.

A NEW NOVEL by SARAH GRAND.

SAINT IVES. By ROBERT LOUIS STEVENSON. In One Volume.

A NEW NOVEL by HALL CAINE. In One Volume.

THE REDS OF THE MIDI, an Episode of the French Revolution. Translated from the Provençal of Félix Gras. By Mrs. CATHERINE A. JANVIER.

THE FOURTH NAPOLEON. By CHARLES BENHAM. In One Volume.

A NEW NOVEL by E. W. PUGH.

CHUN-LI-KUNG. By CLAUDE REES. In One Volume, 6s.

BELOW THE SALT. By C. E. RAIMOND. In One Volume.

WITHOUT SIN. By MARTIN J. PRITCHARD. In One Volume, 6s.

THE WORLD AND A MAN. By Z. Z. In One Volume, 6s.

THE FAILURE OF SIBYL FLETCHER. By ADELINE SERGEANT. In One Volume.

EMBARRASSMENTS. By HENRY JAMES. Crown 8vo cloth.

A NEW NOVEL by HENRY JAMES. Crown 8vo.

THE DANCER IN YELLOW. By W. E. NORRIS. Crown 8vo, cloth. 6s.

THE MALADY OF THE CENTURY. By MAX NORDAU. Crown 8vo, cloth, 6s.

MR. HEINEMANN'S LIST.

Popular 6s. Novels.

THE FOLLY OF EUSTACE. By ROBERT HICHENS. Crown 8vo, cloth, 6s.

AN IMAGINATIVE MAN. By ROBERT HICHENS. Crown 8vo, cloth, 6s.

THE ELEVENTH COMMANDMENT. By HALLIWELL SUTCLIFFE. Crown 8vo, cloth, 6s.

ILLUMINATION. By HAROLD FREDERIC. Crown 8vo, cloth, 6s.

HERBERT VANLENNERT. By C. F. KEARY. Crown 8vo, cloth, 6s.

CORRUPTION. By PERCY WHITE. Crown 8vo, cloth, 6s.

MR. BAILEY MARTIN. By PERCY WHITE. A New Edition, uniform with "Corruption." Crown 8vo, with portrait, cloth, 6s.

A SELF-DENYING ORDINANCE. By M. HAMILTON. Crown 8vo, cloth, 6s.

A COMEDY OF SENTIMENT. By MAX NORDAU. Crown 8vo, cloth, 6s.

THE ISLAND OF DOCTOR MOREAU. By H. G. WELLS. In One Volume. Crown 8vo.

STORIES FOR NINON. By ÉMILE ZOLA. Crown 8vo, with a portrait by Will Rothenstein. Cloth, 6s.

THE YEARS THAT THE LOCUST HATH EATEN. By ANNIE E. HOLDSWORTH. Crown 8vo, cloth, 6s.

IN HASTE AND AT LEISURE. By Mrs. LYNN LINTON. Author of "Joshua Davidson," &c. Crown 8vo, cloth, 6s.

A DRAMA IN DUTCH. By Z. Z. Crown 8vo, cloth, 6s.

BENEFITS FORGOT. By WOLCOTT BALESTIER. A New Edition. Crown 8vo, cloth, 6s.

A PASTORAL PLAYED OUT. By M. L. PENDERED. Crown 8vo, cloth, 6s.

CHIMÆRA. By F. MABEL ROBINSON, Author of "Mr. Butler's Ward," &c. Crown 8vo, cloth, 6s.

MISS GRACE OF ALL SOULS'. By W. EDWARDS TIREBUCK. Crown 8vo, cloth, 6s.

A SUPERFLUOUS WOMAN. Crown 8vo, 6s.

TRANSITION. By the Author of "A Superfluous Woman." Crown 8vo, cloth, 6s.

TERMINATIONS. By HENRY JAMES. Second Edition. Crown 8vo, cloth, 6s.

OUT OF DUE SEASON. By ADELINE SERGEANT. Crown 8vo, cloth, 6s.

Popular 6s. Novels.

SENTIMENTAL STUDIES. By HUBERT CRACKANTHORPE. Crown 8vo, cloth, 6s.

THE EBB-TIDE. By ROBERT LOUIS STEVENSON and LLOYD OSBOURNE. Crown 8vo, cloth, 6s.

THE MANXMAN. By HALL CAINE. Crown 8vo, cloth, 6s.

THE BONDMAN. A New Saga. By HALL CAINE. Crown 8vo, cloth, 6s.

THE SCAPEGOAT. By HALL CAINE. Author of "The Bondman," &c. Crown 8vo, cloth, 6s.

ELDER CONKLIN; and other Stories. By FRANK HARRIS. 8vo, cloth, 6s.

THE HEAVENLY TWINS. By SARAH GRAND, Author of "Ideala," &c. Crown 8vo, cloth, 6s.

IDEALA. By SARAH GRAND, Author of "The Heavenly Twins." Crown 8vo, cloth, 6s.

OUR MANIFOLD NATURE. By SARAH GRAND. With a Portrait of the Author. Crown 8vo, cloth, 6s.

THE STORY OF A MODERN WOMAN. By ELLA HEPWORTH DIXON. Crown 8vo, cloth, 6s.

AT THE GATE OF SAMARIA. By W. J. LOCKE. Crown 8vo, cloth, 6s.

A DAUGHTER OF THIS WORLD. By F. BATTERSHALL. Crown 8vo, cloth, 6s.

A COMEDY OF MASKS. By ERNEST DOWSON and ARTHUR MOORE. Crown 8vo, cloth, 6s.

THE JUSTIFICATION OF ANDREW LEBRUN. By F. BARRETT. Crown 8vo, 6s.

THE LAST SENTENCE. By MAXWELL GRAY, Author of "The Silence of Dean Maitland," &c. Crown 8vo, cloth, 6s.

APPASSIONATA: A Musician's Story. By ELSA D'ESTERRE KEELING. Crown 8vo, cloth, 6s.

THE POTTER'S THUMB. By F. A. STEEL, Author of "From the Five Rivers," &c. Crown 8vo, cloth, 6s.

FROM THE FIVE RIVERS. By FLORA ANNIE STEEL. Author of "Miss Stuart's Legacy." Crown 8vo, cloth, 6s.

RELICS. Fragments of a Life. By FRANCES MACNAB. Crown 8vo, cloth, 6s.

Popular 6s. Novels.

THE TOWER OF TADDEO. By OUIDA, Author of "Two Little Wooden Shoes," &c. New Edition. Crown 8vo, cloth, Illustrated, 6s.

THE MASTER. By I. ZANGWILL. With Portrait. Crown 8vo, cloth, 6s.

CHILDREN OF THE GHETTO. By I. ZANGWILL, Author of "The Old Maids' Club," &c. New Edition, with Glossary. Crown 8vo, cloth, 6s.

THE PREMIER AND THE PAINTER. A Fantastic Romance. By I. ZANGWILL and LOUIS COWEN. Third Edition. Crown 8vo, cloth, 6s.

THE KING OF SCHNORRERS, GROTESQUES AND FANTASIES. By I. ZANGWILL. With over Ninety Illustrations. Crown 8vo, cloth, 6s.

THE RECIPE FOR DIAMONDS. By C. J. CUTCLIFFE HYNE. Crown 8vo, cloth, 6s.

A VICTIM OF GOOD LUCK. By W. E. NORRIS, Author of "Matrimony," &c. Crown 8vo, cloth. 6s.

THE COUNTESS RADNA. By W. E. NORRIS, Author of "Matrimony," &c. Crown 8vo, cloth, 6s.

THE NAULAHKA. A Tale of West and East. By RUDYARD KIPLING and WOLCOTT BALESTIER. Second Edition. Crown 8vo, cloth, 6s.

AVENGED ON SOCIETY. By H. F. WOOD, Author of "The Englishman of the Rue Cain," "The Passenger from Scotland Yard." Crown 8vo, cloth, 6s.

THE O'CONNORS OF BALLINAHINCH. By Mrs. HUNGERFORD, Author of "Molly Bawn," &c. Crown 8vo, cloth, 6s.

A BATTLE AND A BOY. By BLANCHE WILLIS HOWARD. With Thirty-nine Illustrations by A. MAC-NIELL-BARBOUR. Crown 8vo, cloth gilt, 6s.

Five Shilling Volumes.

THE ATTACK ON THE MILL. By ÉMILE ZOLA. With Twenty-one Illustrations, and Five exquisitely printed Coloured Plates, from original drawings by E. COURBOIN. In One Volume, 4to, 5s.

THE SECRET OF NARCISSE. By EDMUND GOSSE. Crown 8vo, buckram, 5s.

VANITAS. By VERNON LEE, Author of "Hauntings," &c. Crown 8vo, cloth, 5s.

Two Shillings and Sixpence.

THE TIME MACHINE. By H. G. WELLS. Cloth, 2s. 6d.; paper, 1s. 6d.

THE DOMINANT SEVENTH: A Musical Story. By KATE ELIZABETH CLARKE. Crown 8vo, cloth, 2s. 6d.

The Pioneer Series.

12mo, cloth, 3s. net; or, paper covers, 2s. 6d. net.

The Athenæum.—"If this series keeps up to the present high level of interest, novel readers will have fresh cause for gratitude to Mr. Heinemann."
The Daily Telegraph.—"Mr. Heinemann's genial nursery of up-to-date romance."
The Observer.—"The smart Pioneer Series."
The Manchester Courier.—"The Pioneer Series promises to be as original as many other of Mr. Heinemann's ventures."
The Glasgow Herald.—"This very clever series."
The Sheffield Telegraph.—"The refreshingly original Pioneer Series."
Black and White.—"The brilliant Pioneer Series."
The Liverpool Mercury.—"Each succeeding issue of the Pioneer Series has a character of its own and a special attractiveness."

JOANNA TRAILL, SPINSTER. By ANNIE E. HOLDSWORTH.

GEORGE MANDEVILLE'S HUSBAND. By C. E. RAIMOND.

THE WINGS OF ICARUS. By LAURENCE ALMA TADEMA.

THE GREEN CARNATION. By ROBERT HICHENS.

AN ALTAR OF EARTH. By THYMOL MONK.

A STREET IN SUBURBIA. By E. W. PUGH.

THE NEW MOON. By C. E. RAIMOND.

MILLY'S STORY. By Mrs. MONTAGUE CRACKANTHORPE.

MRS. MUSGRAVE — AND HER HUSBAND. By RICHARD MARSH.

THE RED BADGE OF COURAGE. By STEPHEN CRANE.

THE DEMAGOGUE AND LADY PHAYRE. By WILLIAM J. LOCKE.

HER OWN DEVICES. By C. G. COMPTON.

PAPIER MACHÉ. By CHARLES ALLEN.

THE NEW VIRTUE. By Mrs. OSCAR BERINGER.

ACROSS AN ULSTER BOG. By M. HAMILTON.

ONE OF GOD'S DILEMMAS. By ALLEN UPWARD.

Other Volumes to follow.

UNIFORM EDITION OF
THE NOVELS OF BJÖRNSTJERNE BJÖRNSON
Edited by EDMUND GOSSE.
Fcap. 8vo, cloth, 3s. net each Volume.

Vol. I.—SYNNÖVÉ SOLBAKKEN.
With Introductory Essay by EDMUND GOSSE, and a Portrait of the Author.

Vol. II.—ARNE.
Vol. III.—A HAPPY BOY.

To be followed by

IV. THE FISHER LASS.
V. THE BRIDAL MARCH AND A DAY.
VI. MAGNHILD AND DUST.
VII. CAPTAIN MANSANA AND MOTHER'S HANDS.
VIII. ABSALOM'S HAIR, AND A PAINFUL MEMORY.

UNIFORM EDITION OF
THE NOVELS OF IVAN TURGENEV.
Translated by CONSTANCE GARNETT.
Fcap. 8vo, cloth, price 3s. net each Volume.

Vol. I.—RUDIN.
With a Portrait of the Author and an Introduction by STEPNIAK.

Vol. II.—A HOUSE OF GENTLEFOLK.

Vol. III.—ON THE EVE.

Vol. IV.—FATHERS AND CHILDREN.

Vol. V.—SMOKE.

Vol. VI., VII.—VIRGIN SOIL. (Two Volumes.)

Vol. VIII., IX.—A SPORTSMAN'S SKETCHES.
(Two Volumes.)

Heinemann's International Library.
Edited by EDMUND GOSSE.

New Review.—"If you have any pernicious remnants of literary chauvinism I hope it will not survive the series of foreign classics of which Mr. William Heinemann, aided by Mr. Edmund Gosse, is publishing translations to the great contentment of all lovers of literature."

Each Volume has an Introduction specially written by the Editor.

Price, in paper covers, 2s. 6d. each; or cloth, 3s. 6d.

IN GOD'S WAY. From the Norwegian of BJÖRNSTJERNE BJÖRNSON.

PIERRE AND JEAN. From the French of GUY DE MAUPASSANT.

THE CHIEF JUSTICE. From the German of KARL EMIL FRANZOS, Author of "For the Right," &c.

WORK WHILE YE HAVE THE LIGHT. From the Russian of Count LEO TOLSTOY.

FANTASY. From the Italian of MATILDE SERAO.

FROTH. From the Spanish of Don ARMANDO PALACIO-VALDÉS.

FOOTSTEPS OF FATE. From the Dutch of LOUIS COUPERUS.

PEPITA JIMÉNEZ. From the Spanish of JUAN VALERA.

THE COMMODORE'S DAUGHTERS. From the Norwegian of JONAS LIE.

THE HERITAGE OF THE KURTS. From the Norwegian of BJÖRNSTJERNE BJÖRNSON.

LOU. From the German of BARON ALEXANDER VON ROBERTS.

DOÑA LUZ. From the Spanish of JUAN VALERA.

THE JEW. From the Polish of JOSEPH IGNATIUS KRASZEWSKI.

UNDER THE YOKE. From the Bulgarian of IVAN VAZOFF.

FAREWELL LOVE! From the Italian of MATILDE SERAO.

THE GRANDEE. From the Spanish of Don ARMANDO PALACIO-VALDÉS.

A COMMON STORY. From the Russian of GONTCHAROFF.

WOMAN'S FOLLY. From the Italian of GEMMA FERRUGGIA.

SIREN VOICES (NIELS LYHNË). From the Danish of J. G. JACOBSEN.

In preparation.

NIOBE. From the Norwegian of JONAS LIE.

Popular 3s. 6d. Novels.

ELI'S DAUGHTER. By J. H. Pearce, Author of "Inconsequent Lives."

INCONSEQUENT LIVES. A Village Chronicle. By J. H. Pearce, Author of "Esther Pentreath," &c.

HER OWN FOLK. (En Famille.) By Hector Malot, Author of "No Relations." Translated by Lady Mary Loyd.

CAPT'N DAVY'S HONEYMOON, The Blind Mother, and The Last Confession. By Hall Caine, Author of "The Bondman," "The Scapegoat," &c.

A MARKED MAN: Some Episodes in his Life. By Ada Cambridge, Author of "A Little Minx," "The Three Miss Kings," "Not All in Vain," &c.

THE THREE MISS KINGS. By Ada Cambridge.

A LITTLE MINX. By Ada Cambridge.

NOT ALL IN VAIN. By Ada Cambridge.

A KNIGHT OF THE WHITE FEATHER. By Tasma, Author of "The Penance of Portia James," "Uncle Piper of Piper's Hill," &c.

UNCLE PIPER OF PIPER'S HILL. By Tasma.

THE PENANCE OF PORTIA JAMES. By Tasma.

THE COPPERHEAD; and other Stories of the North during the American War. By Harold Frederic, Author of "The Return of the O'Mahony," "In the Valley," &c.

THE RETURN OF THE O'MAHONY. By Harold Frederic, Author of "In the Valley," &c. With Illustrations.

IN THE VALLEY. By Harold Frederic, Author of "The Lawton Girl," "Seth's Brother's Wife," &c. With Illustrations.

THE SURRENDER OF MARGARET BELLARMINE. By Adeline Sergeant, Author of "The Story of a Penitent Soul."

THE STORY OF A PENITENT SOUL. Being the Private Papers of Mr. Stephen Dart, late Minister at Lynnbridge, in the County of Lincoln. By Adeline Sergeant, Author of " No Saint," &c.

NOR WIFE, NOR MAID. By Mrs. Hungerford, Author of "Molly Bawn," &c.

THE HOYDEN. By Mrs. Hungerford.

MAMMON. A Novel. By Mrs. Alexander, Author of "The Wooing O't," &c.

DAUGHTERS OF MEN. By Hannah Lynch, Author of "The Prince of the Glades," &c.

Popular 3s. 6d. Novels.

A ROMANCE OF THE CAPE FRONTIER. By BERTRAM MITFORD, Author of "Through the Zulu Country," &c.

'TWEEN SNOW AND FIRE. A Tale of the Kafir War of 1877. By BERTRAM MITFORD.

ORIOLE'S DAUGHTER. By JESSIE FOTHERGILL, Author of "The First Violin," &c.

THE MASTER OF THE MAGICIANS. By ELIZABETH STUART PHELPS and HERBERT D. WARD.

THE HEAD OF THE FIRM. By Mrs. RIDDELL, Author of "George Geith," "Maxwell Drewett," &c.

A CONSPIRACY OF SILENCE. By G. COLMORE, Author of "A Daughter of Music," &c.

A DAUGHTER OF MUSIC. By G. COLMORE, Author of "A Conspiracy of Silence."

ACCORDING TO ST. JOHN. By AMÉLIE RIVES, Author of "The Quick or the Dead."

KITTY'S FATHER. By FRANK BARRETT, Author of "The Admirable Lady Biddy Fane," &c.

A QUESTION OF TASTE. By MAARTEN MAARTENS, Author of "An Old Maid's Love," &c.

COME LIVE WITH ME AND BE MY LOVE. By ROBERT BUCHANAN, Author of "The Moment After," "The Coming Terror," &c.

DONALD MARCY. By ELIZABETH STUART PHELPS, Author of "The Gates Ajar," &c.

IN THE DWELLINGS OF SILENCE. A Romance of Russia. By WALKER KENNEDY.

LOS CERRITOS. A Romance of the Modern Time. By GERTRUDE FRANKLIN ATHERTON, Author of "Hermia Suydam," and "What Dreams may Come."

Short Stories in One Volume.

Three Shillings and Sixpence each.

WRECKAGE, and other Stories. By HUBERT CRACKANTHORPE. Second Edition.

MADEMOISELLE MISS, and other Stories. By HENRY HARLAND, Author of "Mea Culpa," &c.

THE ATTACK ON THE MILL, and other Sketches of War. By EMILE ZOLA. With an Essay on the short stories of M. Zola by EDMUND GOSSE.

THE AVERAGE WOMAN. By WOLCOTT BALESTIER. With an Introduction by HENRY JAMES.

BLESSED ARE THE POOR. By FRANÇOIS COPPÉE. With an Introduction by T. P. O'CONNOR.

PERCHANCE TO DREAM, and other Stories. By MARGARET S. BRISCOE.

WRECKERS AND METHODISTS. Cornish Stories. By H. D. LOWRY.

Popular Shilling Books.

PRETTY MISS SMITH. By FLORENCE WARDEN, Author of "The House on the Marsh," "A Witch of the Hills," &c.

MADAME VALERIE. By F. C. PHILIPS, Author of "As in a Looking-Glass," &c.

THE MOMENT AFTER: A Tale of the Unseen. By ROBERT BUCHANAN.

CLUES; or, Leaves from a Chief Constable's Note-Book. By WILLIAM HENDERSON, Chief Constable of Edinburgh.

THE NORTH AMERICAN REVIEW.

Edited by LLOYD BRYCE.

Published monthly.   Price 2s. 6d.

THE NEW REVIEW.

NEW SERIES.

Edited by W. E. HENLEY.

Published Monthly, price 1s.

LONDON:
WILLIAM HEINEMANN,
21 BEDFORD STREET, W.C.

www.ingramcontent.com/pod-product-compliance
Lightning Source LLC
Chambersburg PA
CBHW021159230426
43667CB00006B/466